THEY CAN'T REPRESENT US!

Acknowledgments

This book, while an incredibly exciting project for the both of us, pales in comparison to the life project to whom it is dedicated—Camilo Turi Azzelini Sitrin—born together with these pages.

We have so very many people to thank, from those who thought together with us about some of these ideas or helped us with editing, transcribing and translating, to others who graciously housed and fed us while traveling, and others who trusted us and brought us into their assemblies and smaller gatherings and then those who patiently read draft chapters and sent us reflections. Since we cannot possibly go into the necessary detail for each person, as it would require another chapter our editors will not permit, we do hope you each know how much we appreciate you. If by chance we have forgotten to list your name, please know it was an oversight and we are sorry. While not nearly sufficient, we have made a list of those people who have supported this project.

Clauida Acuña in Argentina; Alexandros, Anestis, Fani, Marita, Theo, and Vasilis, in Greece; Ana Méndez de Andéz, Ernest Marco, Eva Fernández, Gerardo Tudurí, and Luis Moreno Caballud in Spain; Marisa Holmes, Carolina Cositore, Sherman Sitrin, David Solnit, David Harvey, and the Committee on Globalization and Social Change at the CUNY Graduate Center in the United States; Benjamin Anaya in Mexico.

An extra special thanks to the Verso crew for getting the book out extra fast considering the delay.

And most of all thank you to everyone who agreed to participate in conversations and interviews so that this book could be created and all people who are creating new worlds based on real democracy and freedom every day.

THEY CAN'T REPRESENT US!

Reinventing Democracy from Greece to Occupy

Marina Sitrin and Dario Azzellini
Foreword by David Harvey

CBR

Oct 2016

VERSO

London • New York

First published by Verso 2014
© Marina Sitrin and Dario Azzellini 2014
Foreword © David Harvey 2014

1 3 5 7 9 10 8 6 4 2

Verso
UK: 6 Meard Street, London W1F 0EG
US: 20 Jay Street, Suite 1010, Brooklyn, NY 11201
www.versobooks.com

Verso is the imprint of New Left Books

ISBN-13: 978-1-78168-097-1
eISBN-13: 978-1-78168-237-1 (US)
eISBN-13: 978-1-78168-542-6 (UK)

British Library Cataloguing in Publication Data
A catalogue record for this book is available from the British Library

Library of Congress Cataloging-in-Publication Data

Sitrin, Marina.
They can›t represent us! : reinventing democracy from Greece to Occupy / Marina Sitrin and
Dario Azzellini ; foreword by Eduardo Galeano.
pages cm
ISBN 978-1-78168-097-1 (paperback) — ISBN 978-1-78168-237-1 (ebk)
1. Democracy. 2. Political participation. 3. Protest movements. I. Azzellini, Dario, 1967– II.
Title.
JC423.S62 2014
321.8—dc23
2014007296

Typeset in Minion Pro by Hewer Text UK Ltd, Edinburgh, Scotland
Printed in the US by Maple Press

Contents

Foreword by
David Harvey

Something the last several years have shown, with the rise of new radical movements worldwide, is that people—on the street, in the squares—are what really matter in the end. That's the only political force we've got. They've got the money and can buy politics, media and, really, anything they want. We don't have that. The only thing we have is people. But we have a mass. And the more people that mass in the street, the harder it becomes for them to say, "Your interests are not our interests."

A succession of crises has plagued the economies of the West since 2008. But for whom are these crises? In 2008, Forbes magazine counted 1,125 billionaires worldwide, with a net worth of $4.4 trillion, and despite a dip to 793 billionaires in 2009, the number has risen steadily to 1,645 billionaires in 2014, with a net worth of $6.4 trillion. The crisis has simply provided an opportunity to assemble even more wealth in fewer hands, at the expense of those who are the most vulnerable. At the same time, the real questions we should have asked in the wake of the crisis were not addressed: the questions of global poverty, global inequality of wealth and income, and inequality of political power. We rarely discuss how wealth is being used to buy politics, despite its being (or perhaps because it is) an old tradition. "The United States always has the best Congress that money can buy," as Mark Twain famously remarked.

This is how politics has been evolving over the last thirty years. Money has always bought influence and political power—and structured the media—but it does so now more than ever. It dominates our educational system, and university departments are now little more than sites for spreading neoliberal ideology, or teaching corporate managerial techniques that are essentially strategies for squeezing more money out of those who can least afford it. Meanwhile, the prevailing view on how to resolve the question of global poverty is to set up more NGOs and institutions to provide direct services to people in need, including providing blankets or medical care. This certainly has some benefits, but the problem is that we cannot truly confront global poverty without targeting the accumulation of global wealth. Until we leave the anti-poverty campaigns behind and join the anti-wealth campaigns, nothing's going to be resolved.

I'm old enough to remember the anti-poverty rhetoric of the 1950s and 1960s. Every decade since, this rhetoric has reappeared in slightly modified form; the Millennium Goals promised to eliminate extreme poverty by 2015, but with one year to go, it is clear this goal will not be reached. We hear these statements again and again, even as global poverty deepens, because the solutions we are being sold are the very same set of mechanisms that produce it. In other words: free markets, free trade, free rein for the capitalist class to exploit, to the hilt, everybody that they can get their hands on. But capitalists are no longer restricted to simply exploiting labor. Increasingly, the accumulation of wealth is occurring through the dispossession of others' wealth, through legal means such as "eminent domain" that allow them to drive populations off their land. A worldwide land grab is occurring, which will give a small group of people effective control over all of the resources that allow social life to flourish. We cannot let this concentration of wealth continue. It has to be stopped. It has to be reversed.

How do we do this when we don't have the money to buy political influence or airtime on TV? The answer is to assemble in public places, as countless people have done since 2011, and then to stay put. The answer is not to have a demonstration and then go home. No. You stay. We stay.

The reproduction of Capital (and society) incurs certain costs, including the costs of education, healthcare, basic human services, caring for the elderly, and dealing with the side effects of alienation in terrible work environments. But Capital tries to shed those costs. Economists call them "externalities," a concept which transforms costs that Capital should bear into costs that others—private individuals—are liable for.

Our political task is to force Capital to bear all of those costs. We should have free, decent education for everybody, which is of equal quality no matter what your income or where you live, whether it is the suburbs or the inner city. The same applies to healthcare and social services; they must all be revolutionized. What we want is not simply the re-establishment of a bureaucratic welfare state, but rather the restoration of the right to decent healthcare and decent caring, to be rendered on a popular basis. Popular assemblies, not politicians, should be the bodies that decide on hospital populations. Meanwhile, indigenous populations in particular are bearing the greatest costs of environmental degradation, even while Capital and industry are most responsible. Capital must be forced to bear those costs as well, but will not do so voluntarily.

It seems to me that these are the two big global issues we face, and it's going to take a global movement to deal with them. But a global movement is emerging, and it is building on movements that have been working at a local level for a long time, including the landless peasant movement in Brazil; the student movement in Chile; the Maoist insurrection in Central India; and the indigenous movement in Bolivia. Since 2011, we have seen many popular movements take over public spaces, demanding an end to austerity and Capitalism. All around the world, there is a growing sense that the system in place does not and cannot work. There is also the sense that it must not be allowed to work any further.

A significant step in that direction is to begin thinking about how to organize political movements that actually have a big, not merely local, impact. The movements documented in this volume succeeded in shutting cities down through tremendous shows of force. And when you shut down a city, you can actually stop capital accumulation.

In order to address the gross inequality of wealth and our manifold environmental dilemmas, we must move from the bottom up. These movements are not guided by some top-down ideology; they are guided from the bottom, and that is a crucial fact. Until we know how to create democracy at the local level and then build that democracy into configurations that remain democratic all the way to the top, we will not be able to implement a truly egalitarian program. Until we start building a truly democratic society, we will continue to see our good ideas co-opted by capital.

Introduction

"They Can't Represent Us!" was a slogan heard ringing through the streets of Russia during the democracy movement of 2012, alongside "They Can't Even Imagine Us!" In Cairo's Tahrir Square, it was *Kefaya!* ("Enough!"); in Athens's Syntagma Square, banners declared, in Spanish, *¡Ya Basta!* ("Enough is Enough!"); in Spain, the banner *¡Democracia Real Ya!* was a unifying call. Each country had its own variation on this theme—"We've Had Enough! We Are Fed Up!" in Turkey; *Eles Não Nos Representam!* in Brazil; "Screw the Troika, the People Must Rule!" in Portugal. Perhaps the one English readers will know best is "We Are the 99 Percent!"—the Occupy movement's slogan throughout the United States.

Something new is happening—something new in content, depth, breadth, and global consistency. Societies around the world are in movement. Since the end of 2010 millions of people have been taking to the streets in cities, towns, and villages—assembling in plazas, occupying parks, buildings, homes, and schools. There is a growing global movement of refusal—and simultaneously, in that refusal, a movement of creation. Millions are shouting "No!" as they manifest alternatives to what is being refused. People from below are rising up, but rather than going toward the top, they are moving, as the Zapatistas suggested, "from below and to the left, where the heart resides." Hierarchy and representational democracy are being rejected, ideologically and by default, and in that rejection mass horizontal assemblies are opening new landscapes with horizons of autonomy and freedom. What that means, what these societies in movement "want," is not always clear, but they are walking, and as they walk they are creating new ways of being, new ways of creating in the crisis. The "want" is tied to the walk—it is intentional, it is a refusal of the crisis while opening new possibilities, still to be determined.

The mobilizations around the globe are taking place in a context in which, for over two decades, the mainstream media and many academics have accused the population in general of no longer being interested in politics, casting them as "apolitical," or even "anti-political."

The idea behind the charge of being "anti-political," of political apathy, is deeply ideological, and goes hand and hand with neoliberalism. It is based on the unbreakable link between "modern democracy" and party-like, structured representation. But the huge mobilizations have proved the media and researchers wrong. They are neither apolitical nor anti-political: they are against what has been called "political" in representative democracy, but has been experienced as anti-democratic. The mobilizations we have seen are laboratories for democracy. Countless people we have spoken to and collaborated with have stated repeatedly that they want nothing to do with *this* system of democracy—and while they reject it they are doing things such as taking over their workplace horizontally, forming assemblies to defend people from eviction, and running alternative healthcare clinics.

This is part of a new wave that is revolutionary in the day-to-day sense of the word. It is also without precedent in terms of its consistency of form, politics, scope, and scale. There have been numerous historical epochs in which something massive and new has swept the globe: the revolutions and revolts of the mid-1800s, the powerful working-class struggles of the early 1900s, and the tremendous political and cultural shifts and anticolonial struggles of the 1960s—to name only three. We believe we have entered another significant historical epoch. This one is marked by an ever-increasing global rejection of representative democracy and, simultaneously, a massive coming together of people who were not previously organized, using direct democratic forms to begin to reinvent ways of being together.

Through use of the internet, and especially Twitter and Facebook, many of today's movements are connected in ways not possible in the past. These new technological forms have helped in both mobilizing and communicating. But this should not be confused with a "social network revolution"—a description academics and many in the media have used.[1] The communication tools have helped, but the essence of what is new in today's movements is the collective construction of new social relationships—creating new spaces and territories. That movements use the media available to them as a way to reach out as far as possible is neither new nor surprising. To label the uprisings "digital" or "Facebook revolutions" is in the best case a misunderstanding and in the worst an attempt to downplay them. The 15-M mobilizations answered this suggestion with the slogan, "Digital indignation—analog resistance."

[handwritten margin note: COLLECTIVE CONSTRUCTION OF NEW SPACES]

This is a book about societies in movement, about changing subjectivities, and about the growing dignity and realization of individual and collective identities of people around the world. In these pages we offer the reader a glimpse into what it feels like to be a part of everyday revolutions. Perhaps the reader has been a part of the process, and this book will share the experiences of other people, in other places—distant but uncannily familiar. We hope to share, inspire, and provoke, as well as grounding some of what has taken place since 2011. This book cannot hope to offer a complete account of the inspiring movements around the globe in this period. But we do hope to contribute to a global conversation on what is shared by people in movements, and thereby to pursue the question of the meaning of democracy. It is a question that should be in the hands of the people, where it is being re-created and experimented with on a daily basis. We believe that this discussion will shed light on the lack of democracy in states and governments around the world.

We, Marina and Dario, have been movement participants throughout our lives, beginning in adolescence, as well as during this historic moment. Here we describe these experiences from the perspective of accompaniment, walking together, and thinking together about the many possible meanings of the diverse actions. In many cases, we have been active participants, but we have chosen to use "we" even in cases where

---

1 Eunice Crook, "Tunisia: The Facebook Revolution," *British Council Voices*, February 11, 2011, blog.britishcouncil.org; John Naughton, "Yet Another Facebook Revolution: Why Are We So Surprised?" *Observer*, January 23, 2011.

we were not, as it reflects a collective identity that belongs to all who fight for a new and free world.

Official history, as Howard Zinn perceptively reminds us in the various People's History series, is told by the "victors"—meaning those who end up holding economic and political power. They have no interest in telling the history of people taking their lives into their own hands, and instead rewrite history in their own interests, emptying it of agency and content, editing the past to justify the present, in the hope of conditioning the future. In the same spirit invoked by Zinn's "people's history," this book shares the voices of people in the movements, who are best placed to explain their actions and motivations.

The collapse of Lehman Brothers in the US in September 2008 triggered a chain reaction that provoked a global financial and economic crisis. Banks had packed bad credit into pleasant-sounding non-transparent funds and sold them on international financial markets, promising huge returns. After years of vertiginous growth, property prices had stagnated and debtors could no longer pay their mortgages. The nominal value of the funds grew until the bubble burst. In order to avoid more bank collapses of the Lehman type, the Western economies bailed out the banks, rendering private debt public. Reduced tax revenues, massive bank bailouts, and economic austerity all deepened the crisis, turning it into one of the worst in many decades.

The crisis that began in the industrialized West has deepened into one of the worst in decades.[2] Millions of people around the world have been forced from their homes and lost access to healthcare, millions are malnourished who were not previously—and that is not to mention the millions of young people who now rightly believe that they have no real future if the movements do not succeed.

It was against this backdrop that tens of millions around the world, led by the same young people being told they have no future, have taken to the streets in refusal. Their shouts of "No!" and *Kefaya!* represent a refusal that is just the first step—the first word. These same millions have turned

---

2   Again, this is not a book about crises and how they are interpreted—but we do have to say that the results of these crises, the human costs, are ones that are absolutely unnecessary.

their backs on the system and states that have turned their backs on them. As they refuse, turning their backs on the state, they face one another. It is in this face-to-face encounter that the recognition of possible futures arises—has arisen. Democracy is at the heart of both the new social creation and the refusal. The "No!" is not a shout of protest, but a *"No" of fear?* refusal to be a part of the economic, political, social, and cultural crises we found ourselves in. But, at the same time, this "No!" also marks the beginning of new attempts to create alternatives to the crisis. In some cases, it was an ideological choice or position—a rejection of the state or forms of hierarchical powers; but for millions of others it is the result of a lack of alternatives. The people refuse to pay for the crisis.

For this reason, the emergence of the new movements has been seen by many as a rupture with a past way of doing things. In this break with old forms of organization and social relationships also lies the creation of new ways of being and organizing, of shifts in power relationships within movements and society at large, especially in relation to institutions. This break is at once an immediate, seemingly spontaneous reaction, and also the result of a long accumulation of frustration and anger. It is not a knee-jerk reaction. In fact, this same framework has been used to describe the experience of being part of a movement in the past—from the emergence of the Zapatistas onto the world scene in 1994, with the declaration *¡Ya Basta!*, to 500 years of colonialism and domination, to the popular rebellion in Argentina, which sang on December 19 and 20, 2001, *¡Que Se Vayan Todos!* ("They all must go!").

Each of the movements we discuss in this book arises from different regional contexts, but in our participation in and conversations with movements around the world, we found many common characteristics. The majority of people mobilized had not been politically active before. The mobilizations around the world were all started from the grassroots, not by traditional political actors such as unions or left parties. Governments sometimes responded quickly with repressive measures, as in Turkey and Brazil in June 2013—though in other places, like the US, Spain, and Greece, occupations of hundreds of plazas were allowed to exist for months before violent repression and evictions began.

Within occupied spaces, people then organized new, internal forms of conflict resolution, from the mediation group in Occupy Wall Street to the "security" teams in Egypt and Greece, and a group with a very similar intention in Spain, called Respect. If you were to compare scenes from Tahrir Square in Cairo, Syntagma Square in Athens, Zuccotti Park in New York, and Puerta del Sol in Madrid, to name only a few of the thousands of gatherings, you would see very similar occupations, with elements including free libraries, child care and health services, food, legal support, media, and art. The forms of organization and relationships created in these spaces, all using direct democracy, are peculiar to the needs of each occupation, but at the same time so much alike that they constitute a new global phenomenon.

Each of these movements has brought democracy into question. They refuse to privilege economic interests over political and social ones (or even to accept the conventional separation between economic, political, and social spheres). A uniting agenda is that of challenging rule by politicians: we can govern ourselves. Movement participants around the world believe that representative democracies are not democratic, and that established politicians and political institutions should not be trusted. Instead, most of the new movements practice forms of direct democracy in public spaces, from Tahrir Square in Egypt to the plazas and parks of Spain, Greece, Europe, and the United States. In this way, the political, economic, and social spheres are no longer separated. In fact, this practice is grounded in a long global history that we will recount in Chapter 1, incorporating many of the movements of the 1960s and early 1970s, as well as the Mexican Zapatistas, who emerged in 1994. Nevertheless, this embrace of direct and participatory democracy is one of the most strikingly novel aspects of today's global movements.

Related to this is the fact that the new movements do not look to others to solve their problems, but together are finding ways to take back—recuperate—what they consider to be theirs. In the United States and Spain, one way in which this is being done is through foreclosure defense: the disruption of auction proceedings and the occupation of peoples' homes to prevent eviction orders from being carried out. In Greece, some neighborhood assemblies are organizing the blocking of cash registers, so that people do not have to pay the newly imposed cost of healthcare. Sometimes the result of this is that laws are changed or rules modified, as has occurred in a few municipalities in Spain where the local governments have ordered the police not to carry out evictions—or in a few neighborhoods in Athens, where the local governments have placed a hold on the collection of new taxes in response to neighborhood assemblies' mass refusal to pay. Recuperation is a manifestation of this new way in which the movements are looking at power and autonomy: taking back what is ours. Instead of articulating demands and expecting institutional power to react, people are constructing popular power—much as the Landless Workers' Movement (Movimento dos Trabalhadores Rurais Sem Terra—MST) in Brazil did beginning in the 1980s, when they took over land to create new societies with their own schools and clinics, and growing their own crops. In 2001, Argentinian workers came together in recuperating their workplaces, using the slogan of the MST ("Occupy, Resist, Produce"), and putting their workplaces back to work using horizontal forms of organization. The fact that they do not wait for governments or institutions to respond to them does not mean that no demands are ever made; in fact, many of the movements demand back from the state what they consider to be theirs anyway from their years of labor.

Fourth, the new horizontal social relationships being created are generally forming in public spaces, including neighborhood assemblies, street corners, plazas, and parks. Though this is a relatively new phenomenon in Europe (where, admittedly, there is a long tradition of gathering in public spaces), it goes back decades in Latin America, where those who were not based in workplaces, as was increasingly the case, organized mass protests, often by occupying and blocking major traffic arteries. As the unemployed in Argentina, the landless in Brazil, and indigenous people in Bolivia, Colombia, and Ecuador alike occupied and shut something down, they simultaneously opened something else up, organizing horizontal assemblies and creating prefigurative survival structures for necessities such as food, medicine, child support, and training. These new spaces of autonomous construction are often called *territorios* ("territories")—invoking a new landscape that is conceptual as well as physical.

In many contemporary cases, and especially in big cities, the occupation of public spaces is also a response to the neoliberal privatization of that space—a response insisting that cities belong to the people and not to capital. For example, Turkey's 2013 uprising had its origins in the occupation of Gezi Park, near Taksim Square, in the heart of Istanbul, in opposition to a plan to transform the area into a shopping district as part of a massive urban renewal project. Over time the movements in the plazas began to decentralize—to re-territorialize. Since the intention is to transform not just the occupied plaza but society as a whole, the movements have gradually shifted into spheres more directly related to the lives of their participants, such as neighborhoods and workplaces, where local needs can be addressed. Generally, this is when the media and many on the institutional left tend to declare the movements "dead," but in our view this is no reliable guide to the life of a movement.

This book describes a few of the movements that have been active since 2011, explaining how they have rejected and reinvented the concept of democracy along the way. It is neither a work of straightforward oral history nor a book that describes or explains what is taking place. It is filled with the voices of those involved in the various movements, supported by the elaboration of historical contexts, and it shares the hopes and dreams of its authors.

In Chapter 1, we outline some of the main conceptual categories around which many of the movements can be organized—concepts such as rupture, horizontal relationships, recuperation, and democracy. We then delve a little more deeply into these concepts, and ground them descriptively in similar movements over the past two decades in Latin America—such as that making use of relationship of *horizontalidad* in Argentina, or the assemblies in Chiapas and Oaxaca, Mexico. Chapter 2 is dedicated to the concept of democracy. It gives an account of representative and liberal democracy under capitalism, demonstrating that it was never designed to be democratic, if that term is taken to denote "the rule of the people." It then illustrates some of the contemporary and historical experiments with real, meaningful forms of direct and participatory democracy. Chapters 3 to 5 explore, respectively, the movement in Greece, the 15-M (May 15) movement in Spain, and Occupy! in the US. We spent much of the period from late 2011 until early 2013 participating in the movements discussed, and communicating with those involved.

Finally, we ground the experiences of the new movements and their experiments with democracy in Argentina (Chapter 6) and Venezuela

(Chapter 7). Both chapters are based on interviews we conducted separately while each living intermittently in both countries, from approximately 2002 to 2009. Additional interviews were conducted in 2012 and 2013.

This book does not provide a complete picture, of course, but forms part of a much larger and more inspiring one. We have been organizing locally and traveling globally for some years in order to discuss the emergence of these alternative forms of organization. In 2013 we paused briefly to compile these pages. We have been able to focus on just a few geographic locations, and explain in each of the chapters that follow why we have made the choices we have. If you do not find your own experience recounted here, that is for reasons other than the value of the particular movement you have been involved in—whether in Portugal, Russia, Italy, Iceland, Ireland, the UK, or elsewhere.

One of the many beautiful aspects of the new movements is the multiplicity of paths envisaged and created. There is no single static or predetermined goal, but instead a process of walking toward desires, and manifesting the desired future in day-to-day relationships. This is not to be confused with taking the process and momentary social relationships as themselves the goal—rather, as the movement develops, as assemblies take place, people involved in the process change; and as individuals change, the groups and territories of construction change. In the 1960s, Latin American movements grounded in Liberation Theology used the framework of *Hacer el Camino al Andar* ("Making the Road by Walking"). The Zapatista communities speak of a similar process as *Caminar Preguntando* ("To Walk Asking Questions"). We hope others throughout the world will also record oral accounts of what has been taking place, and find ways to share these stories—our stories—as widely as possible.

CHAPTER ONE

Grounding the "New" Globally

W alter Benjamin wrote of memory and history as a "secret rendez-vous between past generations and our own."[1] The secret is not something known but not told; rather, it is a reflection of its newness to us, as lived experience. Our history and memory are "secrets" kept from us. Many of the "new" practices we describe in these pages in fact have long histories, especially in Latin America. This does not mean that they copied Latin American movements, only that their needs and desires are similar. We see the new global movements since 2010 as a second wave of anti-representational movements, following the first wave of Latin American movements of the 1990s and early 2000s.

We can see this "secret rendezvous" in many of the concepts and terms the movements use to describe themselves. These include: territory, assembly, rupture, popular power, horizontalism, *autogestión* ("self-administration"), and protagonism. Examples of each term may be drawn from various Latin American communities of struggle, from the spreading of *horizontalidad* with the popular rebellion in Argentina, and the concept of "territory" having currency in Bolivia and Mexico, to the construction of "popular power" in the Consejos Comunales in Venezuela, and the vision of interconnected human diversity articulated

---

1 Walter Benjamin, "Geschichtsphilosophische Thesen," in Walter Benjamin, *Zur Kritik der Gewalt und andere Aufsätze* (Frankfurt: Suhrkamp, 1965), p. 88.

in the call for "one world in which many worlds fit" by the indigenous Zapatista communities in Chiapas, Mexico.

This linguistic rediscovery is a part of the process of the people finding their own voices in the new usages of direct democracy. As people recuperate the voices they did not have under representational forms of democracy, they also rediscover themselves. The movements recognize this new agency and protagonism, and name it. This claim to voice and language is part of the claim to real democracy. Today's movements are finding or creating places where the new meets the old, offering spaces of *encuentro*—encounter and meeting—where new and emerging social relationships mix creatively with many hundreds, if not thousands, of years of collective experimentation with the various forms of relating, rebellion, and struggle.

RUPTURE

Imagine this scene. *Families sitting at home before their television sets, on an evening that began the way so many others had: what to watch, what to make for dinner, the regular nightly questions. Then a TV newscaster appears on every channel and announces that, from that moment on, all bank accounts are frozen. The economic crisis has fully arrived. People sit in silence, staring at the TV. They wait. Suddenly, outside the window:* tac!—tac tac!—tac tac tac! *Families run to their windows and balconies. The sound comes from people banging spoons and spatulas on pans—the sound of the* cacerolazo.[2] *The sound becomes a wave, and the wave begins to flood the streets.*

The government does not know what to do. It declares a state of emergency in the morning, falling back on what has always been done: law and order. But the people break with the past, no longer staying at home in fear but filling the streets with even more bodies and sounds. The tac tac tac turns into a song—one of both rejection and affirmation. ¡Que se vayan todos! *("They all must go!"). It is a rupture with obedience, with not being*

---

2   *Cacerola* literally means "kitchen pan," and the *cacerolazo* is the collective banging of pots and pans. This tactic has now spread to the student struggle in Quebec, as well as to New York and other cities around the world.

together, with not knowing one another. It is a rupture that cracks open history, whereupon vast new histories are created.

A rupture is a break that can come from many places, always shifting both the ways people organize, including power relationships, and the ways people see things. Sometimes the detonator is external, like an earthquake or economic collapse, which can inspire thousands, even hundreds of thousands, to come together and help one another—especially when formal institutions of power also collapse. At other times, the rupture is facilitated by movements, such as the Zapatistas or Occupy. Whichever is the case, people look to one another and begin to try and find solutions together, often doing so in ways that are more *effective* and definitely more empowering—*affective*—than if the rupture had come from an external source.

In the movements that we describe, which arose in 2010 and 2011, rupture came upon us seemingly as a surprise, though in many places around the world there was some organization in advance. This included the New York City General Assembly organizing throughout the summer in response to the *Adbusters* call, and ¡Democracia real ya! in Spain meeting and gathering others for the first assemblies, before the occupation of Puerta del Sol—yet not imagining that there would be such a lasting and massive occupation. Many movement participants around the world in 2012 used the same language to describe what took place with the Plaza and Park occupations—the same word, even, translated everywhere as "rupture." From *ruptura* in Spanish (literally "rupture") to *kefaya* ("enough") in Arabic.

HORIZONTALIDAD, HORIZONTALISM, HORIZONTAL

A bonfire is burning at the intersection of Corrientes and Federico Lacroze in the city of Buenos Aires. More than one hundred people of all ages are gathered around it, some still in work clothes, others in housecoats, T-shirts, and flip-flops. The noise of the city hums in the background, but around the bonfire it is quiet.

An older woman is discussing how to organize the upcoming weeks' free medical service, which will be offered by a doctor from another neighborhood assembly. Where will the medical services take place, and how will they get the necessary supplies? The health of the neighborhood children is at stake.

People take turns speaking. Some talk over others, and the facilitator is often ignored. Yet all manage to speak and to be heard. This is the quiet insurgent noise of horizontalidad. *Eventually the group reaches a consensus and the quiet is overtaken with song—the same song sung on the first days of the popular rebellion.* Oh, que se vayan todos, que no quede ni uno solo (they all must go, not one should remain). *This is* horizontalidad *in Argentina.*

Participating in any of the assemblies taking place throughout the world generally involves standing or sitting in a circle, with a handful of facilitators, and speaking and listening in turn, observing general guidelines and principles of unity, and then discussing whatever issue has been raised until a consensus is reached. If one were to ask a participant about this process, they would most likely explain the need to listen to one another, feeling that in society they are excluded from meaningful participation, and perhaps they might use the language of direct or participatory democracy. In these conversations, some version of the horizontal often will arise, whether as the description or desired goal.

Horizontalidad, horizontality, and horizontalism are words that encapsulate the ideas upon which many of the social relationships in the new global movements are grounded. The idea that they express is based on affective and trust-based politics. It is a dynamic social relationship that represents a break with the logic of representation and vertical ways of organizing. This does not mean that structures do not emerge, as they do with mass assemblies and autonomous governance, but the structures that emerge are non-representational and non-hierarchical. (Spokescouncils, the Zapatista form of self-governance, and the communes in Venezuela are three examples of this.) But because social relationships are still deeply marked by capitalism and hierarchy—especially in terms of how people relate to one another over economic resources, gender, race, and access to information—*horizontalidad* has to be understood as an open-ended social process, a positive act of seeking, rather than a final end. It would be an illusion to think that a "happy island of horizontalism" could be created in the middle of the sea of capitalism.

The word *horizontalidad* was first heard in December 2001, in the days after the popular rebellion in Argentina. No one recalls where it came from or who might have used it first. It was a new word, and emerged from a new practice of people coming together and solving their problems without anyone being in charge or asserting power over one another. Significantly, the experience of *horizontalidad* has remained prevalent among the middle classes organized into neighborhood assemblies, the unemployed organizing in neighborhoods, and workers taking over their workplaces. *Horizontalidad*, with its rejection of hierarchy and political parties, became the norm. In 2012, the assumption that people often began with in organizing is that any new movement or struggle will be horizontal. This can be seen today in the hundreds of assemblies up and down the Andes fighting against international mining companies, and the thousands of *bachilleratos*—alternative high school diploma programs organized by former assembly participants, housed in recuperated workplaces.

But this process is not without challenges, as new movements aspiring to horizontal forms of organization have begun to discover. In Spain, Greece, the UK, and the United States, participants have noted that simply naming the practice is not enough to conjure the behavior; treating it as an identity—"I am horizontal" or "We are horizontal"—obfuscates the fact that *horizontalidad* is only made real in practice, and that any competition that develops between groups over who is more horizontal necessarily reproduces a hierarchical structure. But this is part of the learning process—we make the road by walking.

PODER POPULAR—POPULAR POWER

Sala de Batalla Alicia Benítez is the community center of the Eje de MACA commune under construction in the Greater Caracas area. The neighborhood is Petare, which is one of Latin America's largest poor neighborhoods, and thirty communities organized in communal councils have united to create a commune; all decide from below, in their local assemblies, what to do in their neighborhoods. The barrios—the informal and marginalized neighborhoods—make up about 70 percent of Caracas. Infrastructure in the barrios is precarious; they lack basic services, there is little to no public space, and most of the dwellings are built into the hillside and connected to one another through unevenly built narrow staircases and walkways.

A government employee has arrived, offering to build a place to store and sell food at far below market price by eliminating intermediaries and speculation.

"Look," says Petare resident Pablo, "one thing has to be clear, we decided in the community that we will administer this place."[3]

Yusmeli also chimes in. "We also have to be able to sell other food, for example by connecting directly with producers."[4]

The government official agrees. He will bring maps to discuss the construction with the community. The commune already has two enterprises of social communal property: a passenger transport system with six four-wheel-drive jeeps, and a center for the distribution of liquid gas for cooking. Most of the communal councils have small community enterprises such as bakeries, cobblers, and even small agricultural production. To set up the communal enterprises, first all the communal councils held assemblies and discussed what they needed most. Then they held workshops with a facilitator from the Ministry of Communes and discussed the project in detail, including the organizational and decision-making structure for the enterprises. The result was approved by the neighborhood assemblies of the communal councils.

Popular power is the capacity of the marginalized and oppressed to organize and coordinate structures to govern their own lives, parallel to capitalist or state-run institutions and services such as schools, hospitals, and decision-making bodies, but in ways that do not reflect the logic of capital. Unlike historical revolutionary socialist movements, these groups—first in Latin American and then beyond—see these autonomous structures, not as transitional phenomena on the way to the "takeover" of the state and the consolidation of the revolutionary party. Understood as both a path and a goal, popular power is the central element in building a new society in the shadow of the old structures.

The forms that popular power can take differ radically. Anything that enables the people to administer aspects of their lives on their own, and gives them the power to make their own decisions and improve their own

---

3 Pablo Arteaga, Comuna de MACA, interview with Dario Azzellini, Caracas, Venezuela, August 8, 2011.

4 Yusmeli Patiño, interview with Dario Azzellini, Caracas, Venezuela, August 8, 2011.

autonomous processes for constructing new social relations, can be seen as part of popular power. It can be expressed through the creation of a community soup kitchen, the recuperation of a workplace, or the formation of a network of community-controlled radio stations. It can also been seen in new forms of local self-administration—a local assembly of people debating their own needs, or an assembly discussing public initiatives and taking a collective position on them.

In Venezuela, the Communal Councils are the most advanced mechanism of local self-organization and popular power. They are non-representative bodies with direct democratic participation, parallel to the elected representative institutions. In 2005, the Communal Councils began forming from below. In January 2006, President Chávez adopted the initiative and began to help it spread. A law of Communal Councils followed in April 2006. The Communal Councils encompass between 150 and 400 families in urban areas, twenty families in rural zones, and ten families in indigenous regions. In 2013 there were approximately 44,000 Communal Councils in Venezuela.

Given the exceptional situation in Venezuela, with a government partly engaged in supporting forms of popular power, popular organizations have a different and stronger relationship with the state than in most other countries. A central question is whether structures of popular power can maintain their own spaces for debate, decision, and construction, or whether they will become co-opted by the state and lose their own agency and agenda. This is an ongoing tension in the process of construction of a new society in Venezuela. The government and its institutions are simultaneously both supportive and an obstacle. And the relationship between institutions and self-organization is characterized by cooperation and conflict. Institutions tend to consolidate and expand their power; by institutional logic, the development and growth of parallel powers and structures is seen as a threat to their existence. In Venezuela this contradiction is especially sharp, with large segments of the institutions of power supporting the autonomous development of the movements, while other large sectors resist this development, even creating obstacles and trying to control them.

In today's movements, the construction of popular power takes many forms. As of May 2012, there were forty-five neighborhood assemblies in

will the state overtake systems of popular power and they become successful?

Athens, each focusing on the needs of its local population (for instance, barter networks and direct exchanges with agricultural producers and consumers), as well as on broader issues such as refusal to pay a new housing tax charged together with the electricity bills. This refusal has become more coordinated citywide, partly through the weekly "assembly of assemblies," in which all the neighborhoods participate, and as a result a number of municipalities have now declared a "hold" on the increase of this tax. This collective organization within and between neighborhoods—establishing what people need directly rather than asking for an external authority to take action—is a demonstration of popular power.

POPULAR POWER doesn't rely on authority

ASSEMBLIES AND ENCUENTROS

In 2007, in an autonomously controlled community, a Junta de Buen Gobierno (Good Government Junta) facilitated the first ever Zapatista Women's Encuentro. The indigenous rebel women explained, among other things, the following:

> *We are going to speak, we women Zapatistas, with* compañeras *from Mexico and the world, and you will be able to ask questions about how we organize ourselves, the women Zapatistas, more directly with women. We are going to ask that the* compañeros *[men Zapatistas] help us with logistical questions.* Compañeros *from Mexico and the world may also come to hear us, but remain silent, the same as our* compañeros.
>
> *This Third Encuentro, as it will be especially of the women Zapatistas, will be dedicated to Comandanta Ramona, and will take her name. Thus its name is this: Third Encuentro of the Zapatista Peoples with the Peoples of the World: Comandanta Ramona and the Women Zapatistas.[5]*

And that is what it was—a gathering of women from around the world, with hundreds of women Zapatistas presenting and discussing what they had been creating together for fourteen years. The space was open and free,

---

5   "Convocatoria al 3º Encuentro, por la Compañera Everilda, candidata al CCRI," Zezta Internazional, August 8, 2007, zeztainternazional.ezln.org.

a true gathering and meeting of women from around the globe, talking about what had been impossible but was now possible.

An integral part of creating direct democracy and *horizontalidad* is the moments of gathering, of intentional coming together in such a way that all can speak and be heard, and so that decisions can be made. For autonomous movements in Latin America and the globalization movement, an assembly is a place where participants seek common ground. Consensus is sometimes the goal, but not always; the most fundamental thing is that agreement is sought in a directly democratic manner, meaning that attempts are made for all voices to be heard, using various tools for speaking, as well as active listening, to be as open and inclusive as possible.

This is often achieved through the use of facilitators who have been trained in whatever democratic form the group has chosen, though sometimes it is more of a collective effort, with the group taking responsibility for facilitation and participation. At other times, a group has a prior agreement for forms of participation, such as the establishment of a speaking order that alternates between male- and female-identified people speaking during assemblies. Occupy Wall Street used a modified speakers' list ("stack"), in which the list of speakers changed so that those people more "historically marginalized" got moved up higher on the speakers' list; in many other groups, a person can only speak once until all those who wish to speak have also spoken.

But even seeking consensus is a flexible process of decision-making that is modified in each location to reflect the needs of the people, sometimes referring to a synthesis of ideas based on all opinions shared during the gathering, and at other times arrived at through voting, as was the case in many of the neighborhood assemblies in Argentina.

Another term that originated in Latin America and in Spanish, and is now used around the world is *encuentro*. Though it also signals a coming together, generally with horizontal relational forms, it is unlike an assembly in being unconcerned with reaching a decision or consensus; the gathering, the process, is the end. The use of *encuentro* became more widespread following the Zapatistas' First Intergalactic Encuentro for Humanity and Against Neoliberalism, in 1996. During this *encuentro*, thousands of people met in liberated Zapatista territory to share their

ENCUENTRO: gathering without a necessary consensus — a moment just to speak and be heard experiences and learn what the Zapatistas were doing, as well as to strengthen international solidarity with the autonomous communities.

The Zapatista concept of *un mundo donde quepan muchos mundos* ("one world in which many worlds fit") has also been brought into the meaning of *encuentro*, so that, rather than being thought of as a place to make a single unifying program, a gathering is instead a place where all can come together in their diversity.

In some Latin American countries—especially Venezuela, but also Colombia, Bolivia, Argentina, Guatemala, and Peru—the term *encuentro de saberes* ("knowledge encounter") is widely used for gatherings to exchange experience and knowledge without creating a hierarchy from the different forms of knowledge. For example, in an *encuentro de saberes ancestrales indígenas y campesinos de agroecología* ("ancestral indigenous and peasants' knowledge encounter on organic farming"), indigenous people and peasants, as well as agronomists and ecologists, might take part and share their knowledge. In an *encuentro de saberes pedagógicos* ("pedagogical knowledge encounter"), teachers, academics, and employees of institutions in the field of education might discuss and share their knowledge with parents, students, and activists engaged in popular education.

RECUPERATE

Located on Avenue Callao, at the corner of Corrientes, in the center of Buenos Aires, the Hotel Bauen could not be more centrally located. It is a five-minute walk to the Congressional building, across from which is the school and bookstore for the Madres de la Plaza de Mayo. Corrientes is one of the main avenues in Buenos Aires, known for all its shops and restaurants, and this section of Corrientes is also home to many bookstores, theaters, and art centers. It is a perfect central place for an occupation, and even better for a recuperation.

When the workers of Hotel Bauen took the plywood off the lobby window and entered the hotel, their intention was to have the entire hotel up and running within the year. Formerly a four-star hotel, the Hotel Bauen has more than 200 rooms, two swimming pools, a massive bronze-filled lobby that includes a grand piano, a full theater, two restaurants, two cafés, two bars, a small print shop, and countless offices and other facilities.

The owners had laid off the remaining workers and shut the doors to the hotel in late December 2001 after months of staff downsizing, and almost immediately a few of the unemployed workers had met with workers from some of the other recuperated workplaces and the network of the National Movement for Recuperated Workplaces (MNER). Together they made the decision to take over their workplace and run it in common. They began meeting more regularly, and gathered a few dozen of the previous workers to join in the process. In March 2003 they took back their workplace, together with hundreds of supporters from other workplaces, recuperated and not, as well as neighborhood assemblies and the community at large. There are now more than 150 workers running the Hotel Bauen.

The night of the takeover was one filled with tension and fear, but at the same time incredibly joyful. People were ready to fight and resist, but they were simultaneously giddy. Many dozens of workers and neighbors stood and sat around, many chain-smoking, waiting to see if the scouts had any news of police movement. Nothing, nothing, nothing. Hours passed. At one point, a man sat at the piano and played a song. It was an unforgettable moment, the sort of event that can create chills even now, thinking back on it. Years later, on another trip to Argentina and the Hotel Bauen, there in the hotel music room we found the very same man who had played the piano for all of us in the occupied lobby. He had changed a little physically; his hair whiter—the result, he jokes, of "all the struggle in fighting for the hotel." But his energy and passion were the same. That night, as we all sat waiting in the lobby, with no electricity except for the few lanterns people had brought with them, Guillermo sat at the piano and began to play a tune, which at that point was little-known. It was a song he had written—a song that is now known throughout the country:

> *We are the present and the future*
> *To resist and occupy,*
> *The factory will not be closed*
> *We are going to raise it together*
> *The factory will not be closed*
> *We are going to raise it together.*
> *To resist and resist and occupy*
> *To resist and resist and produce.*

The "new" global movements are known for occupying public space, but the idea is not just to take it over, but to make it useful.

In the 1980s, the Brazilian MST movement inaugurated the slogan "Occupy, Resist, Produce"; over the past decade, it has become the battle cry for movements recuperating workplaces across Latin America. Argentina now boasts more than 300 worker-recuperated workplaces (*empresas recuperadas por sus trabajadores*), including traditional factories such as metal, ceramics, and print shops, alongside other workplaces such as grocery stores, medical clinics, daily newspapers, schools, bakeries, and hotels. The process of workplace recuperations in Argentina arose from economic necessity and a total lack of response from bosses, management, owners, and the state. Workers simply took the situation into their own hands.

Worker recuperations have been occurring throughout Latin America, with dozens in Brazil, Uruguay, and Venezuela, and a few in Colombia and Mexico. The organizational structure they adopt varies, from processes of worker control using directly democratic assemblies to ones that resemble more traditional cooperatives with less direct participation in day-to-day decisions. During recent years it could be seen how the practice of workplace recuperations made its unexpected appearance in other countries. In 2011, Chicago saw the recuperation of Republic Windows and Doors, which reopened as New Era Windows under workers' control in early 2013. In the same year the factory for industrial cleaning products, Vio.Me, in the Greek city of Thessaloniki, began production as a recuperated factory under workers' control. Only one year earlier, a number of our Greek interview subjects told us they could not imagine workplace recuperations taking place in Greece. Since then, further recuperations have happened or are under discussion among workers in Spain and Italy.

"Recuperation" has also been used in a broader sense, in relation to workplaces or geographic spaces. In Mexico and Venezuela, for example, movements speak of the recuperation of memory, history, knowledge, and dignity. Before the march of 1,111 unarmed Zapatistas to Mexico City in 1997, Subcomandante Marcos declared on behalf of the Indigenous Revolutionary Clandestine Committee General Command of the Zapatista Army of National Liberation: "We are going to recuperate national history for the ones from below. Today it is hijacked by the ones governing, to be killed and buried under the economic indices. We will shout out: Never again a Mexico without us!"[6]

But rather than being a nostalgic return to an idealized past, the recuperation of memory and history is a collective process meant to enrich the present and build a common future. In many places in Latin America, especially poor urban areas, the recuperation of the history of one's own neighborhood has often been the starting point in the construction of community and collective consciousness.

PROTAGONISM AND SOCIAL PROTAGONISM

I think the best lesson we, and especially the young people, have learned from the Water War in Cochabamba is that it is possible to change things without having to follow anyone, without depending on the political parties, without needing political parties to mediate. For eight days, every sign and even symbol of the state disappeared in Cochabamba. The army was barracked and the police asked the people for permission to leave the police station. There was no political party, there was not any leader telling anyone what to do. Nobody was telling people what they should do or had to do. That is where people really began to feel that they were the real protagonist in this collective action, one based on a collective horizon, but also built together, in common . . . and that we were doing everything among equals.[7]

The idea of protagonism, as it has been used by movements over the past two decades, is strongly related to social agency, and therefore to direct democracy and participation. In Venezuela, protagonism became more prominent over the course of the 1990s, when movements stopped asking political parties and institutions to solve the problems they faced and began struggling for direct participation and control in their neighborhoods.

People in the movements and neighborhood organizations speak

---

6   Communiqué, August 8, 1997.

7   Oscar Olivera, from the Coordinadora del Agua, interview with Marina Sitrin, Cochabamaba, Bolivia, 2007.

regularly about the difference in their participation now, feeling that they were previously not involved in, or allowed access to, the processes and politics that affect their lives. They now call themselves protagonists because they fought and won their political agency; but this also means that people have to organize in order to make things happen. People's self-identification as protagonists—especially those without any previous organizing experience—became widespread during the first years of the Chávez government, through government social programs called Missions, in which self-organization of the population was a central element. One example was the literacy campaign Yo Sí Puedo, organized with support from Cubans, who helped train volunteer facilitators. The literacy process took place in communities where people who desired basic literacy education organized to make it happen. Within the first two years, 1.5 million people achieved literacy. Overcoming marginalization through their own protagonism led people to organize themselves around other questions concerning their own lives and communities. Meanwhile, through the active participation of grassroots organizations, a new constitution was drafted in 1999 in which Venezuela was defined as a "participatory and protagonistic democracy," to be distinguished from its liberal and representative form.

In Argentina, the terms "protagonism" and "social protagonism" took root after the popular rebellion of 2001. They refer to the newfound agency people felt in acting together to reject long-established patterns of representational politics. Cándido, a worker from a recuperated print shop in Buenos Aires, once explained in a conversation that he is not "political," but rather a "protagonist." Many in the autonomous movements in Argentina do not call themselves activists, but rather "protagonists." It is an understanding based on the experience of various relationships, rather than an overarching theory. Through this collective protagonism also arises the need for new ways of speaking of the *nosotros* ("we/us") and *nuestro* ("our"), as they relate to the *yo* ("I"). As each individual changes, that change has an effect on the group, thus changing the group, and as the group changes, this change is then reflected on the individuals, creating new ways of thinking about the individual self and collective selves.

When workers in the recuperated workplace movements in Argentina and Venezuela refer to the workplaces as "theirs," they do not invoke the notion of private property, but a broader collective sense of ownership.

The workers of Zanón in Argentina—now Factory Without a Boss (Fábrica Sin Patrón, or FaSinPat)—say, *Zanón Es del Pueblo* ("Zanon is of the people"), meaning that it is the community mobilized that makes Zanón exist, and that it exists for the people.

AFFECTIVE AND TRUST-BASED CONSTRUCTION

We can have really difficult discussions and disagree, but we all stay part of the organization. We try to love each other. It's difficult. Imagine being in a neighborhood like La Matanza, which is full of really tough men, men who have lived, and still live, a violent, macho life, and we're talking about new loving relationships. No, it isn't easy, not even to talk about, let alone practice. This is part of our changing culture, and as we change, we notice how much we really need to.[8]

The current global movements are not only attempting to create the most horizontal and directly democratic spaces, but are also creating new subjectivities. A part of the grounding for these changing relationships is a base of trust and a growing feeling of care and mutual responsibility, with the goal of building a movement and society based in a relationship of mutual trust and concern for the other and for the collective.[9]

In Argentina, the movements began speaking of *política afectiva* ("affective politics") as a way of discussing these new forms of relationships, which they saw as necessary to building a new society. This was not without challenges. Organizing a movement based in love met with some resistance from the many people who do not take the concept of love seriously in a movement, particularly in a macho society. Nevertheless, many participants saw affective politics as one of the most important foundations of what was being created in their movement, and this was especially true in the movements of the unemployed, where participants live in the same neighborhoods, know

---

8   Toty Flores, from the Unemployed Workers Movement La Matanza, interview with Marina Sitrin, outside Buenos Aires, Argentina, January 2004.

9   This is not to be confused with creating intentional communities "outside of society," such as alternative communes, or with creating relationships that are not linked to the idea of acting together for the transformation of society.

one another's histories and families, and generally share similar life challenges, from a lack of basic resources to police repression.

This does not mean one needs to be friends with all of the people in the movement, or that politics is only engaged in with people for whom one has affection. However, in the recuperated workplaces or the unemployed movements in Argentina, it is certainly the case that those workplaces where people have the longest history of working together, and then reflect on their close relationships to one another, are also the ones that have seen the most militant resistance to the police, and to eviction attempts. Participants often reflect on how their basis of trust and affect is what helps to keep them going in difficult times of organizing and struggle.

Affect and emotion are too often relegated to the politics of gender and identity, and thus not seen as "serious" theory or as a potentially revolutionary part of politics. This argument denies the fact that responsibility for the other and solidarity are basic conditions of a future society not grounded in capitalist principles. In fact, relegating affective politics to the feminine realm simply reinforces gendered roles in patriarchal societies. Affective politics is not an expression of "maternal responsibility," but a social responsibility to build a new society based on cooperation and mutual aid rather than competition.

At the same time, we cannot write about affect-based politics without acknowledging the political role of anger, rage, and even hatred. It is not only the love or affect for one another and for society that drives organizing, but also an anger and hatred for those who make a free society impossible, and who create the conditions of total desperation and crisis for many millions around the world. So, while affect is our creative base, it is also tied to a rage against those who work to prevent our freedom.

AUTOGESTIÓN

San Luís Acatlan is one of ten municipalities formed by sixty-five communities that comprise the region controlled by the Policía Comunitaria (Community Police). It is also located in Guerrero, one of the poorest, most violent, and most repressive states in Mexico. Most of the communities are indigenous—Mixtec, Tlapanec, and Nahua—but there are also seven Mestizo communities that have joined together with the Community Police. Beginning in the early 1990s in response to government and police indifference to widespread assault and armed robbery, community members began organizing and coordinating for their own safety, and have policed themselves ever since.

For this reason, communities supporting the Community Police have been under constant attack by state authorities. The army has moved in several times to disarm the police, and community police officers have been arrested on false charges. Their goal was to put a halt to the communities' self-organized police. But since the inception of the Community Police, the crime rate has decreased 95 percent in the region controlled by the community, which includes approximately 100,000 people. And this was achieved by just 600 women and men serving as police officers, armed only with small rifles and without any sophisticated technology, or even patrol cars. All police are accountable to the community—officers are elected by them directly, and are only able to serve for a limited time.

After the people began running their own police force, they then found the need to create their own justice system. They founded one based on re-socialization, and not on retribution and vengeance. In the case of minor offenses, if someone breaks the law they are judged by people in their region who have been elected in local assemblies. If it is a more serious offense, then there is a regional body that judges the accused person.

Those found guilty are imprisoned in a jail at night; during the day they work on community projects. After a few weeks, the imprisoned person is moved to another community. Each community writes reports about the person, which are then used by the assemblies to decide whether he or she should be released early. Up until now, most of the people from outside the region who have been apprehended by the Community Police have chosen to be judged by the community justice system, rather then handed over to state authorities. It is also quite common, after these individuals have served their time, for them to ask to remain in the communities and be assigned land in order to become local peasants.

Autogestión literally means "self-administration," but more broadly refers to collective democratic self-management, especially within local communities, workplaces, cultural projects, and many other entities. *Autogestión* is usually mentioned in the context of workers running their workplaces—for example, the cooperatives and recuperated workplaces of Argentina and the surrounding region of South America. Some of these are simply self-administered workplaces, organized in whatever way makes the most sense, and without any organized resistance to the capitalist market; others seek to foster horizontal processes and subvert the boundaries of capitalist value-exchange, in order to create less alienated workplaces, and to barter and exchange with other workplaces based more on needs than on market dictates.

Guerrero can seem like a far-reaching example of *autogestión*, but similar autonomous institutions can be found in other parts of Mexico—for example, in the Zapatista communities in Chiapas and other indigenous communities in Oaxaca, Hidalgo, and Veracruz. In each case, to a differing extent, the community organizes itself in a variety of ways through the creation of autonomous collective institutions, ranging from food production and community radio to community governance. The Good Government Juntas in Chiapas are an example of this, as is the provision of medical care, education, and alternative adjudication and security processes.

The practice can be found throughout Central and South America. In the highlands of Colombia the Nasa communities have organized an "indigenous guard" through community-based assemblies, and the Regantes,[10] in the areas around Cochabamba, Bolivia, have been organizing their own security forces and autonomous governance since the Water Wars of 2000. Perhaps one of the best-known cases is that of the Brazilian MST. With over 1 million participants, the MST takes over unused land, which they use collectively to cultivate crops, develop schools, and provide medical care. To support this process, they organize assemblies and administer alternative forms of adjudication and security that do not involve the police or other formal institutions of Brazil. Forms of local self-administration are also developing in Venezuela, with the emergence of Communal Councils and Communes.

Groups and collectives outside Latin America are practicing all kinds of self-administration, including social spaces in Europe, collectives and

---

10 Literally the "irrigators"—the agricultural producers depending on and taking care of irrigation systems. These were parts of the communities that organized autonomously as a result of the Water Wars.

independent media projects and groups, and all sorts of alternative education practices, from Free Schools to alternative high school diploma projects (as in Argentina). The Occupy movements, as well as the movements in Turkey, Spain, Greece, and Egypt, have all used *autogestión* as a way of coordinating within the plazas. Within these spaces (as with all kinds of spaces), internal conflicts do arise, and the methods of dealing with them are imperfect, but the attempts do reflect a growing seriousness with which people are taking *autogestión*, one that begins to envision a more complete autonomy along with self-administration projects.

AUTONOMY

The state exists. It's there, and it won't leave even if you ignore it. It will come to look for you however much you wish that it didn't exist. I believe that the assemblies and movements are beginning to notice that something important is being forgotten… We began to think of a strategy for constructing an alternative autonomous power, forgetting the state, but now we see it isn't so simple.[11]

The language of autonomy is used in the Occupy movements, as well as by many of the movements in Latin America, from the recuperated workplaces and unemployed movements in Argentina to the Zapatista communities in Mexico, and many of the grassroots organizations in Venezuela. It refers to the capacity to make decisions about one's own life without having to subordinate these decisions to external forces, the only real limit being a recognition of the autonomy of others. In this way, it reflects the politics of self-organization, *autogestión*, and direct participation—hence, these movements use the term "autonomy" to distinguish themselves from others movements, groups, or organizations subordinated to external interests, including the state, political parties, and other groups and institutions.

The idea of autonomy can be found animating many struggles in history. Following the Italian Autonomia movement of the 1960s and

---

11 Ezequiel, from the assembly Cid Campeador, interview with Marina Sitrin, Buenos Aires, Argentina, April 2003.

1970s, and the autonomous movements in central and northern Europe in the 1980s, it was from the 1994 Zapatista uprising in Mexico that these ideas regained widespread currency. The Zapatistas invoked autonomy in an indigenous context—not as a concept of territorial separation, but as the right to decide and exercise their own forms of social, political, and economic organization. The Zapatistas set up their own form of self-government, which has evolved over time into the constitution of "autonomous municipalities." They have set up their own primary schools, health system, and regional planning system for agricultural production, as well as a network of community-controlled radio stations that broadcast in the indigenous languages Chol, Tojolabal, Tzeltal, and Tzotzil. The new structures are based on the culture, experiences and collective decisions of the Zapatista communities. It is not a question of reviving folkloric habits, but of creating something new based on one's own reality, needs, and wishes. In the Zapatista schools, for example, the classes are bilingual, so the children learn Spanish, but they also learn in their own language, and the learning materials are also based on the reality the people live and not state-imposed textbooks that refer to a different history, lifestyle, and culture.

But autonomy is not autarchy—a total independence from everything and everybody else. Rather, it simply means that decisions are not subordinated to other forces. This entails an increasingly complicated relationship to the state. The problem is that the capitalist state is based on territorial hegemony and homogenization. It sometimes allows parallel structures, but usually only if they do not challenge its absolute authority. As soon as autonomous self-organization threatens state power (implicitly or overtly), it becomes the object of repression, violence, and destruction.

Local autonomy in Venezuela is not being built in isolation from the state, or as a "counterweight" to it, but through a complicated network of self-administration. But even there, where the leftist government officially supports the movements and their self-organization, the movements constantly struggle against subordination to the state and its institutions. This struggle, like all such struggles for autonomy, is still to be determined.

"TODOS SOMOS . . ."

Yes, Marcos is gay. Marcos is gay in San Francisco, black in South Africa, an Asian in Europe, a Chicano in San Ysidro, an anarchist in Spain, a Palestinian in Israel, a Mayan Indian in the streets of San Cristóbal, a Jew in Germany, a gypsy in Poland, a Mohawk in Quebec, a pacifist in Bosnia, a single woman on the Metro at 10 p.m., a peasant without land, a gang member in the slums, an unemployed worker, an unhappy student—and, of course, a Zapatista in the mountains.

Marcos is all the exploited, marginalized, oppressed minorities resisting and saying, "Enough!" He is every minority who is now beginning to speak, and every majority that must shut up and listen. He is every untolerated group searching for a way to speak. Everything that makes power and the good consciences of those in power uncomfortable—this is Marcos.[12]

"Todos somos . . ." means "We all are . . ." and is meant to express solidarity between struggles and movements in various situations. In the United States, it has been widely used in the formulations: "We are all Trayvon Martin," "We are all Troy Davis," and "We are all Bradley Manning." Seeking to organize around values of acceptance and recognition, this phrase conveys a linking together of struggles, rather than their hierarchization. We recognize one another and our diversities, but we also see ourselves in the other, and the other in ourselves. This does not imply that there are not power differentials, or that all people experience life in the same way (for example, with oppression or without access to resources), but that only by recognizing all of these diversities and differentials, and not giving power-based priority to one over another, are we able to create a foundation from which to organize together.

Many guerilla movements have employed the slogan "Todos somos . . ." —adding the name of a fallen comrade. In Latin American human rights movements such as the Madres de la Plaza de Mayo in Argentina, many refer to those who were murdered by the dictatorship in the "we" form—a

---

12   Quoted in Naomi Klein, "Farewell to the End of History: Organization and Vision in Anti-Corporate Movements," *Socialist Register* 2002 (London: Merlin Press), pp. 1–14.

sort of collective identification with "our" children who were killed, or a way of saying that those who were killed are also us: *El otro soy yo* ("I am the other"). "Todos somos . . ." was picked up by movements around the world after the Zapatista uprising that began on January 1, 1994. Support for the indigenous rebellion was so strong in Mexico and internationally that the Mexican government did not risk using military force to crush the insurgent communities after the short period of combat had ended. Instead, the government developed a massive propaganda campaign against the Zapatistas, and in particular against their most charismatic spokesperson, Subcomandante Marcos, publicizing his alleged previous identity and attacking him in an attempt to damage his image. When this campaign began, throughout Mexico and then the world, people took up the slogan "Todos Somos Marcos." In 1995 the Mexican press joined the government's campaign to discredit the Zapatistas, and Marcos in particular, and accused him of being gay. The statement above was Marcos's response.

TERRITORY AND SPACE

Since there are no institutions, not even a club, a church, or anything, the assembly meets on any corner, and even in the street. When this new form of politics emerges it establishes a new territory, or spatiality . . . In the beginning, the assembly consisted of people from all walks of life, ranging from the housewife who declared, "I am not political," to the typical party hack. But there was a certain sensibility. I don't know what to call it, something affective . . . It's as if we live in flux, moving at a certain speed, like little balls bouncing all about, and then suddenly, the assembly is our focus. Our intention is to establish a momentary pause in time and space, and to say, "Let us think about how to avoid being dragged and bounced about, and simultaneously attempt to build something new ourselves."[13]

The growing commodification of territories has raised the need to claim territories for the construction of spaces with alternative values and

---

13   Martin K., from the Assembly of Colegiales, interview with Marina Sitrin, Buenos Aires, Argentina, May 2003.

practices. This has generated different, sometimes contradictory uses of the terms "territory" and "space" in different movements. Nevertheless, the meanings are quite similar, and are being articulated more and more around the globe.

The Zapatistas have made the autonomy of indigenous territories in Chiapas one of the central points of their struggle, and they have declared the territory in which the Zapatista construction of a different and democratically self-administered society takes place a *territorio zapatista*—words we see written on large roadside signs when we enter the regions of Chiapas, where the Zapatista communities are based. Sometimes they relate to other "rebel territories" in their process of construction, and sometimes to the whole territory of Mexico (meaning the people within the boundaries of Mexico), regardless of the level of conflict or cooperation with the governments in power. Over the last two decades, the "demarcation of indigenous territory" has become a core question of indigenous struggles around the globe. In these territories, claimed by dispossessed indigenous groups, they have begun processes of self-administration under their own rules, based on their own cultures.

The relationship of movements to territory has also been important in urban areas for the construction of alternative social relationships, as well as for the interruption of capitalist business-as-usual. The unemployed workers' movements in Argentina began as a protest, demanding an unemployment subsidy from the state, but the movement transformed into something different. In the absence of a workplace within which to base the struggle, the protest took the form of a *piquete*—a blockade. Bridges and major intersections were transformed into spaces of struggle, with the intention of shutting down major transportation arteries. Along with blockades, horizontal assemblies were created, opening conversations about what to do next, but also facilitating an entire infrastructure of food, healthcare, media, and child care. This space came to be referred to as free *territorio*. From these new territories on the *piquete*, the same practices were expanded into the neighborhoods, often taking over land and building homes, growing crops and raising animals together, and generating a wide range of projects in areas, from clothes production to healthcare. These projects were always organized with horizontal assemblies, creating a new community and a new territory.

Finally, in the context of movements, territory and space are about the construction of autonomous community. And "community" is not a given "place," but a set of social relations that has to be built actively. Trust, affect, care, and responsibility for the other are the base of this set of social relations, and the community also strengthens these values.

Whatever the differences between the various understandings of "territory," each of them is a reaction against the ever-increasing commodification of spaces and social relations under capitalism. In each of these cases, participants look to reclaim territory in a way that builds social relations that are not subjected to commodification.

POLITICS OF WALKING AND PROCESS

Many stories ago, when the first gods—those who made the world— were still circling through the night, there were these two other gods—Ik'al and Votán.

The two were only one. When one was turning himself around, the other would show himself, and when the other one was turning himself around, the first one would show himself. They were opposites. One was light like a May morning at the river. The other was dark like night of cold and cave.

They were the same thing. They were one, these two, because one made the other. But they would not walk themselves, staying there always, these two gods who were one without moving.

"What should we do then?" the two of them asked.

"Life is sad enough as it is," they lamented, the two who were one in staying without moving.

"Night never passes," said Ik'al.

"Day never passes," said Votán.

"Let's walk," said the one who was two.

"How?" asked the other.

"Where?" asked the one.

And they saw that they had moved a little, first to ask how, then to ask where. The one who was two became very happy when the one saw that they were moving themselves a little. Both of them wanted to move at the same time, but they couldn't do it themselves.

"How should we do it then?"

And one would come around first and then the other and they would move just a little bit more and they realized that they could move if one went first, then the other. So they came to an agreement that—in order to move—one had to move first, then the other. So they started walking and now no one remembers who started walking first because at the time they were so happy just to be moving . . .

And they were going to start walking when their answer to choose the long road brought another question—"Where does this road take us?" They took a long time to think about the answer and the two who were one got the bright idea that only by walking the long road were they going to know where the road took them. If they remained where they were, they were never going to know where the long road leads.[14]

The concept of walking and questioning, or making the road as one walks, has been used throughout history. Most recently, it was popularized by the Zapatistas through the story above, the "Story of Questions," which has now been passed along, read, and performed at countless global gatherings and *encuentros* everywhere. It captures the spirit of questioning as we walk, our need for one another, and that only through constant discussion and debate can we define the meaning of emancipation.

The global movements, particularly since 2011, organize from a very similar spirit of walking and questioning, not trying to force everybody to sign up to the same program, or the same master plan on how to make the program a reality. Hence Occupy's insistence against demands. The practice is rather to open democratic spaces for the convergence of ideas and practices. As for the Zapatistas, and many of the movements in Latin America over the last two decades, there has been a real break in particular forms of organizing—forms that are hierarchical and have the answers and the "program" predetermined.[15]

---

14   There are countless versions of this story. The one included here is the one most widespread in English, due mainly to Subcomandante Marcos's retelling it and having it translated, first on the internet and then in Domitilia Dominguez, Antonio Ramirez, and Subcomandante Insurgente Marcos, *Questions and Swords: Folktales of the Zapatista Revolution* (El Paso, TX: Cinco Puntos Press, 2001).

15   In this context, it is important to underline that democracy and horizontalism do not mean that every single space and situation is organized following these principles, but that the process of horizontal democracy opens the conversation about what forms are most

Instead, what movements are creating is a multiplicity of paths toward an ever-changing end.

Nevertheless, these are very concrete paths, such as taking over hundreds of workplaces and pushing the boundaries of capitalist value-production in places such as Argentina and Brazil. The projects are concrete and militant; it is only that the "goal" is a multiplicity, and one discovered as people struggle and create together. Another example of the end as a process can be found in Venezuela. People in the communities and movements there refer to what is taking place as a "process." While there is a stated "goal" of creating "Socialism of the 21st century," it is not an ideology predetermining a certain structure or form. It is a search, a "work in progress," based on a set of values that include solidarity, mutuality, community, equality, self-administration, democracy, freedom, and so on. The motor behind what is developed and constructed is meant to be the neighborhoods, communities and workplaces; thus the meaning of this twenty-first-century socialism is an ever-changing one, and one that is itself also the walk. This does not mean that there are not different and conflicting visions of what should be done or how, or that there are not people who have more power to impose themselves than others do. But the idea is to have an open process of creation, and to understand that even deep structural changes such as revolution are not acts but processes.

No one is able to tell where the various directly democratic and participatory movements for change around the globe will go on their walk. That remains to be determined. But they have, without a doubt, created, and continue to create, huge and exciting social laboratories, spaces of participation and creation of the new. *Caminando preguntamos . . .*

---

appropriate. And in certain cases it has been found that it is not always possible to maintain horizontal decisions. For example, the EZLN is a military structure that is generally subordinated to the democratic decisions of the supporting Zapatista base communities. But, as a military structure, it also needs a chain of command, and cannot submit every step and action to an assembly. The same can be said about certain production processes that might decide horizontally that they need a chain of command.

CHAPTER TWO

It Is About Democracy

NO NOS REPRESENTAN! NO TO REPRESENTATIVE DEMOCRACY!

Almost every country in the world claims to be democratic. Democracy is used to argue for everything from wars, repression, control, and spying to the right of people to carry weapons, shoot home intruders, evict families, and deforest the land. Democracy, while a seemingly broad term, is generally used with a very specific meaning—generally as a synonym for liberal democracy. But liberal democracy is far from being the only possible form of democracy.

They don't represent us

Among broad sectors of the world population, the multiple crises that began in 2008 have caused and strengthened the feeling that they have no influence over decisions made regarding their lives, that they are not heard or taken into account in any way by those making the decisions, and that these "representatives" do not act in the people's interest. "The general feeling is that, here is this whirlwind that now is called *crisis* just to name it, and then this crisis goes on, making decisions over your life, things about which you have no control at all,"[1] explains Ana Méndez from Madrid.

---

1   Ana Méndez de Andés, Observatorio Metropolitano, Madrilonia, Traficantes de Sueños, Madrid, Spain, author interview, April 2012.

"Democracy has lost its initial meaning," says Fani from Thessaloniki, Greece. "It is said that we have democracy right now in Greece. This is not democracy. We have no real power. We don't make decisions. So democracy is a concept that has been destroyed to such a degree that, if we're about to use it again, we should completely reinvent it."

It is no coincidence that "They don't represent us" has emerged as a powerful slogan in mobilizations all over the world. We hear it in the US, Italy, Spain, Greece, Brazil, Turkey, Slovenia, and even Russia, where *вы нас даже не представляете!* (*vy nas dazhe ne predstavlyayete!*) means not only "You don't represent us" but also "You cannot even imagine us." The slogans are not phrased as rejections of specific political representatives, but as expressions of a general rejection of the logic of representation. The "representation of interests" does not work. It is perceived as undemocratic; people mobilizing do not feel "represented," and they no longer believe that "representation" by those in power is possible.

Pablo García, a 15-M activist from Madrid who also studied in Thessaloniki, says, "This democracy does not represent us, nor facilitate or help in the expression of citizens, for them to be consulted or taken into account beyond the elections. The system created after the Franco regime only permits us to elect representatives, and they then have the power to make whatever decisions they want during four years. That's it! There's no more control by the citizens, only that."[2]

In liberal or representative democracy, the "representatives" do not have to comply with what they or their party promised during elections, or what their party program says. Once they are elected, they do whatever they want (or the economic elites want), and do not have to justify themselves to the people who voted for them. There is no accountability for decisions, even not if they do the exact opposite of what they promised while campaigning. Supporters of liberal democracy try to hide these circumstances by saying that the elected representatives should act "according to their conscience" regardless of the stance of their electorate or their party. This not only turns the supposed "representation" into a

---

2 Pablo García, PhD student (ecology), 15-M activist in Madrid, then Occupy Mount Desert Island in Maine; since mid-2012 student of the University of Thessaloniki, Greece, author interview June 2012.

joke, but obviously also transforms the campaigns into fairytale contests. And, worst of all, until more recently with the new movements, most people in society acknowledge this fact, and might simply shrug and say, Well, what can we do? And so it continues.

Liberal and representative democracy were never meant to be democratic

The logic of representation has always been at the foundation of modern democracy—but not of classical democracy. In liberal democracy, "the economic," "the political," and "the social" are constructed as three separate spheres. The economic and social spheres are excluded from democracy. Stanley Moore wrote that, "when exploitation takes the form of exchange, dictatorship tends to take the form of democracy."[3] Today this separation of spheres is simply taken for granted in public discourse. But if we do not accept the whole idea of the autonomy of economy, the difference between those who govern and those who are governed, the autonomy of the political sphere, and so on, the whole edifice simply collapses like a house of cards. The rationale for wielding power over others, and for making decisions against the will and interests of the majority without consulting them, lies in the construction of a separated political sphere that follows its own logic. The separation of spheres is grounded on the idea of representation.[4] While abstraction is often important in the construction of collective decisions, representation is simply not possible, since it is based on homogenization and the necessary negation of diversity. The crisis of representation is a crisis of liberal democracy.

French philosopher Jacques Rancière stresses that

> representation was never a system invented to compensate for the growth of populations. It is not a form in which democracy has been adapted to modern times and vast spaces. It is, by rights, an oligarchic form, a

---

3   Stanley Moore, *The Critique of Capitalist Democracy* (New York: Paine Whitman, 1957), p. 85.

4   The modern effort to find a universal generalization of the specific, which emerged with the Enlightenment.

representation of minorities who are entitled to take charge of public affairs . . . Nor is the vote in itself a democratic form by which the people makes its voice heard. It is originally the expression of a consent that a superior power requires and which is not really such unless it is unanimous. The self-evidence which assimilates democracy to a representative form of government resulting from an election is quite recent in history. Originally representation was the exact contrary of democracy.[5]

In fact, a look at the "founding fathers" of modern liberal democracy shows that fundamental democratic values, such as participation and popular sovereignty, have never been on its official agenda.[6] Liberalism and democracy have been fierce enemies for hundreds of years. It was the exclusion of the social question from democratic decision-making that made the liberals accept democracy and create liberal democracy as the new form of governance of the emerging production model. As Karl Marx noted,

> The parliamentary republic was more than the neutral territory on which the two factions of the French bourgeoisie, Legitimists and Orleanists, large landed property and industry, could dwell side by side with equality of rights. It was the unavoidable condition of their common rule, the sole form of state in which their general class interest subjected to itself at the same time both the claims of their particular factions and all the remaining classes of society.[7]

Nevertheless, the idea of democracy, as Marx argued, is a constant threat to the rule of the bourgeoisie, since it might be used by critics of the existing order against the ruling interests. That is the reason why the bourgeoisie, especially in times of crisis such as we are witnessing now in

---

5   Jacques Rancière, *Hatred of Democracy* (London: Verso, 2009), p. 53.

6   *The Federalist Papers*, written by the crafters of the US Constitution to convince people to ratify it, demonstrates the clear intention to use the idea of participation to maintain economic control. Madison argued in *Paper* 10, that a government of thirteen states would be able to "control class conflict" and help prevent a "majority faction," as quoted in Howard Zinn, *Declarations of Independence: Cross-Examining American Ideology* (New York: Harper Perennial, 1990), p. 152.

7   In *The Eighteenth Brumaire of Louis Bonaparte*, Marx analyzes the historical events in the French Republic leading to Napoleon's coup d'état of 1851 from the viewpoint of a materialist conception of history. The *Eighteenth Brumaire* is considered the main writing of Marx on the capitalist state.

Greece, Turkey, the US, and elsewhere, tend toward authoritarian rule and the suspension of civil and democratic rules and rights. It is therefore important to take a closer look at the origins of the critique of liberal or parliamentary democracy, and at its potential goals. During the last few years, the crisis of liberal democracy has become so evident that even bourgeois intellectuals cannot deny or ignore it anymore. But their goal in criticizing liberal democracy is to pave the way for authoritarian and less democratic forms of decision-making, for the sake of efficiency.

We are taught that there are certain generally shared assumptions and rights that we have as a fundamental part of liberal democracy—things such as limitations on the government's ability to restrict citizens' movements and ideas, on the government's ability to exercise arbitrary power; the holding of fair and free elections, and respect for civil liberties such as freedom of speech, thought, religion, assembly, and so on. We are taught that these things exist and are grounded in the very nature of this democracy. But it is important to make clear that those civil liberties and rights we do have are not at all an inherent part of liberal democracy. In fact, they were won in long, hard struggles going back to the nineteenth century and earlier, and took effect only after the enforcement of the new model of production. Upon closer examination, one can see that, just as soon as almost all of these "rights" or "liberties" were won, governments set to work trying to dismantle them—from the right to an eight-hour work day to the right to be free from unlawful search and seizure. Volumes have been written about the encroachment on rights in modern democracies, and while many are outraged, and should be, the fact remains that these rights were never a fundamental part of the conception of liberal democracy.

As Beth, an activist in the San Francisco anti-foreclosure mobilization Occupy Homes Bernal put it, "The metaphor of democracy and the story that's woven around it is I think a very beautiful thing, but it never has been put in effect. It's really been used as a kind of decoy to keep people's attention and their fury away from the injustices that happen around democracy."[8]

---

8   Beth Stephens, professor at UC Santa Cruz, arts and environmental activist, Occupy Homes Bernal, Bernal Heights, San Francisco, CA, author interview, May 30, 2012.

The neoliberal turn: back to the roots of modern liberal democracy

The form of political organization corresponds to the form of economic organization, as Karl Marx wrote in the third volume of *Capital*. The bourgeois democratic republic is the ideal type of capitalist state for economies that rely primarily on trade in free markets and capitalist commodity-production. Modern liberal democracy as a space of conquest and the extension of rights, always limited by its compatibility with capital, can be considered the political form of the Keynesian national welfare state. Globalization undermined the conditions for the Keynesian national welfare state and for liberal democracy. And neoliberalism undermined those conditions even further, since its attendant financialization and supranational institutions threaten the core of both the nation-state and liberal democracy.

The increasingly deteriorating work conditions under neoliberalism also undermine democracy. Precarization means the generalization of insecurity and fear—and fear is not a good basis for democracy. It reduces the possibilities to speak up, complain, get organized, and express solidarity. Those who are subject to these precarious work relations often also lack energy for democratic participation. At the same time, the ongoing precarization of work, and the fear it inspires even in those not currently subject to it, has had a disciplining effect on workers with supposedly stable jobs.

The increasing transfer of decisions to supranational and international institutions has further deepened the "crisis of representation." This is due on the one hand to the undemocratic nature of these actors (none of which—the UN, European Union, European Central Bank, IMF, G8, and so on—have been elected), and on the other hand to the fact that the ability to represent decreases with the distance (geographic and scale) from the represented. It was therefore no accident that the precursor movements to the current movements for real democracy—the global justice or anti-globalization movements—came about in the mid-1990s, precisely against the undemocratic nature of these very institutions.

Much has been published on the general incompatibility between democracy and capitalism, especially in the 1970s and 1980s.[9] These

---

9 See Samuel Bowles and Herbert Gintis, *Democracy and Capitalism: Property, Community, and the Contradictions of Modern Thought* (London: Routledge & Kegan Paul,

positions have gained greater popularity in the current global crisis, in the context of nearly three decades of increasingly rapid dismantling of rights and social security mechanisms. Alex Demirović notes that it is difficult to believe that the structural deficiencies we experience "are not systematically connected with the known form of political democracy," but just contingent phenomena that will be corrected over time.[10] A look at the development of liberal democracy since the golden era of Keynesianism confirms this doubt. The fundamental historical contradiction within liberal democracy—the mediation between the rights of capital and the rights of human beings—has definitely shifted to the advantage of capital, and the social achievements won over the last 160 years are being steadily dismantled.

Through the worldwide implementation of neoliberalism since the 1980s and the enshrining of "efficiency" at the core of neoliberal thought, democracy experienced a roll-back to the form it had immediately after World War II in the core countries of liberal democracy. The main theorists of that model, Joseph A. Schumpeter (*Capitalism, Socialism, and Democracy*, 1942) and Karl Mannheim (*Freedom, Power and Democratic Planning*, 1951), placed their focus on results—on creating efficient bodies of leadership legitimated through elections. As Schumpeter explains, "Democracy is a political method, that is to say, a certain type of institutional arrangement for arriving at political—legislative and administrative—decisions and hence incapable of being an end in itself."[11] In order to achieve that, modern liberal democracy concentrated on eliminating any element of direct democracy or participation from "representative" democracy. Even for critics of liberal democracy, it is difficult to be clearer than Schumpeter himself:

1986), and Philip Green, *Retrieving Democracy: In Search of Civic Equality* (London: Methuen, 1985).

10   Alex Demirović, "Ein langanhaltender Prozess," *Fantomâs* 8 (2005). Regarding the critique of liberal democracy, see for example Johannes Agnoli and Peter Brückner, *Die Transformation der Demokratie* (Frankfurt: Europäische Verlagsanstalt, 1968); Crawford Brough Macpherson, *The Real World of Democracy* (Toronto: CBC, 1964); Crawford Brough Macpherson, *The Life and Times of Liberal Democracy* (Oxford: Oxford University Press, 1977). Herbert Marcuse, Barrington Moore, and Robert Paul Wolff, *A Critique of Pure Tolerance* (Boston: Beacon Press, 1965).

11   Joseph A. Schumpeter, *Capitalism, Socialism and Democracy* (New York: Harper, [1942] 1976), p. 242.

First of all, according to the view we have taken, democracy does not mean and cannot mean that the people actually rule in any obvious sense of the terms "people" and "rule." Democracy means only that the people have the opportunity of accepting or refusing the men who are to rule them . . . [by means of] free competition among would-be leaders for the vote of the electorate. Democracy is the rule of the politician . . . The voters outside of parliament must respect the division of labor between themselves and the politicians they have elected . . . they must understand that, once they have elected an individual, political action is his business and not theirs.[12]

In terms of its theoretical definitions, institutional assets, and practices, liberal democracy has little or nothing to do with what is usually understood as democracy. One might be surprised how simplified even many academic definitions of liberal democracy are. Mainstream political science has eliminated one of the central pillars of the original idea of democracy: people's sovereignty. "Popular sovereignty—the idea that a government should do what most citizens want it to do—is the oldest and most literal definition of democracy, although not necessarily the best one. Contemporary theorists now consider popular sovereignty neither sufficient nor strictly necessary for democracy."[13]

Giovanni Sartori, also considered one of the main modern theorists of liberal democracy, claims that democratic stability and quality increase as the level of competition between parties, and therefore the extent of their ideological differences declines.[14] The idea that fewer choices provide a higher quality of democracy needs little in the way of explanation to show how absurd it is. And yet, it is one of the main characteristics of the reigning liberal democracies—a characteristic that is increasingly being rejected worldwide. In the US, for example, many people came into the Occupy movement having worked for "Hope and Change" with the Obama campaign, only then to realize that in fact there was no real difference between the two parties in policy terms. Similarly, the largest

---

12   Ibid., p. 284–5.
13   Michael Coppedge, "Venezuela: Popular Sovereignty versus Liberal Democracy," Kellogg Institute Working Paper No. 294 (Notre Dame, IN: Kellogg Institute, 2002), p. 6.
14   Giovanni Sartori, *Parties and Party Systems: A Framework for Analysis* (Cambridge: Columbia University Press, 1976).

non-parliamentary protest movements in Europe and Latin America under representative democracy took place while broad government coalitions were in power, or parties sharing the same politics alternated in office.

How liberal democracy can see political parties as a central pillar of democracy is something of a mystery. Belarusian political scientist Moisey Ostrogorsky (1854–1921), who lived and worked in Paris, the US, Great Britain, and Russia, and is considered to have founded the sociology of political parties after decades of comparative party-system analysis, came to the conclusion that democratic parties carry an almost pathological tendency to transform into bureaucratic and oligarchic organizations. The concept of "party democracy" thus becomes an oxymoron. As Rancière notes,

> what we call democracy is a statist and governmental functioning that is exactly the contrary: eternally elected members holding concurrent or alternating municipal, regional, legislative, and/or ministerial functions and whose essential link to the people is that of the representation of regional interests; governments which make laws themselves; representatives of the people that largely come from one administrative school; ministers or their collaborators who are also given posts in public or semipublic companies; fraudulent financing of parties through public works contracts; business-people who invest colossal sums in trying to win electoral mandates; owners of private media empires that use their public functions to monopolize the empire of the public media. In a word: the monopolizing of *la chose publique* by a solid alliance of State oligarchy and economic oligarchy.[15]

In most liberal democracies the main parties have usually alternated in power or shared power for half a century or more (even if they have undergone a few name changes, as in Italy), providing some kind of "political stability," albeit at the expense of democratic content. While the creation of a certain social consensus necessary to sustain the system has been the main pillar of stability in liberal democracies, we should not forget that selective as well as massive repression, structural violence, and wars have always been recourses of liberal democracies.

---

15   Rancière, *Hatred of Democracy*, pp. 72–3.

In most countries, there is little or no difference between the political positions and practices of the main parties. Since all governments respond increasingly to the dictates of economic actors, most parties in most countries agree on all fundamentals. Tariq Ali fittingly named this the "extreme center." Anestis, from Athens, tells us that the center-right and center-left parties of Greece, along with the fascists, are called the "united party of the markets." Amador Fernández Savater, a 15-M activist from Madrid, describes the common perception of party politics in Spain as follows:

> It's not any more just a truth for the more radical political groups or leftists . . . politics of politicians are increasingly a simple management oriented to the necessities of the global economy. Management, not politics, not decision, nor direction, but just a management of a power that surpasses, and overpasses the political power: that of the market—the financial market first of all. A widespread perception is: we don't live in a democracy, we live in a "market's dictatorship," although that dictatorship still respects some liberal rights and liberties. Power is concentrated in political and economic elites, but not as a dictatorial power, but rather one that allows some liberties that are often put forward and promoted spite of that power.[16]

The Rule of Goldman Sachs

"Spain's problem, as in the rest of the world, is that we're under the rule of Goldman Sachs," says Ana Méndez, also from Madrid. The Goldman Sachs Group is a US transnational investment banking firm engaged in global investment banking and financial services, doing business primarily with institutional clients. For any clear-thinking and reasonable person, this should automatically exclude any Goldman Sachs employee or advisor from any public office. But one look at the Eurozone decision-makers confirms in an alarming way how right Ana Méndez is, as the presence of Goldman Sachs technocrats in crucial decision-making positions in the Eurozone before and after the 2008 economic crisis showed. Although Goldman Sachs had played a crucial role in provoking the European

16   Amador Fernández Savater, journalist, editor, 15-M activist, Madrid, Spain, author interview, January 2012.

crisis—the systematic cover-up of the true size of the Greek national debt between 1998 and 2009 occurred through derivative deals with Goldman Sachs[17]—Greece's debt management agency has been headed since 2010 by Petros Christodoulou, who began his career with Goldman Sachs.

But the rule by Goldman Sachs is hardly restricted to Greece. When Italian Prime Minister Silvio Berlusconi was forced to resign in November 2011, Mario Monti, an international advisor to Goldman Sachs who did not hold an elected public position, was called upon to build a new government. Creating a technocratic cabinet based entirely on unelected professionals, Monti also took over the post of minister of economy and finance, in addition to his role as prime minister, and proceeded to govern Italy without democratic legitimacy until April 2013, when a new government was formed. Monti ran in the 2013 elections, winning only 10.5 percent of the vote.

And the list goes on. Mario Draghi, who is a former vice-chairman and managing director of Goldman Sachs International, was appointed to head the European Central Bank in 2011; Otmar Issing, former board member of the Bundesbank, who was crucial in creating the euro and developed the approach to monetary policy the European Central Bank adopted, has been an international advisor to Goldman Sachs since 2006; Peter Sutherland, former advisor to the Irish government, attorney general of Ireland, head of the General Agreement on Tariffs and Trade, and first director of the WTO, has been part of the Goldman Sachs International Directors' Board since 1995; Mark Carney, who became governor of the Bank of England in July 2013, and was previously the governor of the Canadian Central Bank and the chairman of the G20's Financial Stability Board, built his career working for thirteen years for Goldman Sachs in various parts of the world; and Henry "Hank" Paulson, secretary of the US Treasury Department since 2006, was formerly the CEO of Goldman Sachs. When Tim Geithner replaced Paulson in 2009, he appointed Goldman Sachs lobbyist Mark Patterson as his chief advisor and chief of staff—not long after Obama had promised during his presidential election campaign to reduce the influence of lobbyists in politics.

---

17   Beat Balzli, "How Goldman Sachs Helped Greece to Mask its True Debt," *Der Spiegel*, February 8, 2010.

In this context, it is instructive to recall what Thomas Jefferson wrote in a letter to John Taylor 200 years ago in 1816:

> the mass of the citizens is the safest depository of their own rights . . . the evils flowing from the duperies, of the people, are less injurious than those from the egoism of their agents. . . . And I sincerely believe, with you, that banking establishments are more dangerous than standing armies.[18]

In fact, the tendency of liberal representative democracy toward oligarchy is a fundamental one, not simply the result of inadequate regulation. Modern democracy being founded upon the separation of the economic, political, and social spheres, the economy and society are excluded from democratic governance. Yet this separation of spheres is inextricably linked to the idea of representation: the government's powers being limited to the political sphere and focused primarily on guaranteeing individual rights and civil liberties (including the right to private property), political participation is kept at arm's length from economic and civic life. Political participation is necessarily indirect. Thankfully, other forms of democracy are possible.

PRACTICING NEW FORMS OF DEMOCRACY

The most obvious shared characteristic of the various popular mobilizations around the globe in recent years is their deeply egalitarian and democratic character. But there is no single model of people's democracy that can be applied indiscriminately in the various contexts of mobilization as a counter to liberal democracy. The movements do not have a detailed proposal to institutionalize. And in fact, as Amador from Madrid comments in relation to the 15-M, neither do they want one:

> What does the movement propose? That's unclear. We do not know exactly what "Real Democracy Now!" means. Everyone has their own version of what "Real Democracy Now!" means. That opens a space for a lot of

---

18 Thomas Jefferson to John Taylor, May 28, 1816, in Thomas Jefferson, *The Writings of Thomas Jefferson*, ed. Paul Leicester Ford (New York: G.P. Putnam's Sons, 1892–99), vol. 10, p. 31.

people. A lot of people share a discomfort regarding the idea that what we have is supposed to be democracy. But if we start asking ourselves what a "Real Democracy" would look like, it is not very clear.

Mariana, from Rio de Janeiro, tells us: "There is a crisis of representation. Some sectors discuss participatory democracy. People talk about a lot of different things. It is very pluralistic."[19] The experiences are similar around the world, as a statement by Debbie from the Solidarity Health Clinic in Thessaloniki explains:

> We are very used to delegating responsibility to somebody else and giving them the power to make decisions over what is happening. We don't think of that as democratic. We don't want to have representatives, we want to represent ourselves. Of course, this raises several problems . . . how do you structure or organize decision-making? As a process of decision-making it's much more democratic and much more useful to have all voices heard. It is interesting that when people gather they automatically, instinctively adhere to the principles of direct democracy. This is because, essentially, when something is very important to you, you want to make the decision for yourself and not have somebody else decide for you.

Vassilis, from Athens, says, "They cannot represent us anymore. It's impossible. So it's like recuperating a factory, the factory here is democracy. It's like the bosses left the factory and you have to make the factory work because you have to make decisions, because you have to be recognized, you have needs and want to cover them, you have desires."[20]

All over the world people are finding one another and together engaging in building democratic processes, and under many different names. "I don't know what this process should be called," says Sandy from OWS, "it's just like, my voice is heard, everyone's voice is heard, and we come together and we decide what to do with that. I don't even know what that actually is termed. It just is something that's powerful.

---

19   Mariana Bruce, academic and activist, Rio de Janeiro, Brazil, author interview, July 15, 2013.

20   Vassilis, social worker, employed as clerk, Assembly for the Circulation of Struggles (SKYA), Athens, author interview, June 2012.

If it's direct democracy, localized democracy, or localized direct democracy, I'm not really sure."[21]

Radical, direct, participatory, or real democracy?

Although the idea of direct, radical, participatory democracy (or whatever one wants to call these forms of non-representative democracy) is much older than many other widely theorized concepts, it is generally not linked to prominent theorists, at least nowhere near as intimately as liberal democracy. Some support for complete democracy can be found from Jean-Jacques Rousseau, Thomas Jefferson, Tom Paine, Karl Marx,[22] and Rosa Luxemburg. But the topic of unlimited democracy has generally been avoided by theorists. This is certainly one of the reasons why we do not find extensive academic debates or widely discussed and shared models of a form of democracy other than liberal democracy.

Several scholars have theorized ideas and concepts using the term "radical democracy." German critical theorist Alex Demirović classifies modern conceptions of radical democracy as deliberative (Habermas, Benhabib, Bohman), associative (Hirst, Cohen, Rogers), civil society-based (Arago/Cohen, Frankenberg, Rödel), hegemonic (Laclau, Mouffe), or "coming democracy" (Derrida).[23] A closer look at the various theoretical approaches shows that their concepts are either not very radical or still so abstract that they are not helpful in the construction of an alternative. Despite their names, the first three categories are not radical at all, and "view democratic institutions as a long-term revolution."[24] Derrida describes democracy as "coming," placing the normative dimension of its promise at the center; he considers its open character to be constitutive of

---

21   Sandy (Sandra) Nurse, 29, political scientist, OWS direct action working group, also runs the youth employment project BK ROT (compost collection service in Bushwick), New York, NY, author interview, December 13, 2012.

22   In his *Critique of Hegel's Philosophy of Right* (1843), Marx defends democracy over monarchy and makes some basic declarations, but then puts the question of democracy aside.

23   Demirović, "Ein langanhaltender Prozess," p. 1.

24   Alex Demirović, "Radikale Demokratie und der Verein freier Individuen," *Indeterminate Kommunismus!*, eds. DemoPunK and Kritik & Praxis Berlin (Münster: Unrast Verlag, 2005), pp. 56–68, p. 56.

democracy itself.[25] But he refuses to define democracy because, he claims, any definition would impose a meaning.[26] So the basic problem with most theories of radical democracy starts to become clear: "the lack of consideration of concrete day-to-day experiences and the failure to connect with common practices."[27]

Chantal Mouffe and Ernesto Laclau are among the internationally better-known theoreticians of radical democracy.[28] Laclau and Mouffe argue for a radical and pluralistic democracy. The former term refers to the radicalization of the democratic revolution by expanding political spaces through the extension of the ideals of liberty and equality to more of the social spaces where relations of domination exist.[29] They see their poststructuralist approach as a non-economistic, post-Marxist extension and an updating of Gramsci's concept of hegemony. At the same time, they view democracy as perpetually incomplete: "Incompleteness and preliminarity are part of the essence of democracy."[30] The inclusion of many traditional socialist assumptions within the normative orientation of liberal democracy (human rights, equality, and so on) created a new point of departure for left criticism, which largely transformed from a plea to introduce democratic principles into a plea to deepen them.[31] Beyond the frequently expressed critique that Mouffe and Laclau omit the questions of the democratization of property and the administration of means of production, and that their concept of considering all voices democratically does not distinguish between people defending their privileges and people fighting for equality, Mouffe and Laclau's radical democracy lacks concrete proposals for how to deepen democracy, make democratic decisions, and build a radical-democratic society.

In light of the possibility of plebiscites and referenda that has been introduced into the constitutions of various Latin American countries over the past two decades, a number of scholars have dealt with alleged

---

25   Jacques Derrida, *Rogues: Two Essays on Reason*.

26   Ibid.

27   Dirk Jörke, "Wie demokratisch sind radikale Demokratietheorien?" eds. Reinhard Heil and Andreas Hetzel (Frankfurt am Main: transcript, 2006), pp. 253–66, p. 258.

28   Ernesto Laclau and Chantal Mouffe, *Hegemony and Socialist Strategy* (New York: Verso, 1985).

29   Ibid.

30   Ernesto Laclau, *Emanzipation und Differenz* (Vienna: Turia & Kant, 2002), p. 41.

31   Demirović, "Radikale Demokratie."

direct democracy in the region.[32] Their analyses generally refer exclusively to elections and referenda beyond the basic structure of liberal democracies—in other words, beyond the election of representatives. From that perspective, direct democracy only complements representative democracy, and is not a possible form of organizing unto itself.

Something similar happens with the concept of participation, which has had a wide range of interpretations. It may be linked to representation, but it arises from a principle that is diametrically opposed: actions that anyone can perform and are not delegated combine in political participation. Anyone can participate in assemblies, elections, demonstrations, and so on, but the logic of the principle indicates that not just anyone can represent others politically. The issue becomes controversial when we try to define the limits of participation, and in particular the limits of direct political participation in decision-making. From a liberal-democratic perspective, there is no place for civic, individual, or collective participation in the (separately constructed) political sphere; these are intentionally confined to the "civil society sphere," and reduced to the periodic act of electing representatives so as not to hinder the efficiency of the democratic processes, and so that democracy is not overloaded with social demands that might endanger the pride of place granted to the accumulation of capital, as against the social distribution of wealth and labor.[33]

During the 1960s and 1970s, concepts of political participation were given greater social importance in liberal democracies and in the social sciences.[34] This did not happen because liberal-democratic regimes or

---

32   David Altman, "Democracia directa en el continente americano: ¿Autolegitimación gubernamental o censura ciudadana?," *Política y Gobierno*, 12;2 (2005), pp. 203–32; Monica Barczak, "Representation by Consultation? The Rise of Direct Democracy in Latin America," *Latin American Politics and Society*, 43:3 (2001), pp. 37–59; Alicia Lissidini, *Democracia directa en América Latina: ¿Amenaza populista o una voz que evita la salida?*, Paper at XI Congreso Internacional del CLAD sobre la Reforma del Estado y de la Administración Pública, Guatemala City, November 7–10, 2006; Daniel Zovatto, "Las instituciones de la democracia directa a nivel nacional en América Latina: Un balance comparado, 1978–2004," *Democracia directa y referéndum en América Latina*, eds. Daniel Zovatto, Iván Marulanda, Antonio Lizarazo, and Rodolfo González (La Paz, Bolivia: Corte Nacional Electoral, 2004).

33   Boaventura de Sousa Santos, *Democracia de alta intensidad: Apuntes para democratizar la democracia* (La Paz, Bolivia: Unidad de Análisis e Investigación del Área de Educación Ciudadana de la CNE, 2004), p. 28.

34   Macpherson, *The Life and Times of Liberal Democracy*.

academia suddenly recognized that liberal democracy excludes popular participation. Participation became a concern of governments and states because huge movements were questioning their legitimacy and demanding profound changes. Participatory mechanisms that were introduced thus never questioned the liberal-democratic model or the logic of representation (they never questioned the separation of spheres—the ascription of "politics" to a "political sphere" separate from the "social sphere"), but were seen as attachments to them, aimed at gaining greater legitimacy for representative politics. Participatory mechanisms were mostly situated within the framework of electoral politics,[35] regarding the activities that accompany elections or electoral campaigns, individual and personal dialogue with political representatives, or organizing with others to influence government action.[36] In some liberal democracies the possibility of a popular referendum has been introduced, usually either without any obligation on governments to respect the result or imposing formidable obstacles to achieving meaningful participation in the referendum. A minimum participation rate of 50 percent of the electorate has often been established as a condition for recognition of the referendum result, while no such condition applies to any election of political representatives.

While outside the mainstream debate, either in scholarship or in society, a number of social movements—beginning in the late 1950s, and in some cases still in existence— both practice more alternative and participatory forms of democracy and reflect upon that practice. In the US these forms are referred to as participatory democracy.[37] While it is not peculiar to the US—for example, Latin American popular movements over the past few decades, especially those based in indigenous regions and movements, have also practiced alternative and participatory forms of democracy—we focus here on the US case. Many of these scholars

---

35   See the famous participation scholars, Sidney Verba and Norman H. Nie, *Participation in America: Political Democracy and Social Equality* (Chicago: University Of Chicago Press, [1972] 1987).

36   Verba and Nie, *Participation in America,* p, 46.

37   Wini Breines, *Community and Organization in the New Left, 1962–1968: The Great Refusal* (Piscataway, NJ: Rutgers University Press, 1989); Barbara Epstein, *Political Protest and Cultural Revolution: Nonviolent Direct Action in the 1970s and 1980s* (Berkeley, CA: UC Press, 1993); Jo Freeman, *Tyranny of Structurelessness,* jofreeman.com/joreen/tyranny.htm, 1971–73.

themselves emerged from the feminist, civil rights, anti-war, and anti-nuclear movements. Most of the best-known writers on the practice of participatory democracy during this period were women, while the theorists of liberal democracy have tended to be men. Beginning with the Student Nonviolent Coordinating Committee, attempts were made to create a more participatory atmosphere both in decision-making and in day-to-day relationships. For example, the idea of beloved community emerged in the SNCC as a way of talking about the importance of participation based in affect and trust. The beloved community was intended to prefigure the society being fought for, one without hierarchy or difference based on race, and organized using radical forms of participatory democracy. The anti-war movement, and particularly Students for a Democratic Society, also spoke a great deal about the need for participatory democracy—though whether it in fact took place within the movement is a different question. It was from there that the radical feminist movement in the US emerged. It is this movement that has most often been credited with experimenting with forms of radical and direct democracy, which in turn had an affinity with forms and practices of the anti-nuke movement, known especially on the west coast of the US for its direct-democratic structure and mass-consensus decision-making.

While there are numerous books and articles describing the forms of organizing within movements, including portrayals of participatory and direct democracy, these are not works specifically studying democracy, but rather addressing movements that use other democratic forms. Francesca Polletta is an exception to this, though even though she pays some specific attention to participatory democracy as a form itself, as in her book *Freedom Is an Endless Meeting* (2002), it is still a book tracing the history and uses of participatory democracy, not an exploration of its meanings.[38]

Since the 1980s, the hegemonic discourse has usurped the concept of participation and used it in a neoliberal bid to outsource the state's collective responsibilities to individual citizens and strengthen the power of markets. But it is definitely not "participation" if you have to choose between different private health insurance companies because the public

---

38 Della Porta has taken up the question of democracy in movements in her more recent work.

health system has been dismantled, or if parents have to take over various tasks in schools or neighborhoods because the state does not perform them anymore. The decentralization of services to a local level without the necessary financial resources has also been presented by neoliberal politics as "local participation." It is obviously neither participatory nor democratic if, for example, social services are handed over to communities while the resources to finance them are cut to a level that no longer guarantees a fundamental level of quality.

Participation as understood and practiced by movements all over the world does not mean participation in a system that someone else established and which is regulated by someone else, but participation in defining the goals and rules. The goal is democracy, not integration (which means inclusion into something existing). As the Mexican philosopher Enrique Dussel puts it, "Excluded persons should not be *included* (which would be like introducing the Other into the Same) in the *old* system. Rather they should participate as equals in a *new institutional moment* (the *new* political order). The goal is not *inclusion* but *transformation*."[39]

Ayelen, from Madrid, comments that collective thinking "is not that everybody is thinking different things and we just join it all together. It must be something built together from the start, something that previously did not exist which has to be created. It doesn't consist in convincing, but building."[40] This description could easily have emerged from many of the other square movements around the world.

A common element in many processes of liberation and democratization in the Global South is participation by diverse social actors in the decision-making processes that make change possible,[41] and popular participation cannot be reduced to certain sectors or predetermined structures. "The scorched-earth policy that neoliberalism brought about generated 'integrated social antibodies' in such a way that the responses to it have occurred in every field and regarding various aspects (economics, politics, normativity and identity, and culture). The main characteristic

---

39   Enrique Dussel, *20 Tesis de política* (Mexico City: Siglo XXI, 2006), p. 106.

40   Ayelen Lozada, physiotherapist, 15-M, Reflection Working Group, Madrid, Spain, author interview, January 8, 2012.

41   de Sousa Santos, *Democracia de alta intensidad*, p. 28.

of the political changes in Latin America is related to that renewed participation."[42]

As C. Douglas Lummis notes, "'Democracy' was once a word of the people, a critical word, a revolutionary word. It has been stolen by those who would rule over the people, to add legitimacy to their rule. It is time to take it back, to restore to it its radical power. Democracy is not everything, but something."[43]

Historical references

For many movement participants in Europe, the occupied squares resembled the Greek *agora*—literally "gathering place" or "assembly"—the central place of ancient Athens, the center of urban life, where the citizens' assemblies were held.[44] The Agora in Athens is considered the birthplace of democracy.[45] For Ayelen, from Madrid, "Sol turned into an *agora*. I understood that day and could imagine what a Greek *agora* was like."

Since the term and concept "democracy" comes from ancient Athens, and since even liberal democracies, especially in Europe, insist on presenting themselves in a democratic philosophical tradition going back to ancient Greece, it is worth taking a closer look at the Athenian democracy.

---

42   Juan Carlos Monedero, "En donde está el peligro . . . La crisis de la representación y la construcción de alternativas en América," *Cuadernos del Cendes* 24: 64 (Caracas, Venezuela: UCV, 2007) p. 1–21.

43   C. Douglas Lummis, *Radical Democracy* (Ithaca, NY: Cornell University Press, 1996).

44   In the context of autonomous collective historical experiences, movements in Latin America bring back democratic practices that existed in some indigenous cultures or among African-American populations—former slaves who, after escaping, set up autonomous communities.

45   The first reforms and institutions pointing toward the Hellenic model of direct democracy occurred under Solon, in 594 BC, and democracy is considered to have come into existence by 462 BC. During the years of 462 and 461 BC Greece underwent political turmoil, members of the Areopagus (the council of elders of the city, similar to the Roman Senate, composed only by "honorable" individuals who had held high public office) were brought to trial. A group of politicians under the leadership of Ephialtes managed to pass some reforms in 462 BC taking away almost all functions from the Aeropagus and shifting the center of power to the Demos—the citizens' general assembly. The Athenian democracy lasted almost 140 years, and was defeated from the outside with the victory of the Macedonians over the Athenians in 322 BC. See Kurt A. Raaflaub, "The Breakthrough of Demokratia in Mid-Fifth-Century Athens," in Kurt A. Raaflaub, Josiah Ober, and Robert W. Wallace, *Origins of Democracy in Ancient Greece* (Berkeley, CA: University of California Press, 2007), pp. 105–54.

Before looking at some of the central aspects of Athenian democracy however, it is important to make some general clarifications. Ancient Greece, as well as the following history of democracy, clearly demonstrates the absurdity of the idea that democracy is brought by governments or states. In Athens, "democracy" had to be imposed by the masses against fierce resistance from noble and rich families. Moreover, even if Athenian democracy is the best documented among the ancient Greek democracies, the inconvenient fact remains that most of what we know about Athenian democracy today is based on Aristotle and Plato, who both rejected democracy in favor of an elitist ideology.[46] The people developing and practicing democracy in Athens, as far is known, did not theorize it. And, for reasons that are generally apparent, we do not propose Athenian democracy is a model to follow. It included only the native, white, male citizens of Athens. The majority of the population—women, freed slaves, slaves, and "metics" (foreigners residing in the city doing business), making up some 80 percent of the inhabitants—were excluded from democratic participation of any kind, since they were not considered citizens.[47] All in all, some 43,000 men out of approximately 315,000 inhabitants were allowed to participate in the citizens' assembly. The number of men assisting at the monthly assemblies is estimated at 6,000.[48]

Nevertheless, it is worth examining some of the basic concepts of Athenian democracy.[49] To begin with, ancient democracy explicitly

---

46   Aristotle and Plato were also wrong in their critique. Both were convinced that Athens's democracy would collapse for internal reasons, because it was simply not feasible. But that did not happen. The democracy proved to be very stable, and was overthrown only by external forces. The critique of today's conservative liberal democrats concerning people's participation in politics and elements of direct democracy is still more or less the same as that of Aristotle and Plato concerning Athenian democracy.

47   This has to be seen in the overall context of those times, when practically all other existing administrative entities were authoritarian empires, kingdoms, and so on. And it is also worth recalling that, more than 2,000 years later, the US considered liberal democracy compatible with slavery, while women in most liberal democracies were only allowed to participate in elections beginning in the twentieth century, and in the US the exclusion of poor people and minorities from electoral participation through property tax laws was a widespread practice until the early 1960s.

48   Richard Saage, *Demokratietheorien. Eine Einführung* (Wiesbaden, Germany: VS Verlag für Sozialwissenschaften, 2005), pp. 50–1.

49   Many more legitimate critiques of the Athenian democracy can be raised—for example, that the prosperity of the city was based on imperialism. Here we simply point out

rejected the principle of representation. All citizens could attend the highest political body, the assembly, held once a month (the year had ten months). The principle of representation and the idea that elected representatives could make decisions—concepts at the heart of liberal democracy—were considered incompatible with the idea of democracy, since they would only disconnect politicians from common citizens, nourishing corruption and patronage networks. Since representation did not exist, and the citizens' assembly was the highest authority, there was also no such thing as a government in the liberal-democratic sense. Nor did anything like parties exist, which in representative democracies came to assume the function of structuring representation through packages of interests and opinions. In ancient Athens, the process of structuring interests and opinions took place in the Assembly around speakers defending different positions. These people, with better communication skills, were called "demagogues"—a term that did not then carry any negative charge, but came to acquire a pejorative character in the writings of Aristotle and Plato because of their rejection of democracy.

The Citizens' Assembly enjoyed complete sovereignty. It would only follow its own rules, decided by itself, and it had neither a constitution nor laws that could override the political process—nor did it create a separate professional justice system. Justice was managed by the Assembly itself. Jurors chosen by lottery from among the participants of the Citizens' Assembly functioned as judges. To avoid corruption, Athens had a complex scheme for assigning jurors to cases. No public prosecutors or lawyers existed. The parties would present their case on their own, though they could ask for support, and the "people," in the form of a popular jury, would decide how to handle the case.

Democracy in ancient Greece meant direct democracy, and nothing else. The citizens gathering for the Assembly decided on laws, institutional employees, military leaders, war and peace, religious questions, and everything else they chose to bring within their authority. The most important questions were usually treated in the first assemblies of the year, after which every citizen had the opportunity to suggest their own issues to the assembly. Obviously, an assembly of such magnitude had to be prepared, which

---

some of the basic principles of democracy at its origins.

was managed by the Council of 500. It would prepare the sessions of the assembly, set up an agenda proposal, and draft the bills to be discussed by the assembly. The members of the Council of 500 were selected by lot, served a maximum of two one-year terms, and were subordinated to the Citizens' Assembly. Every proposal issued by the Council of 500 had to be ratified by the Citizens' Assembly, which had the power to dismiss anything presented by the Council of 500. Apart from military leaders—whose functions were reduced to leading troops in wars, while decisions on troops and military objectives were taken by the Assembly—some financial experts, and the head of the water system, which were elected by the Citizens' Assembly, all public officers were chosen by lottery. This was a corollary of democratic principle that Athenians clung to so firmly: since democracy was the rule of the people (citizens, in this case), every citizen was able to fulfill the tasks assigned in the interest of society.

The similarities between many principles of ancient Athenian democracy and the democratic practices of the new global movements are evident. We are not arguing that this is a consequence of the movements' knowledge of Athenian democracy. We can find direct-democratic and egalitarian practices and principles throughout history in various geographic and cultural settings, and they do not depend on any knowledge of previous democratic practices or councils. These practices and principles are the expression of a search for a truly democratic society of equals. Humans are social beings who evolve collectively through cooperation. Nevertheless, as Walter Benjamin emphasizes, historical consciousness of the role of past generations is a crucial element in building emancipatory paths.

We have encountered very little in the way of direct references to the practices of the Assemblies in ancient Greece, aside from those to the *agora* and the loose grounding of the idea of direct democracy. But there is one exception to this: Greece. On several occasions, people did refer to specific aspects of the Assemblies in Athens, used some of the ancient Greek words for things like direct democracy, and even sometimes borrowed their tactics. For example, when there were thousands of people in Syntagma Square who all wanted to speak, and it would have been impossible to hold an assembly with so many on the speaker's list, the facilitators proposed using a lottery system, which was met with broad support. It was subsequently one of the reasons many decided to organize in the neighborhoods, so that more could speak and for longer periods of time; but the fact remains that ancient Greece exerted a powerful hold on the imaginations of many in the Square.

Beyond the example of ancient democracy in Athens, many more references can be found to historical experiences in the movements. In many cases these historical references became stronger over time. In Spain, at the beginning of the 15-M movement, many participants and activists took their distance from all historic experiences, insisting on the uniqueness of the 15-M. This was true even though, for external observers, the strong link to the Spanish revolution of 1936–39 seemed more than obvious, and the activists with long political histories would share the ideals of the Spanish revolution. With time, more and more Republican flags of the Second Spanish Republic, 1931–39—which was overthrown by the fascists—appeared on demonstrations, and at the same time the reference was so powerful that the ruling right-wing party, the Partido Popular, asked the social-democratic PSOE to ban their party members from displaying the Republican flag.

Tradition and myth have a persistent function in Latin American popular struggles.[50] Thus, throughout the centuries, embodiments of past struggles against the established order have been fashioned into banners for current struggles.[51] This is not a matter of nostalgia or folklore, because it requires in each case an adaptation to the present, but more like a "secret rendezvous between past generations and our own."[52] Moreover, every such adaptation "contributes to a collective, historically grounded composition of the utopia which thus consists of superimposed layers and strata."[53]

Latin America also has a long tradition of practices of direct democracy, self-government, and collective organization, with which contemporary debates and practices in the region reconnect. Various

50   Miguel Mazzeo, *El sueño de una cosa: Introducción al Poder Popular* (Caracas, Venezuela: El perro y la rana, 2007), p. 56.

51   Examples include Túpac Amaru, Túpac Katari, José Martí, Farabundo Martí, Ricardo Flores Magón, Augusto Cesár Sandino, Emiliano Zapata, Pancho Villa, and so on.

52   Walter Benjamin, "Geschichtsphilosophische Thesen," *Zur Kritik der Gewalt und andere Aufsätze* (Frankfurt am Main: Suhrkamp, 1965), pp. 78–94, p. 79.

53   Mazzeo, *El sueño de una cosa*, p. 57.

degrees and models of direct democracy, or even of some sort of communal egalitarian socialism, can be found in historical, popular, indigenous, and African-American experiences throughout Latin American history, as well as traditional forms of indigenous collectivism and communitarianism. This can be seen in the historical experiences of the Maroons, former African-American slaves who escaped to remote regions and built self-administered communities, as well as settlements called Cumbes in Venezuela and Palenques or Quilombos in various Latin American countries. In some countries—Bolivia, Ecuador, Mexico, and Colombia, for example—the practices of self-organization, self-administration, and direct democracy are rooted especially in indigenous communities.

Current movement democratic practices

The new global movements continue to experiment with a wide range of mechanisms, trying to build a democratic process in which everyone can participate in decision-making. We witnessed democratic mass assemblies emerging all over the world, from the US to Spain, and most recently in Turkey and Brazil. As many participants in movements all over the world noted, the assembly model developed intuitively. Marianna, from Athens, told us, "The assembly is something many of us knew from the university. It's something that we do, something close to us—even with all its problems. So it came up naturally: we discuss now and decide what we want to do."[54] Gülşah Pilpil, an activist in Istanbul's Gezi Park movement reflected that, "Since Gezi Park was evicted, people gather in other parks to talk, share and to produce new ideas. In the universities, forums and assemblies have been set up by academics, students, and workers."[55] And Marianna Bruce wrote to us from Rio de Janeiro, "Here in the eastern part of the city we do popular youth assemblies in the plazas."[56] And, as Amador from Madrid notes, "Democracy

---

54   Marianna R., welfare worker, Assembly for the Circulation of Struggles (SKYA) and Workers' Union of the Municipality of Tavros, Athens, author interview, November 2011.

55   Gülşah Pilpil Yöney, academic and Gezi Park activist, Istanbul, Turkey, author interview, August 16, 2013.

56   Mariana Bruce, academic and activist, Rio de Janeiro, Brazil, author interview, July 15, 2013.

will start to include something like this, an open space for everyone, not a privatized space for those who have economic or political power, and certainly not a privatized space for professional politicians or activists, but a space open to everyone. Democracy would be to ensure that that space stays constantly open to everyone."[57]

In the plazas, people have adopted and developed numerous mechanisms and practices to ensure broad and vibrant democratic participation. The examples we have encountered include the famous hand signals, which have spread throughout the world's various movements. They help enormously to capture tendencies of opinion during debates involving huge numbers of people. The sign for liking or not liking something, often called "twinkling" or "jazz hands," is based on the sign in American Sign Language for applause. Assemblies have also introduced various mechanisms to ensure that discussions are not dominated by individuals, and to encourage better gender, race, or other identity equality in participation, such as alternating speakers based on their self-identification, or asking people quite specifically to wait to speak—to "step back" in Occupy language. Facilitators are often empowered to shuffle the "stack"—the list of those who are in line to speak—so as to balance the list. The handling of disruptive behavior, and other mechanisms to achieve more open participation—avoiding the "tyranny of the eccentric," as Gopal from Occupy Farms in Berkeley refers to it—is one of the larger challenges movements have faced, and each has dealt with it differently. In Berkeley, speaking was governed by predetermined agreements on active participation. In Spain, many of the squares included teams of people—often called "peace makers," from the group "Respect"—who went directly to the disruptive individuals, and tried to support them without letting them dominate the space. None of the movements we encountered made decisions by simple majority; rather, they aimed for some sort of consensus. This was defined in different ways from one location to another. Madrid used a model of absolute consensus, and New York struggled with a consensus-minus-one rule, meaning one person could block and a consensus could still be reached. New York did also have a fall back

---

57 Amador Fernández Savater, journalist, editor, 15-M activist, Madrid, Spain, author interview, January 2012.

plan of a vote needing 90 percent to pass, but this was so unpopular it was only used in one general assembly. As far as the meaning of consensus, many people who observed the process in the squares assumed that democracy was a series of hand signals, or that decisions were only ever made with a 100 percent consensus. This was not true: each location in these movements, as with similar preceding movements, decided in their specific location what form of direct decision-making worked best for them. In general principle, this kind of consensus is outlined clearly by Rafael, from Caracas: "Consensual democracy, not the majority rule. Not the type of democracy that smothers, where there is a loser and a winner, but a consensual democracy that enables us all to see ourselves in the decisions that are made."[58] Amador, from Madrid, provides an example of two different models adopted in Sol, in Madrid:

> In the beginning, organization in Sol had a lot in common with the chain model, which means several collective assemblies function like a chain and are advancing all together, when all have achieved consensus. That model has its virtues, but it is very slow. [There is] another model: network, based on connection and disconnection, and the ability of some part of the people to create something without waiting for the consensus of the rest. We do this and don't pretend to represent. Many decisions were taken this way toward the end: blocking foreclosures or occupying a hotel, or rallies, including the one held on June 27. Many times a singular autonomous node said we are going to do this, and then suddenly if that node's proposal allied with the common spirit, everyone supported it. Consensus doesn't mean everyone must vote and approve what you want to do, but that we share the general sense of what [we] are doing.
>
> The chain model has that beauty of togetherness. But with the chain model the problem is that the kinds of lives we lead are complex, and therefore it is difficult to spend six hours in an assembly meeting and then having drinks, partying—you almost have to put your real life in parentheses. It was a miracle that scenario occurred for three weeks, but people

---

58   Rafael Falcón, facilitator for the construction of Enterprises of Communal Social Property during a workshop in the Commune of MACA in Petare, Caracas, Venezuela. Dario Azzellini and Oliver Ressler, *Comuna en construcción*, Caracas/Berlin/Vienna, 2010, 94 min (film).

have now returned to their normal lives . . . The political forms that we have are not connecting well with people's ways of living. You have to become an activist to do politics. That way spaces turn into "activist spaces" and the 99 percent is lost.

The network model is more connected to the reality we live. It's flexible but at the same time it is pretty fragile. It does not require you to participate in seventeen meetings every week—you can connect, disconnect, come and go, contribute, while a nucleus exists. That's what happened at Sol.

One feature that all historic and contemporary experiences have in common is that the starting point for participation and democracy is rooted in the local. That is not surprising, as Douglas Lummis states: "Democracy generally depends on localism: the local areas are where the people live. Democracy means not putting power any place other than where the people are."[59] This can be seen in the movements in terms of how they have related internally, with a focus on horizontal relationships, as well as in the shifts from organizing in the large central squares and plazas to the move to the neighborhoods. This is reflected by Anestis, along with many others:

People thought that this is a natural way to organize if I want to do something for my neighborhood. For example, Kesariani was controlled by the Communist Party for many years. The party told people all you have to do is elect our mayor, our representatives, and we will support you, and support you against the central state. But over the last ten or fifteen years people experienced that this did not happen. So a lot of people in the neighborhood thought it is better to have a direct relationship between us, and to self-organize. They know that the model of representative democracy in regions is ineffective.[60]

---

59   Lummis, *Radical Democracy*, 18.
60   Anestis, physics teacher, Assembly for the Circulation of Struggles (SKYA) and Open Assembly of Peristeri, Athens, Greece, author interview, June 2012.

CHAPTER THREE

Greece

In 2013, the Canadian government extended a three-year-old travel warning for Greece, stating that, while it was not dangerous for travel,

> Strikes and demonstrations in Athens are a common occurrence due to austerity measures imposed by the government . . . Avoid all public gatherings and demonstrations and stay away from areas where they can occur as they may turn violent without notice . . . Strikes and demonstrations affecting public health services and transportation, such as trains, buses, taxi, metro, ferries and cruise ships, are usually announced in advance. Road closures may occur at short notice, particularly in Athens. Flights may be disrupted and access to airports and ports may be difficult.[1]

May 2010 marked the beginning of a series of austerity measures forced upon Greek society by the so-called Troika—the tripartite committee under the leadership of the European Commission, and with the participation of the European Central Bank and the International Monetary Fund, as a requirement for new loans. As had been the custom for the past decades in Greece, the population responded by emerging onto the streets en masse. These protests would often take the form of strikes, or even a general strike, and would conclude with confrontations with the

---

1   Available at travel.gc.ca.

police. A series of such demonstrations would sometimes force the government to adapt their proposals or policies slightly, or might at least force them to respond to the populace. Thus, when the first austerity measures were proposed, the population mobilized throughout the country in their millions. The government ignored them and enforced the cuts. When a second round of austerity was proposed, millions again took to the streets, and, again, the people were ignored and austerity imposed—a pattern that recurred from April 2010 to January 2011. Five general strikes occurred in this period, as well as major workplace struggles. Still, the government completely ignored the will of the people, except of course in terms of police repression. In May 2011, something different happened. People broke with the traditional forms of protest— including making demands of parliament—and instead began an open, ongoing assembly in front of the parliament building in Syntagma Square, literally turning their backs on the building and facing one another. Inspired by the events in Tahrir Square in Cairo, and in Puerta del Sol and many other cities in Spain, movement participants, most of whom, like their models, had little to no prior political experience, took over the center of Athens, where they opened ongoing assemblies, discussing alternatives in a directly democratic way, as well as feeding and taking care of those participating in the square.

Since the beginning of the crisis in 2008, the Greek economy has been steadily shrinking, starting in 2009 with 2.3 percent and reaching 6.4 percent in 2012.[2] The cumulative decline in Greek GDP over the last six years of recession (2008–2013) amounts to 25 percent.[3] Since the beginning of 2011, 68,000 businesses have closed down, and another 36,000 were to follow by June 2013; collective bargaining agreements, once common in Greece, have practically ceased to exist; and unemployment rose from 7.7 percent in early 2009 to 16.8 percent in mid-2011 and 27 percent in 2013. And there are further planned austerity measures aimed to lay off another 150,000 public sector workers. In 2013 over 44 percent of the Greek population had an income below the poverty line of €7,180

2 Figures available at indexmundi.com.

3 INE/GSEE-ADEDY (Labour Institute of the General Confederation of Greek Workers), *Greek Economy and Employment—Annual Report 2013* (Athens: INE/GSEE-ADEDY, September 19, 2013), available at www.etui.org.

per year.[4] This situation has been compounded by cuts in the health sector, where the crisis presents itself literally in the form of questions of life and death. Cuts to public health spending have driven people to experiment on themselves with reduced drug dosages, or by choosing not to take prescribed drugs at all, which has already led to a higher death rate, particularly among the elderly. Elsewhere, this tremendous increase in poverty has also led to the return of child labor. The ombudsman for children's safety estimated in 2013 that approximately 100,000 children under the age of fifteen are working. While most of them were Roma immigrants from the Balkans, increasing numbers of Greek children were also now begging on the streets, working in bars and restaurants,[5] or singing and playing music on the street for customers of restaurants and cafés.

The first Memorandum (bailout deal) for a loan of €109 billion, signed with the Troika in May 2010, cut health spending by 10 percent. The second Memorandum, for a loan of €172.7 billion, signed in March 2012, took another €1 billion out of the health budget. And a package of cuts passed by the government in September 2012 reduced government spending by a further €11.9 billion—€4.6 billion in pensions alone, and €1.387 billion in public health.

The Greek financial crisis should not have come as a surprise. Greece was maneuvered into its current situation by local elites, international financial actors, EU politicians, and transnational companies. All of these actors intentionally ignored the approaching disaster, as they now ignore the fact that the austerity measures imposed on Greece can only prolong the ransacking of the country.

THE ROOTS OF THE NEW MOVEMENTS

This is the context in which anarchism has gained new visibility in Greece, especially over the past few years. While it is not the majority sentiment or form of organizing within the new movements, anarchism has played a

---

4   "Nearly half of incomes below poverty line," *Ekathimerini*, January 6, 2014, ekathimerini.com.
5   "Schuldenkrise: Mehr als 100,000 Kinder arbeiten in Griechenland," *Spiegel Online*, June 11, 2013, spiegel.de.

very real role in the movements, as well as in the imaginations of radicals interested in Greece around the globe. While the tradition among individuals, small groups, and a few printing houses goes back to the late 1800s, and persisted in a small way fairly consistently for the next hundred years or more, it was not until the late 1980s and 1990s that anarchism began to assume a prominent role. As in other countries in Europe, anarchists, inspired by black bloc tactics and a confrontational attitude to the state and police, organized around squatting and in opposition to numerous events and policies, including the Olympics, international banking and financial institution meetings, and education cuts.

Those networks and groups that existed before 2005 expanded, deepened, and renewed their networks, now occupying buildings and creating social centers and other bases of support and defense for the movement. Growing student struggles and occupations since 2006 practiced inclusive and non-politically biased or predetermined assemblies, distinct from assemblies organized by a left party or their student organizations. Soon thereafter, residents of Keratea, outside Athens, began to come together in assemblies to discuss how to prevent the building of a landfill site in their small town. They organized protests and other events, from petitioning to direct actions, until ultimately they were forced to occupy parts of their own town to prevent the construction of the site. These blockades and actions were all organized and facilitated by the local assemblies, foreshadowing both the forms of organization as well as the form of action beginning to take place more widely. The most recent example that many provided was the blocking of toll booths—something that has turned into a full campaign, called "Can't Pay, Won't Pay," in which people refuse to pay tolls on major roads. This began in 2008, not as a national campaign but as a local initiative in response to increasing tolls.

Many of these groups and networks emerged in the Athens neighborhood of Exarchia, where the Polytechnic University is located alongside numerous cafés and small parks. It is both a gathering point and a "safe space" from police, since the high density of organized anarchists ensures a regular street presence. In the spot where the fifteen-year-old Alexandros Grigoropoulos was killed by police on December 6, 2008, there is a memorial wall, including a painting donated by the Zapatista community of Chiapas with an inscription of solidarity signed by Subcomandante

Marcos. After Alexandros was killed, massive unrest had broken out, with banks and other buildings burned, and all-night battles fought with the police. In many neighborhoods, the police found themselves surrounded by rioting youth, and were forced to lock themselves inside police stations. Many saw this as a new stage in youth rebellion in response to their empty future and the growing crisis. It has also been seen as the beginning of the extension of struggle and organization to the neighborhoods.

ELECTIONS AND PARLIAMENTARY POLITICS

In the parliamentary elections of June 17, 2012, the Coalition of the Radical Left (SYRIZA), which rejects the austerity Memoranda, won 26.9 percent of the vote. This made them the second-strongest party, after the conservative Néa Dimokratía (ND), with 29.7 percent, and left them with more than double the votes of the "socialist" Panhellenic Socialist Movement (PASOK), which received 12.3 percent of the vote. However, despite SYRIZA's popularity, the Greek electoral system assigns fifty extra seats to the party with the highest number of votes. Thus the ND, PASOK, and the small liberal leftist party DIMAR (which had received 6.3 percent of the vote) formed a coalition and elected ND leader and economist Antonis Samaras as prime minister on June 20.

Neither the rise of SYRIZA nor the slight majority that allowed the formation of a pro-austerity government points to a rehabilitation of electoral politics, or a newfound trust in parliamentary democracy. Most people over forty who voted for the pro-austerity parties did so out of fear that had been stirred up by politicians and the media. A massive campaign was launched before the elections claiming that they would lose their pensions, savings, and belongings if they did not elect a government who was loyal to the decisions of the Troika. But most people under forty voted for SYRIZA, despite government leaders and politicians from all over Europe threatening the Greeks before the elections that if they did so they would be abandoned by the other EU countries. Young people in Greece, feeling they had nothing to lose, voted for SYRIZA anyway, hoping there might be a chance to challenge the conditions imposed by the Troika.

As of 2014, the future of SYRIZA is not clear. SYRIZA continues along the electoral path, consolidating itself into a political party and losing its identity as a coalition. But it is also trying to build bases in the neighborhoods and with the movements. Despite its participation in elections, SYRIZA's electoral base has no hope of positive outcomes resulting from parliamentary routine.

At the other end of the political spectrum is the fascist Golden Dawn, which won nearly 7 percent of the vote in the elections, and has increased its violent attacks against immigrants—attacks that are often tolerated, if not actively supported, by the police. Golden Dawn is attempting to build a broader social base by, on the one hand, offering services and support for "pure" Greeks, and, on the other, by brutally attacking immigrants and political opponents, in a strategy reminiscent of the German SA[6] or the Italian Blackshirts.[7] Golden Dawn's tactics have been largely successful in gaining support among segments of the Greek population through the fomentation of racism and an irrational fear of "the other," arguing that immigrants are taking Greek jobs and are the source of violence in society. At the same time, Golden Dawn broadcasts its determination to take action to "solve" this "problem" that it has, in fact, created.

Nevertheless, the crisis brings about opportunities, as Theo from Thessaloniki describes:

> I have hope because I get hope from our social movements and our autonomy. We can be autonomous to an extent, and self-sufficient to an extent . . . the economic crisis in some ways is also a good thing, because it is not just a crisis of our capacity to feed ourselves, but it is a crisis of an economic model that was destructive—destructive for the planet and for people. So this is a great opportunity to create new values and to create a new system. So this is my hope—that we find a new way to look after ourselves, take over our lives, and make decisions in collective ways—to regain a sense of collectivity that we have lost in the past couple hundred years and create a new economic system and decide what our needs are.[8]

---

6   *Sturmabteilung* means "Assault Division." The Nazi paramilitaries were also known as "brown shirts."

7   The Italian fascist paramilitaries.

8   Theo, Micropolis, Thessaloniki, author interview, June 2012.

VOICES

We conducted interviews with eighteen movement participants in Greece between November 2011 and June 2013. A number of people were interviewed several times over the course of those twenty months, as is reflected in the interview index. We remain in regular contact with many movement participants, exchanging experiences and receiving regular updates and evaluations of the situation in Greece. All interviewees are movement participants, and none belong to any political party. All interviewees were living either in Athens or Thessaloniki—the two biggest cities in Greece, as well as its main centers of economic and political power. These two cities were also the main sites of anti-crisis mobilization. Eighty percent of the interviewees have university degrees or are professionals, even if they do not work in their professions or—as is the case for some—have no regular paid work at all. Unlike in Spain, all Greek interviewees had political and social organizing experiences prior to their experiences in Syntagma Square in 2011. People in Greece seem more politicized than their Spanish counterparts, and clearer about the substance and political orientation of their rejection of the existing political system. State repression against movements is much more intense here than in many other Western countries, and has been historically. For this reason, of the eighteen people interviewed, only one felt comfortable using his full name, all others asked to be identified by first name only. This alone should already be cause for concern regarding the state of Greece's supposed democracy.

CRISIS

When asked about the crisis, leaving the nature of the crisis an open question, people in Greece generally began by describing the overall economic situation, though that quickly flowed into the question of day-to-day survival, with people discussing the crisis of healthcare, employment, access to food, electricity cuts, and the rise of fascism. Crisis became a sort of overall state of being. We have divided the following material thematically, following what people shared with us.

The economy

Vassilis, thirty-six, from Athens, studied social work and considers himself lucky to be employed as an underpaid clerk after lengthy unemployment. He was also a participant in the Assembly for the Circulation of Struggles (SKYA), in which participants from different struggles exchange experiences and sometimes co-produce written material for the movements.

Vassilis, Assembly for the Circulation of Struggles (SKYA), Athens: What is happening is a war. It is a war without guns. It is conducted by other means. In Europe we had many wars, but now it's not possible to destroy the whole infrastructure with a massive war and then rebuild it. It is a different kind of war.

Anestis, thirty-six, works on a contractual basis as a physics teacher, and is part of the Open Assembly of Peristeri in Athens. He participated in political collectives, workers' unions, and local assemblies, and is also a participant in the SKYA.

Anestis, Peristeri Assembly, Athens: There is no way to survive with this amount of money right now at the end of 2011. Families especially are facing huge problems. A lot of them have taken out bank loans in order to buy a house. In the last two decades in Greece, when you started a family it was easy to get a loan and buy a house. For example, a teacher in public school earned €1,200 per month, about a year ago. Now, after all the cuts in the salaries, a teacher earns about €700 a month. If you have to feed your children and repay your loan to the bank, you are destroyed! This also causes depression for many of the women between thirty and thirty-five, because they realize that they cannot have children. My sister is thirty-seven years old and has been unemployed for a year and a half . . . so that's the end for her, you know?

Since the capitalist crisis continues, maybe soon you will hear that in Greece there are marches outside the local tax offices. They lowered the income limit for paying taxes. Now it is approximately €5,000 per year, so if you earn €500 a month you will have to pay taxes. Even people who get unemployment benefits will probably have to pay taxes! A lot of people do not have the money to pay. I earn about €600 a month. In three months, in September 2012, the Greek state will tell me: "You owe us 500." As the capitalist crisis continues, there will be new issues people will organize around.

Vassilis, SKYA, Athens: From 1974 to 2000, most people in Greece worked in the public sector. They had good salaries, a steady job, and everything was fine. In the private sector many workers also had steady jobs and good salaries. For example, in the '80s my parents raised a family with my father only working during the tourist season, which is five to six months. It was a hard job with no days off, etc., but it worked. In the '90s my mother also started working, because our needs increased.

In the beginning of this fascinating century, neoliberalism started to get into the workplaces and, of course, in the workplaces the younger people were doing all the bad jobs. Most young people in Greece are well educated. They study for years to enter university, then they study in university, and finally they end up making hamburgers or delivering pizzas—after ten years of studying.

Marita, thirty-eight, is a doctor working for the national health system and was part of the formation of a health workers' assembly and the assembly of Ano Poli in 2008 in Thessalonki.

Marita, Ano Poli Assembly, Thessaloniki: In the '90s we had a period of "democratic capitalism" in Greece. There was money for a lot of people, many who also had cars and loans from the banks. It was something like "the American dream." So many people did not see social injustice—they couldn't see what the capitalist system produced. Now, in a way, there is equality in the cutting of rights and salaries. The middle class has been destroyed!

Work

Afrodite, Eleftherotypia *newspaper*: More than 800 employees have been laid off, without compensation and while being owed six months' outstanding wages. *Eleftherotypia* is part of the Greek crisis. More than 5,500 media employees have been laid off during the last four years, just from major print and broadcast outlets. And many more if you count the thousands of part-time uninsured workers in smaller media and the fast-expanding news portals. And that is without the 2,600 employees who were fired when the government shut down the public TV and radio network Elliniki Radiofonía Tileórasi (ERT) in June 2013. Some of them were then hired again with two-month contracts in a new government TV channel. The layoffs in the media sector are just a drop in the ocean of almost 1.5 million unemployed in Greece.

Vassilis, SKYA, Athens: People in workplaces were, and still are, very frightened. After being unemployed, I finally started working again in November 2011 and thought, "OK, head down and moving on." I had a good job, because I was paid. I remember last winter, when you met someone the first question was, "Are you working?" and if the answer was "Yes, I am," then the second one was, "Are you getting paid?" with the usual response of, "No, I haven't gotten paid for two months or so."

Though there wasn't any general open disobedience in workplaces, people were still much angrier than before, so there was a general secret disobedience—productivity dropped. Many people in workplaces were just doing the least amount of what they were supposed to. Everyone was stealing from the boss—in small amounts, so that the boss couldn't check it. We are not talking about big money. We are talking about €5, for example, which is what you need to buy a bus ticket, a coffee, something to eat or a phone card.

Health

Marita, Ano Poli Assembly, Thessaloniki: During the last two years the government has cut everything, and Greek society has suffered all these inhuman measures. It's not only in the healthcare system, it's like being in a war and you're shot at from everywhere.

Anestis, Peristeri Assembly, Athens: In the last six months the situation has gotten worse and worse. There are not enough doctors and nurses in many hospitals, and they are planning to close some hospitals. There is a big problem with medical supplies in the hospitals, since the Greek state owes money to the pharmaceutical companies and many stopped delivering for lack of payment. What they do not say is that for all these years the pharma industry sold its products at a totally inflated price to the hospitals. Now, people go to the hospital and cannot have their treatment since there is no medicine. The shocking thing is that doctors told us that there are hospitals in Athens where they do not have basic stuff to do their jobs—needles, for instance, and they have to buy needles themselves.

Debbie, in her early thirties, is a molecular biologist in Thessaloniki. She participates in the Solidarity Clinic and has a background in autonomous horizontal assemblies and grassroots movements.

Debbie, Solidarity Clinic, Thessaloniki: A lot of international pharmaceutical companies also stopped selling medicine to Greece because they were very afraid that this "radical" (no, it's not that radical) new party SYRIZA would come into power, Greece would drop out of the Eurozone and not be able to pay it back. We had a lot of shortages; a lot of medication was not even available.

Marita, Ano Poli Assembly, Thessaloniki: Before the crisis there were different forms of public insurance. Some of the patients paid, but some other patients who belonged to the "poorest" didn't have to pay. Now the ticket is for everyone, and more expensive. Month after month, they want more money from the patients in general. They want you to pay when you have an emergency if you don't have insurance. That did not exist in Greece. If you didn't have insurance, you were unemployed or you were an immigrant, and you had an urgent problem, you could go to the hospital and never pay.

At work I see that, because drugs are more expensive for patients now, the older patients stop taking their drugs or they take them one day and not the next day. They do these small experiments on themselves, or come and ask if it is necessary to take this or that drug—it's awful. This situation could lead to a drop in life expectancy. Also, many young people have died in the last two years. It's not an official statistic, but we know it since we see it—there are many sudden deaths, and if you live in a small place and you ask what happened you'll hear that it was somebody who was unemployed or in debt. We have many sudden deaths. Heart attacks are a result of anxiety and stress, and that has been widespread during the last two years.

The fascists

Alex, twenty-six, is a student at the University of Economics and Commerce, and a participant in the Assembly of Immigrants and Locals in Solidarity, and SKYA.

Alex, Assembly of Immigrants and Locals in Solidarity, Athens: After December 2008, when the crisis started to hit, many of us say the social state went away and the police state came. It was a major issue in the media, and politically convenient for them to say, "We want a safe city center, no criminality, no illegal selling." We had more controls, more attacks, more pogroms by the police. They started to show they were acting against illegal immigrants—supporting the fascists. Now there are new policemen with motorbikes, who are always in the city center. This made it impossible for the immigrants to be in Victoria Square, since the police can easily attack and arrest them there and did so many times. Now there are less immigrants in the center and only around the university.

Theo, in his mid-thirties, is a translator and editor in Thessaloniki, and participates in the Micropolis community center and the Vio.Me Solidarity Initiative.

Theo, Micropolis, Thessaloniki: So, now you have a totally different response as well, which is fascism. And always, as historically, it is something that comes up in times of great uncertainty—and fascism, as always, is the long hand of the state. It pretends to be anti-system, against exploitation, but at the same time its only role is to protect the status quo. And now, you have an enormous rise in fascism in Greece—the parliamentary rise of fascism is only the tip of the iceberg, there are many people in Greek society that are now going back to the basic values of "family, nation, and religion," and the opinions that are pushing for violence for anyone who goes against the grain in society are growing. For example, here in Thessaloniki we had the first gay pride parade last week, and the response was extreme: "Perverts—they are even parading in the streets! Why don't you keep your perversion to yourself?" And they were not all voters for the fascist party, but that is fascist society, and now fascism wants to restore some sense of certainty.

SURVIVAL AND SOLIDARITY IN CRISIS

Solidarity Clinics have begun to be set up all over Greece. Most are run by volunteer doctors, nurses, and other staff, and survive on donations of supplies and medicines from people in that region. The Solidarity Social Practice Clinic was one of the first ones, set up in Thessaloniki.

Debbie, Solidarity Social Practice Clinic, Thessaloniki: We attend people who have been excluded from the social medical system—for example, because they are immigrants who don't have a legal job, and therefore no insurance. The Solidarity Social Practice Clinic started from a hunger strike of 300 immigrant workers. It was a need of a lot of immigrants who live in this country and are excluded by the hospitals. Unfortunately, what happened is that we coincided with the huge economic crisis in Greece and, although we were expecting more immigrants here, 60 percent of the people we treat are Greeks. Of course, everybody excluded from the medical care system is welcome here, but it is something we didn't expect.

In six months of activity here we had more than 1,000 people coming to the dentist, and that actually means that they did not go to the dentist just once, but multiple [times]. More than 700 people have been attended by the other specialists we have, which include pediatricians, neurologists, psychiatrists, psychologists, general practitioners, cardiologists, dermatologists, and ear-nose-and-throat specialists. And if you need a specialized doctor we give you a referral paper and you go to external doctors and to their private practices, or to hospitals where we have people working that have shown their solidarity. Everything is free here and wherever we send you.

If we have the medicine you need, we will also give it to you for free. Our expenses are €3,500 per month—€1,500 is for the dental practice and the rest mostly for the vaccination for children. We cannot afford to buy more specialized medication unless it's something very very important and people cannot get it from the hospitals or anywhere else—for example, anti-epileptic drugs. We are very happy that a lot of people are actually donating their old medication. Anything you don't need, as long as it hasn't expired, you can leave it here and we will use it.

Even though people are giving, and we provide a service, this is not an NGO—we decided quite consciously that we didn't want to be an NGO—we don't get any corporate funding, we don't get any state funding: it is all self-funded by people's donations, and we try to have social spaces, like the social center Micropolis, help with monthly donations. Others organize soup kitchens, where people donate money, or a concert or any other event to raise money.

We are self-organized and operate in a horizontal way. We have a general assembly where everyone—no matter whether it is a medical practitioner, a secretary, or a technical engineer—is equal in the decision-making. We also try to empower the patients so that they do not actually feel that they are victims, and what we do is philanthropy. We show them the way they can get involved, whether it is in cleaning, or maybe you are an electrician. We tell our patients that we are all equal and what we do has nothing to do with just helping them. It is something they are entitled to, because all humans are entitled to medical care and this is something the state should provide anyway. We are not trying to help the state out in this time of crisis. We are trying to show a different path by being quite autonomous in the way we operate.

What we are trying to do now is to organize ourselves, people of the movement generally in Thessaloniki and our patients, to go and demand from the hospitals hospitalization of more severe and serious cases. If someone needs to have surgery we go to the hospitals and inform the people that work there that it's something they have to do. It's not a choice: you work in a hospital, you have to care for people and you can't let the management or government decide who is to be treated or not. Being silent and not taking a stance toward this injustice makes you equally responsible. We are trying to make them see what they are doing is wrong, how they should go against their hospital policies and help us by letting people know. We mobilize for demonstration inside and outside hospitals, occupy them, try to pressure people who work there and the administration to take a stance and say, "Yes, we will do this free of charge."

In the Solidarity Social Practice we have all sorts of people, from autonomous people, people from SYRIZA, to people who don't belong anywhere and are strongly against any political organization or party. We don't want any party agendas within our group, and everybody agrees and respects that. Of course, ways of thinking differ, and that is why it is important to discuss and decide collectively what we do. A lot of us think we need to overthrow the system, and all of us can decide on how to tackle the issue of capitalism or the state, but here our first and only common ground is that every human being, no matter where from, needs and is entitled to health-care. A lot of people say, "What you're doing is not revolutionary, because you are not actually trying to change the system." But now we have to fulfill basic needs first. We will see how we can progress in the future.

One of the many shifts taking place in Greece is the relationship one has to one's community beyond the immediate family. In particular, this has emerged as economic and social needs have grown, and the ability of families to support themselves has diminished. The result is a changing political culture as to need and the social question of poverty.

Vassilis, SKYA, Athens: When the welfare state finally came to Greece in the '80s, it was mostly based on the family—the core family and the grand-parents. The trick of the Greek welfare state was to have in each family at least one person with a steady job—which meant in the public sector. In general, families kept helping all their members. Parents gave their children money or a house to live in, or children helped their parents when they were in need. But it always stayed in the family. I would ask my father or my brother for help, but not my neighbors or friends. I would not act in a way that people could see that I have a problem and can't make a living. This was people's perception of what helping each other meant . . .

People are ashamed of asking for money and help. They are even ashamed to tell the welfare office, "I'm poor, I have no money. Can you give me the very small amount that I'm entitled to?" When I was a social work student there was a social worker whose job was to give the benefit to poor people, and often it was their neighbors or their distant relatives who came and said "Check this family." Although in small towns and in the countryside it is very common for the village or the neighborhood to take care of an old man or woman, giving him a plate of food, cleaning his house, or keeping him company. But it is not exactly solidarity. The idea is more, "I'm a good Christian, I must do it," or, "This old man once helped me," or "He was a good neighbor."

This family focus on help has begun to shift to be more social. For example, with what happened with the sharing of public transportation tickets. For many years you could buy a ticket for €1. Then the subway ticket price rose to €1.40. The fine if you get caught without a ticket went up to €60, and if you don't pay it, they pass it to the tax office and you pay a €600 fine. So it could happen that you don't find an open kiosk to buy a bus ticket and end up paying a fine that is a whole salary, although the transportation in Athens is public and paid by us through taxes! People started to discuss the matter in assemblies and came up with the plan of passing on the used ticket to the next passenger. The tickets last for ninety minutes.

Some more political transportation assemblies formulated demands like "Free transport for everyone," "Don't raise the ticket price," or "Make a fund to cover the fines." Originally the idea of passing tickets came up organically, not straight from the assemblies. Someone wrote in his blog, Let's do this, more bloggers followed, and the "Pass your ticket to the next one" idea spread. And, of course, there was lots of propaganda against it, claiming it was illegal. Some lawyers claimed that it was not, based on the argument that if someone goes to a restaurant he can have just one dish and share it with his companion and it is legal. It is a service provided as a whole and the client has the right to offer it to someone else. Now, on the back of the tickets it says that giving or taking a used ticket, or even asking people to give or take one, is forbidden by the law . . . Before, it was very common to find two or three tickets on the validation machines, and choose the one valid for the most time. Now people pass them hand to hand. The only reason you cannot see it happening as often now is because most people don't even buy tickets anymore. Very few people pay, or they pay just sometimes. If you are a resident you know when or where the controls are done.

Electricity cuts and direct action

New taxes on electricity bills have led to thousands having their power cut every month.[9] People in neighborhoods throughout the country are organizing through their local assemblies, as well as spontaneously, both to physically

---

9   Andy Dabilis, "Electric Bills Up 9%, Government Agencies Won't Pay," *Greek Reporter*, January 13, 2013, avgreece.greekreporter.com.

resist the power company coming to shut off the electricity and to reconnect homes when it is cut. In Athens alone, the refusal to pay the new tax is over 40 percent, with a high rate of reconnections when the electricity is cut.

Anestis, Peristeri Assembly, Athens: The first and very basic problem was the new tax on houses, which must be paid together with the electricity bill. It was introduced in October 2011. From October until Christmas most of the assemblies tried to mobilize on this issue. Not all the assemblies did the same thing, however. For example, in Peristeri we produced a leaflet explaining that people should not pay the tax on the electricity bill, and if the electric company came to cut off energy supply, we would come and support them to try to stop the electricity workers or help them to reconnect it if it was cut. We put a number at the bottom of the leaflet so that people could call us if they needed support. Most assemblies did something like that at first.

But it did not have a huge effect—only a few people contacted us. We don't know how many did not pay the tax, but we do know they are many. Then, assembly participants went together to the local office of the electricity company, and we took all the lists of people who had not paid their bill and so would have had their electricity cut off. Many records you see are still kept only on paper.

Other assemblies were more effective. For example, the assemblies from the East—Kesariani, Vironas, and Pagrati—organized two or three daily occupations of some electricity company local offices, and achieved that in those neighborhoods people pay only the electricity and not the tax. There were also mobilizations organized by several assemblies on different days against the subcontractor cutting off electricity. The electricity company has outsourced the job. When we eventually found out who ran that company, we went to their offices and closed the office of the manager and told them, "Don't even think of coming to our neighborhood to cut off our electricity." We also went to the central offices of the electric company, along with other local assemblies, when they had an open bidding for the job of cutting off electricity, and we stopped it. All we did was walk in, start yelling, and they have this fear that we will beat them up at the end—so they stop. You can do that without a lot of people, we were only, maybe, fifty.

Some assemblies managed to have a better relationship with the neighborhood and helped a lot more people reconnect their electricity. It is not so hard to reconnect, especially in a single house. Many people in the neighborhoods have done it without help from the neighborhood assemblies. It also happens to many people that they start to pay, and then realize they cannot pay and ask the electricity company to renegotiate the debt. That also caused a problem for the electricity company because they lost money or had to wait for it. Many assemblies tried to deal with this issue. Some were more successful than others. Here in Peristeri, after one month of trying to mobilize people, some of us, along with others from the neighborhoods, decided to create smaller assemblies within neighborhoods. In Peristeri, for example, four more assemblies were created to mobilize around only electricity. People did not participate for any other reason. These assemblies gather about twenty to thirty people each, mostly older people.

The Greek state claims that, all in all, 60 percent paid—so 40 percent did not pay. But a lot of the people who did not pay did not organize at the same time, so this is what I am concerned about. OK, so you did not pay, but if they really want to start to cut massively you need to be organized to resist that.

Resisting fascism

Since the crisis began, and increasingly, fascists have played an almost daily role in society, from their formal political role within the political structure with the Golden Dawn Party, to their organized attempts to win over supporters among very young people in the schools and the elderly in the neighborhoods, to their violent attacks on immigrants and participants in movements and left groups.

Theo, Micropolis, Thessaloniki: The answer we give to neo-fascism through the movements is clear—because fascism has a very strong component of creating a lost sense of community. Fascism is not only hate speech in the mass media, but it is also working at the level of the neighborhood. This party that won so many seats in the parliament did so by going to the neighborhoods and listening to the people and what they had to say, and in many cases they presented themselves as the defenders of the weak.

They organized food and gave resources to people, taking old women across the street, etc. This is part of why the fascist party succeeded. What we—the movements—say to this is that, against this fake social relationship, we want to create real social relationships. We are talking about those movements that are working for more liberty and equality—those movements that work for more autonomy in society. Autonomy for society means a society that can take care of itself and has real social relationships—not virtual relations, as we have right now.

We want to promote the establishment of real communities. People now are governed by fear and don't know their neighbors. We are told by the media that if we go out in the street we will be robbed and killed. So our biggest fight is against this fear. This takes place on different levels—within us and in the neighborhoods. Fighting against fascism means getting out into the neighborhoods, getting to know our neighbors, getting organized with them, creating assemblies with them, and building small struggles for our rights in the neighborhoods. This is the first step to creating real social relationships. And yes, this also means self-defense against the fascists. Sometimes this means violence. The violence of fascism is enormous—we cannot stop this by asking them to please stop.

NEW RELATIONSHIPS OF CONSUMPTION AND PRODUCTION

The crisis has forced new ways of thinking about consumption upon most people. For many this just means less consuming, but for others it has led to creative ways of exchanging products that are needed to survive, and others have even begun to think more deeply about what is consumed and produced, and how.

Vassilis, Athens, 2012: People are trying to build small producer networks that send their products to those who want them. For example, ten to fifteen producers in an area in the countryside gather, say "You produce potatoes, I produce tomatoes, wine, honey, etc.," and sell it all together to consumers in the city—Athens mainly, which is a very big city. It was common years ago, for example, as a small wine producer, to have your own customers in the city, three or four taverns, and a few individual customers, nothing big. Most people involved in agriculture do not own much land and have more than one product, such as wine, some vegetables, or something else, in small quantities, but they can make a living out of this. This is now becoming more formal and more solid as a network. It is happening not only on the small scale, but larger, where, for example, some potato producers came with trucks to the cities to sell their potatoes directly.

There is a general change compared to how it was before—now it is happening in a different frame and with a different meaning. It used to be a tradition for small producers, but now it is more of a conscious political thing. If it becomes more widespread, it could pull the carpet out from under the big companies.

Theo, Micropolis, Thessaloniki: We would like to have this principle of horizontality and direct democracy applied to all areas of life, and a very important area is consumption. Right now the market is organized in a hierarchical way, so our relationship is as consumers. But here we want to promote a different sort of consumption. So we are in touch with people who produce food and all different types of things, and we want to have a direct relationship with them, and we want to know what sorts of things they are producing, how they are producing it, and to have as much control over what we consume as possible. We want it to be as wholesome as possible, so as to eat good food, and we want to have a direct relationship with those who produce it, so we put that in practice here by creating a space that does this, where there is no intermediary, no middle man, and this works in many different ways. It also helps us to create new productive cooperatives so as to help meet our needs. So we begin with our needs, and from there we decide what we want. Maybe we will have to redefine our needs, but now, starting from these needs, we create worker cooperatives to satisfy these needs from the community. For example, we have a bread and detergent production cooperative, others that produce herbs and spices, and so on.

When I speak of community, it is people who participate in this space and the areas around this space. It is an open sense of community, and does not revolve around any sort of identity, but it is just a community that shares certain basic principles.

Barter Networks

Anestis, Peristeri Assembly, Athens: There are also barter networks. The consumer must realize that he is also a producer, and must give something back. He may produce a service in the city, he may be a call center agent and can help with internet, or a teacher can give lessons . . . I'm also a producer, a teacher or whatever, in a wider sense . . . of social and political consciousness. This is the frame in which these things will happen more.

Theo, Micropolis, Thessaloniki: The barter network, aside from meeting real human needs, is meant to make the economy a human thing again. It is a matter of scale, and what the economy is is a way of meeting our needs—it does not have to be something abstract that takes place out there, and the only way I can participate is from out there, as a worker who gets a wage, or a consumer. No, I can be all of these things and have a face-to-face relationship with people, and have a way to measure value that is not necessarily the way that the global economy dictates. I can use a currency that cannot turn into capital, that cannot be accumulated, where there is no interest on this currency so all this value that determines the global currency cannot hold in the local barter economy. We have more human values, and our material needs become human again.

In 2008 it was a magical moment—it was a moment when we realized that there are so many of us and we think alike—not the same, but alike—and that if we come together we can create communities. And Micropolis was a space that was born then, and is trying to be a real community, which means proximity. It means some way of communicating with each other and making decisions together, and also geographic space so that we can come together.

It is a three-story building, with loads of different activities, like the child care center where we are right now, a store that exchanges directly with producers and consumers, a bar; there is also a social kitchen with food every day, a free shop, a furniture restoration project, ceramics, a wild animal rescue center, classes, a library, a space for public activities—there are many, many things here.

The intention behind organizing this space comes from people who had begun to meet one another as part of the 2008 uprisings, and they realized that what was before a marginal form of organization now suddenly became more mainstream, and people were starting to take their lives into their own hands. So there was a great need for the social movements to come closer to society. And we saw a need to create a space where people could meet one another as we do this—a place where people do not have to be a part of the movements to come, but a place that is open and anyone can come, as long as they respect certain values that are behind this space. For example, we do not accept any sort of hierarchy here—the assemblies and general assembly decide all things through a democratic procedure. We do not want any relationship with the forces of the state or the market, so we do not accept any form of sponsors or companies. We value our autonomy. But apart from that, any sort of activity can take place here if they respect these principles.

Anestis, Peristeri Assembly, Athens: When the assembly in Syntagma started [in 2011], a lot of people came and participated in the assembly because they were tired of the fragmentary character of the general strike, or because some of them, especially people working in the private sector, could not easily participate in the general strike. One of the reasons that most of the people were against political parties and unions in the beginning of the assembly in Syntagma was that they were tired of them manipulating the general strikes or other struggles.

There is another very important thing about Syntagma and the local assemblies. During the last year we faced a difficult situation in Greece. We experienced that our lives changed for the worse every single day. At the same time, the basic medium of reaction we had was the general strike. The general strike is called by the bureaucrats of the general confederation of unions, which is controlled by the social democrats. What they did was call a general strike once a month or every two months, and let the people fight with the police so their anger can go away for a while. The general strikes, although they were important and necessary, also operated as a relief valve. For some of us that was a dead end. During the whole year we could not achieve a single goal with general strikes, since the majority of the people in the private sector did not participate. The participants were mainly working in the public sector, and the whole mobilization mainly had a symbolic character. We went to the street and there was always some fighting with the riot police. That was very exhausting for those people, not experienced in fighting the police. In the end we went back home and the next day to our jobs, and every day we saw our lives becoming worse and worse.

The uprising in December 2008 was a turning point. It was the first time that a lot of people from the movement started having political activity that we felt had real concrete results. On the evening of December 6, the fifteen-year-old Alexis Grigoropoulos was assassinated by the Epaminondas Korkoneas special forces of the Greek police. It was a Saturday night, and we went down to the street in Exarchia and fought with the police. The first day of the uprising, the majority of the participants came from the anti-authoritarian movement or the various anarchist groups. The next day there was a big demonstration, and it was the first time in my life that I saw the whole demonstration fighting with the riot police, not just the "black bloc." But it was also the first time I really got scared, because there was so much violence, from their side but also from our side. The riot police had a hard time dealing with us that day—the street fighting lasted for six or seven hours.

The street fighting began outside the central police building on Alexandras Avenue, in the center of the city. By Sunday evening we went home and felt that we had taken our revenge for the assassination. We thought nothing would probably happen tomorrow. The next day most of us woke up in complete shock, because we switched on our computers and we saw that high school students all over Athens had attacked nearly all the police stations. All the police stations! We saw pictures of police cars turned upside down and wondered "How did that happen without us!" In previous years we thought that if something important happened we would definitely be in the front line. But suddenly we were nothing! These high school children taught us that if you want to fight the police effectively, do not fight them in the center of the city, where they now know very well what to do, where they have confronted you 200 times— go and fight them in the neighborhoods, where they don't know what to do. It was unbelievable, the schoolchildren threw everything at the bastards: stones, oranges, bags full of garbage, everything! The cops closed the doors of the police stations and didn't know exactly what to do because outside there were schoolchildren. That day we began to understand that what was happening was larger than us—it was something that surpassed the limits of our understanding as political activists. It was a rupture. Those attacks on the police stations happened on Monday morning. Monday evening there was a huge demonstration, larger than the previous day. It was the second moment of rupture. It was the first time that protesters forced the riot police to surround the parliament to defend it from their attacks. They couldn't attack us effectively. It was impossible, because people were everywhere in the center of the city, street fighting or looting shops. You know Ermou Street? That night all the shops there were destroyed and looted.

The police basically defended the parliament. During the night there were rumors that the government would call the army, while many public buildings were on fire. That night the occupations of the Polytechnic School and Athens University of Economics and Business began. All that, and what happened the following two or three weeks, was a rupture.

We met new people in the assemblies, and we saw an element that was lost in the last two years in the struggles against the crisis. It was that we were not defensive, neither in content nor in practical methods of struggle. People who participated in the uprising were saying, "We want that, we are going to conquer it." We were not only saying that we were against what the state does. In the last two years the state has succeeded in putting us on the defensive; we now say, "We are against this, we are against that." But the uprising of December 2008 and the struggles against the austerity measures are related. Not a lot of people see that, but it was a big problem for the Greek state and for Greek capitalism. When the restructuring of the national debt and the IMF program started, they had to deal with a nucleus of society that was, to some extent, organized because of the December uprising. One week after the austerity measures came into effect we already had huge demonstrations.

In the assemblies and the occupations during December 2008, I felt a big opportunity to change my everyday life. It was the first time I could really dream of a future society while I was participating in a struggle. We were offensive then, not defensive, and there was also a strong creative element in the structures that we built. We said, "Enough with this shit we are living! We want something much better than this." The December uprising was also important for me because it taught me that the political activity I had engaged in all those years was not as important as I thought. The experience proved that you must have a social basis for whatever you do. Another important thing is that I created new personal relationships. I met a lot of new people during the uprising.

Kostas is forty-two, an electrician, and collaborates with the Autonomo Steki Social Center, Dokimi (political/theoretical collective), and Social Solidarity Neighborhood Assembly in Exarchia.

Kostas, Autonomo Steki Social Center, Athens: The events of 2008 led to a qualitative change regarding the anarchist movement. It experienced a gradual decentralization. Before that, the anarchist movement was more or less focused on the Exarchia area. But then people started going back to their neighborhoods. This was the legacy of 2008—small neighborhood assemblies that started, stopped, continued, a lot of different situations. Because of the crisis they started to reassemble; 2008 created this backbone of some sort of a community that never existed before.

Areti, forty-four, is an unemployed teacher, and collaborates with the Autonomo Steki Social Center and Dokimi.

Areti, Autonomo Steki Social Center, Athens: Some of the anarchist *compañeros* made the choice, "We won't do huge assemblies at Polytechnic University, where only the leaders talk—only men, also—but we'll try to do things in our neighborhoods, in order to understand the ordinary people, because perhaps we are ordinary people, too."

SYNTAGMA—AS DIRECT PARTICIPATION AND DEMOCRACY

While the mass assemblies and three-month occupation of Syntagma Square was a turning point in the collective imagination of Greek society, it is also not seen in the same way, taking on the same importance, as, say, Zuccotti Park in New York or Plaza del Sol in Madrid. Hundreds of thousands participated in the various assemblies and working groups over the period of the occupation, and many thousands attended and participated in each assembly. People speak of having been transformed by the experience. Greek movement participants also quickly speak of 2008 and the current neighborhood assemblies, linking all of the experiences on a continuum.

Anestis, Peristeri Assembly, Athens: A lot of people were influenced by what happened in Syntagma last summer. There was a certain political tradition of self-organizing in Greece, mostly by anarchists. But in the Syntagma mobilization a lot of people saw that, organizing this way, you can at least have your opinions heard—you can express your view clearly and express yourself more openly to others.

Here is an example of one of the many resolutions passed [showing us the text below]:

One resolution:

#603. Resolution by the Popular Assembly of Syntagma Square
. . . an assembly attended by 3,000 people.
For a long time now, decisions are taken for us, without us.
We are workers, unemployed, pensioners, youth who came to Syntagma to struggle for our lives and our futures.
We are here because we know that the solution to our problems can only come from us.
We invite all Athenians, the workers, the unemployed and the youth to Syntagma, and the entire society to fill up the squares and to take life into its hands.
There, in the squares, we shall co-shape all our demands.
We call all workers who will be striking in the coming period to end up and to remain at Syntagma.
We will not leave the squares before those who lead us here leave first: Governments, the Troika, Banks, Memorandums and everyone who exploits us.
We tell them that the debt is not ours.
DIRECT DEMOCRACY NOW!

EQUALITY—JUSTICE—DIGNITY!
The only defeated struggle is the one that was never fought![10]

Alexandros, twenty-four, is originally from Thessaloniki, where he became active in autonomous groups and movements in high school. He then moved to Athens for university, and is a participant in his neighborhood assembly, the Autonomous Assembly of Zografou.

Alexandros, Zografou Assembly, Athens: We had been talking about self-organization and these things for many years, but it was just among ourselves. We put it into practice in our groups and squats, but it was never adopted by larger groups of people. With the December rebellion a lot of us felt in an awkward position—so many people in many social spaces, workplaces, universities, etc., were organizing horizontally. Self-organization started to become some sort of instinct in people—you begin a struggle and it's going to be self-organized or nothing. For many of us it stopped being an ideological reference or political project, and it became an everyday experience in our everyday struggles. When we saw it was coming from people almost instinctively, we thought that all those years' long discussions about how self-organization should be, when it is revolutionary and when it is reformist, etc., did not really matter in the process of struggle. What really mattered was to have collective results. People taught us that bringing results through a collective and directly democratic process was the most important thing. And we saw all of this again in Syntagma.

Fani, thirty-three, is a precarious worker in Thessaloniki who has participated in collective social and publishing initiatives, and was a participant in the Ano Poli Neighborhood Assembly, which was formed during the revolt of 2008.

Fani, Ano Poli Assembly, Thessaloniki: People have lost their trust in governments and politicians. Even the people really into political parties, those who vote for them or are members, started losing their trust. Politics in Greece was always based on clientelistic relationships, and when politicians ceased to have the power they used to, because of the

---

10   Available at blog.occupiedlondon.org.

crisis and the external political forces that came into the country, people didn't seem to have a reason to keep trusting them anymore, and their interests weren't met.

If you disagree with the individualist approach, you immediately turn to a collectivist one. Some day the workers realized that they don't have any other power besides their collective one. The same goes for all the political issues, like the austerity measures, pension schemes, educational reforms, etc. Why this reaction? It has to do with a collective feeling and the fact that, as history shows, collective demands are more successful than individual ones. I'm not sure if people are actually consciously thinking, "Ah, we have to act collectively!" I think it just comes naturally. And yes, this is what I think happened with the mass assemblies in the plazas, from Thessaloniki to Athens.

Anestis, Peristeri Assembly, Athens: In Syntagma Square there were some people who had been active in the Peristeri neighborhood before the Syntagma mobilization, but not in an assembly. On the fifth or sixth day of the mobilization, some people from the neighborhood of Kesariani came to the central assembly and said, "There is a problem: we need to organize locally, so whoever comes from Kesariani, let's gather here and start a local assembly." [I] and three or four people from Peristeri I knew said, "We'll do exactly the same." The next day we went to the microphone and said, "Anyone who comes from Peristeri, let's gather here to see what we can do in our neighborhood." The main reason for the creation of the assembly in Peristeri was that we needed to act locally in order to act! The second reason was that, after five or six days in Syntagma, we saw how members of the left parties presented themselves as individuals, and because of the open character of the central assembly they started to dominate it. They tried the same with the working groups. There were many working groups in Syntagma Square: groups for the study of the changes in labor relations, for the legal assistance of the mobilization, for the defense of the people in the square, etc. Another reason was that we voted for many things, but everything we voted for didn't have a concrete end. We voted in favor of the refusal to pay metro or bus tickets, but the next day nobody went to the metro station or the bus station to talk to the people and prevent them from paying. We also voted that we need a new constitution, yes . . . ha-ha, we voted to refuse to pay the national debt, and for the destruction of capitalism—we voted for all those things. So what? We realized that there was too much talking and practically no action.

FROM SYNTAGMA TO THE NEIGHBORHOODS

Partly because of the strong history of neighborhood assemblies and the use of direct democracy, the move from the central square in Athens to the various neighborhoods came about quite naturally and rapidly. In many cases local assemblies developed while the Syntagma occupation was still taking place. In other instances, there were already existing local assemblies, and the participants came to both Syntagma and the neighborhood assembly, with the local assembly then growing significantly after Syntagma.

Anestis, Peristeri Assembly, Athens: A lot of people also experienced problems in the central assembly of Syntagma Square. There were thousands of participants, so if you wanted to speak you only had one or two minutes. Many people understood within the first two weeks of Syntagma that creating smaller assemblies made for better and more concrete participation.

The neighborhood assemblies have far more potential than the Syntagma occupation assembly, because they have the direct relationships we lacked in Syntagma. We can be together every day in the neighborhood, we can talk about our common problems every day—that the prices at the supermarket are very high, that we can't go to the hospital, etc.—and it's in our neighborhood, not somewhere abstract and away from where we live in Athens or in Greece.

I was very enthusiastic at the start of the Peristeri Assembly. We met in the central square, and the first two assemblies were spectacular—about 200 people in the square! We had never experienced anything like that. You could see working-class housewives talking about their problems and twelve-year-old children talking to the assembly. There is a big church on the central square, and some housewives proposed that the assembly should squat the church and take the money from the priests. It didn't happen, but they proposed it. In the beginning it was a bit chaotic—a lot of people spoke in the assembly, but we couldn't find something practical to do, because everybody wanted to speak and speak and share his or her problems with the others. But that changed after a while. It was also very interesting that people who came for a walk around the square stopped to listen and see what was happening.

In the beginning there were also members of the leftist parties participating in the assembly, such as Trotskyites and others. There is Antarsya,[11] the largest left party outside the parliament. They are not social democrats, they are communists. In Peristeri they have two elected representatives in the local municipality, so they have some power in the neighborhood. They were not among the people who called the assembly, but they came. From the start they tried to dominate the assembly. They said, "We are with direct democracy, everybody can speak," but saw the local assembly as a small supplement of the central assembly in Syntagma and didn't recognize the need for independent local action. The first four or five times it was ridiculous—they came to the assembly and told us that the only thing we had to do is to vote for the decisions that had already been voted on in Syntagma, and then distribute a leaflet with these decisions to the people of Peristeri. We said, "OK, we agree with the decisions of the Syntagma assembly, but we also want to do other things here." The people from the neighborhood insisted on specific local actions, because we have concrete problems. For example, we are searching for practical ways to stop the electricity cuts. If people in the neighborhood see that we are successful, they will come and participate in the assembly. As long as they don't see a result, they won't come—it's that simple. In Greece there is a legacy of talking about political issues but not having measurable results for what we do.

In our neighborhood, our internal process is that the person who keeps the notes is also responsible to upload them onto our blog, so those who couldn't participate can read what was discussed. When we finish the discussion the person who keeps the notes reads the practical proposals that are documented for collective action. And then we vote for the proposals one by one to see what we are going to do. During that first summer, a big problem occurred. At the end of the assembly we

---

11   The Anticapitalist Left Cooperation for the Overthrow was founded in 2009 by ten smaller organizations with mainly Maoist and Trotskyist backgrounds.

collectively decided that we were going to do five things, but then people would only show up for two. So we adopted a different procedure. Before voting for an action, we asked who was willing to participate. If there were enough people to participate in the particular action, then we discussed how we would do it. If there weren't enough people, there was no need to discuss it because we weren't going to do it anyway.

We also participated in the Syntagma Square occupation, and created a popular assembly in the central square of Zografou. It was called the Popular Assembly of Zografou, and it still continues. Along with other similar collectives, it has taken an active part in organizing militant events in our neighborhood during general strikes, and supporting other workers' struggles. We're also creating neighborhood solidarity networks such as self-organized community kitchens, bazaars, free classes, etc., trying to take action concerning the rising cost of our social reproduction.

It is a bit contradictory, since it has less political structures than we activists had before. Many of us in the assembly have a political past in the anarchist and anti-authoritarian movement, but all of us developed a strong and somewhat collective critique of the movement, and we decided we wanted to act in the neighborhoods, as neighbors. We don't want to be the conventional anarchists, the black bloc guys in demonstrations, etc. We are also a part of society—we want to act together and develop solidarity with people we meet every day, who we work and live together with in the neighborhood. We are still struggling with this conflict of political and social identity, but we are constantly trying to overcome it by participating in the struggles of the neighborhood.

Fani, Ano Poli Assembly, Thessaloniki: When you're facing so many problems with your social reproduction, you have to find new ways to resist. It is a question of survival. The answer lies in smaller-scale initiatives. Neighborhood assemblies started multiplying exactly because they were trying to cope with the problems of social reproduction. It was difficult for the square movement to get involved with the electricity bills or the electricity cut-offs in different neighborhoods. It was a more central organizational form. In a neighborhood assembly—on the other hand, the neighbor can come and say, "My electricity's been cut off—we have to do something." So we act immediately. It was the decentralized organizational project that helped us confront social reproduction issues.

Anestis, Peristeri Assembly, Athens: I can't tell you how many assemblies there are all over Greece, but there are many assemblies in the countryside and in small towns that are doing great things—not so much in mobilizing people and participating in struggles, though they also do that, but they organize networks of mutual help, which is a lot easier to do in the countryside since people already know each other. There are many assemblies in small towns exchanging services—like, I come to your house and teach your children for two hours, and you come to my house and fix my oven for two hours. Unfortunately, with the exception of a small number of assemblies in Athens, the majority do not have deep relationships with the assemblies in the countryside . . .

Over the winter there were about forty assemblies in neighborhoods in Athens, though some of them don't exist anymore. Most of the assemblies began mobilizing after the events in Syntagma, but a few are older. After Christmas 2011 we tried to set up a coordination of all assemblies called the "assembly of assemblies." We had four meetings in Pantios University. The first and second assemblies were attended by approximately 600 people. We exchanged information about what we were each doing and how we mobilize. A second part of the assembly was a discussion with no specific agenda. In the second meeting, some comrades said the assembly was not very effective, and that it did not make sense to tell others what we were doing since everybody knows through blogs or friends what the other assemblies are doing. The assembly then decided to shorten the first part and to talk about problems we face in our everyday mobilizations during the second part of the assembly. Unfortunately it did not work. The whole meeting was a little chaotic, and some assemblies began to see that they coordinate more effectively with other assemblies in their local regions, since people there already often know each other and the problems they face.

Another problem was that many assemblies—including ours—sent spokespeople to the assembly of assemblies who did not have the right to vote. The assembly could not make decisions without sending people back to their local assemblies to consult. That turned out to be a little bureaucratic. Many assemblies wanted to stay faithful to non-representation, and they were right, but how would we decide what to discuss at the next meeting if we meet just once a month? For example, two assemblies from eastern Athens proposed a joint action about the electricity cuts. After proposing it twice, they saw that the assembly couldn't reach a decision. They proposed it to the other three assemblies in eastern Athens, and ended up occupying the electricity company offices, and were very effective. This failure to have a real coordination through the assembly of assemblies caused a lot of frustration and disappointment.

REPRESENTATION IS NOT DEMOCRACY

People in the autonomous movements in Greece approach the question of democracy with reserve at best, and rejection at the other extreme. It is clear to them that there is no democracy in Greece, and people will immediately tell you so, and why.

Anestis, Peristeri Assembly, Athens: During the last two years, different forms of organizing, struggle, and mobilization have been tested. If you asked people, even from the movement, two years ago, "If we had a massive demonstration in the center of Athens with half a million people, would we succeed in throwing off the government and canceling the austerity measures?" most people would have said yes. We did that four times, five times, and they continued. I am not implying that we should stop having massive demonstrations in the center of Athens. I am just saying that we have experienced the limits of what they can do. The fact that, for eight months, we had a government that no one elected was a message. They were telling us that they will continue to manage the capitalist crisis against us without pretending that the state is democratic.

If you ask people in the neighborhood, "Are you in favor of representative democracy? Do you think this is a good way to solve your problems?!" the majority will say no. But their mentality is contradictory—they will say, "I am with you, I support you, and I may come to the assembly once or twice, but you can do the work." For example, the few people that came to the assembly to ask for help with the electricity cut-offs did not go to their neighbors, they came to us. I am very happy they came, but they saw us as "first aid" from the movements, which looks too much like representation.

People thought that this is a natural way to organize if I want to do something for my neighborhood. So a lot of people in the neighborhood thought it was better to have a direct relationship amongst us, and to self-organize. It is not the majority of the neighborhood, but a strong minority. They know that the model of representative democracy is ineffective.

Konstantino, Ano Poli Assembly, Thessaloniki: Many people in the neighborhoods don't trust anyone, because they have been betrayed by political parties and forms of representation. "Who are you? Are you coming from a political party?" is always the first question. It is an ambiguous situation. Many neighbors are not full members of the assembly—sometimes they say something and participate, and sometimes they want you to do the job.

Vassilis, SKYA, Athens: They cannot represent us anymore. It's impossible. So it's like recuperating a factory—the factory here is democracy. It's like the bosses left the factory and you have to make the factory work because you have to make decisions, because you have to be recognized—you have needs and want to cover them, you have desires. And you don't have money to go to a coffee shop, a club, or a disco to find a girlfriend. So you have to go to the assembly to meet people [laughs]. Yes, it's also a reason! If you are unemployed, how do you find a girlfriend? You don't even have the money for a beer in the park.

Anestis, Peristeri Assembly, Athens: For eight months we had a government that no one elected. The prime minister was an ex-banker, and the left parties were yelling, "This is undemocratic! It is against the interests of the majority!" Before the crisis it was true, and we all experienced that capitalism uses representative democracy in order to function in a more normal way. But at the same time representative democracy, as a friend of mine used to say, "stops at the factory gate." Inside the factory you must do as the boss tells you, and organize work the way capitalism tells you. In workplaces and neighborhoods, when there is a concrete problem there is the objective of capital and there are our objectives—and that has not changed, because now they depend less on representative democracy. The crisis of representative democracy pushes people to look for something else, but in my eyes the crisis of representative democracy is not linked enough to the crisis of capitalism.

After the May 2012 elections, a good friend told me, "Maybe people see a social state with justice as a more realistic perspective than direct democracy and building structures in the community." I answered that, as the capitalist crisis manifests itself a lot of people will see that the welfare state and capitalism in crisis will not coexist. If you talk to people in Greece, what they really want is justice—to have a job with a decent income, a political system that is not corrupt, free healthcare, and a functioning education system. The left says we can do that. But how can you do that in the midst of a global crisis? How can you do that without getting rid of capitalist relations?

If you ask people on the street, many will tell you that in the last two years the Greek political system has made decisions in favor of big foreign banks, but is that the link we want? If our perspective is to create new structures of struggle and mutual help, that kind of link is not helpful. Some call Néa Demokratía, PASOK, and the fascists the "united party of the markets."

The last two parliamentary elections did not mean a resurgence of belief in representative democracy—after all, the number of people who didn't vote has increased. In Greece, after the fall of the military junta in 1974, representative democracy has gone hand in hand with the state giving you a job, giving you some rights, giving you free education and healthcare. During the last two years all of that collapsed, and none of the parties can tell you, "Vote for me because I am going to do this and this for you." They have nothing in their hands they can give you. They cannot promise new jobs in the public sector. On the contrary, they are trying to find a way to lay off workers.

Theo, Micropolis, Thessaloniki: Greece, the same as the squares in Spain, Occupy in the Anglo-Saxon countries, and the Yo Soy 132 in Mexico, all express the same discontent of people with the institutions of representation. In one way or another, we have to overcome representation. It is a recipe that has not worked up until now, so why would it work? And people are aware of this. And people might not have a political background, or know exactly what they want, but they know what they don't like.

Anestis, Peristeri Assembly, Athens: There is a link between all of the movements globally. Two issues link them. One is the common consequences of the capitalist crisis in our everyday lives. If you look at Portugal or Spain, who already have austerity plans, the consequences are very similar. Debt is used as a way of reorganizing society and capital. The second issue is that people understand clearly—I saw that with Argentina—that some old forms of organization are not effective, and cannot express the struggle. No matter if, in New York or in Argentina, people don't go to traditional forms of organization even if everybody knows where their union office or the office of the mayor is.

THE SEARCH FOR DEMOCRACY

Many movement participants are hesitant to use any one word or category to describe the relationships that have been developing in the wake of the rejection of liberal and representative democracy. While direct democracy, self-organization, horizontalism, and participatory democracy are all terms that have currency, there is no single framework, like for example the "Democracía Real Ya!" in Spain, or the use of the word "horizontal" in the US.

Fani, Ano Poli Assembly, Thessaloniki: Democracy? To be honest, I don't usually use the word "democracy" in the leaflets I write or when I speak in public—not even "direct democracy." I prefer terms like "horizontalism," "self-organization," or "*autogestión*" when I'm trying to describe our utopia. Democracy has lost its initial meaning. It is said that we have democracy right now in Greece. This is not democracy. We have no real power—we don't make decisions. So democracy is a concept that has been destroyed to such a degree that, if we're about to use it again we should completely reinvent it.

Anestis, Peristeri Assembly, Athens: During the summer of the occupation of Syntagma, people used the expression "real democracy" or "direct democracy"—a lot of people used these terms. As time passed and participation in local assemblies fell, now you can hear the majority of the participants using the word "self-organizing" or "horizontalism," but "self-organizing" is the most common.

Marita, Ano Poli Assembly, Thessaloniki: The term "democracy" has some limits. We used to say that democracy is that the majority of people decide. I wouldn't like that in the things I do with my friends or with my companion, because I think that all voices should be heard. I would try to do it as we do in the neighborhood assembly, trying to decide together with others, all together, but not by voting. We discuss and we try to reach an agreement that satisfies everyone.

Vassilis, SKYA, Athens: It's the struggle that makes us feel like being a part of something. As a part of a struggle, you see yourself as part of a community, whether it refers to a community of struggle, desires, or needs. You sit down, discuss, and act in an equal way with others. I don't know if this is direct democracy, anarchy, or communism. I don't even care what you call it.

Theo, Micropolis, Thessaloniki: Direct democracy, to us in Micropolis, means that the decisions that affect people are made by the same people who are affected by them. We want to oppose this culture of representation and create structures where everyone can participate—which is the sense of real democracy. What we call democracy, representational democracy, I think is not really democracy, but oligarchy. The real democracy is the political system where everyone is participating directly. What we do here is only the first level of direct democracy. We have our community and our community assembly—so far, so good. But in order to have real direct democracy we would need to have more levels of organization, and to have assemblies of assemblies, and probably some institutions that could help with networking and the making of common decisions between larger bodies of decisions.

Debbie, Solidarity Clinic, Thessaloniki: We are very used to delegating responsibility to somebody else and giving them the power to make decisions over what is happening. We don't think of that as democratic. We don't want to have representatives—we want to represent ourselves. Of course, this raises several problems . . . How do you structure or organize decision-making? As a process of decision-making, it's much more democratic and much more useful to have all voices heard.

It is interesting that, when people gather, they automatically, instinctively adhere to the principles of direct democracy. This is because, essentially, when something is very important to you, you want to make the decision for yourself and not have somebody else decide for you. When there are more specialized issues, of course, some people are more knowledgeable about a certain thing, but it doesn't mean that they are entitled to decide for you. That is what occurs here in the clinic, and how I see the new movements operate around the world. The challenge is to prevent people from taking over, so that we continue to look to each other for questions, answers, and decisions.

It is fantastic to see people that were never politically active get involved organically [in] things that you are passionate about. They actually become more militant than us . . . That's the most gratifying part of what I do. You don't see that in a lot of other movements. You see small groups that have the same ideology fighting for a cause—the cause is what is important. But in what we do now, I see the process as what is important and how it changes you, and I have seen people change through this. It's one of the most amazing things.

Marianna is thirty-five, a welfare worker, participant in SKYA and the Workers' Union of the Municipality of Tavros, Athens.

Marianna, Workers' Union of the Municipality of Tavros, Athens: People don't trust parties anymore, and are hostile toward parties. That's why they didn't want any party representatives to be there in Syntagma. There were some artists who wanted to interrupt the assembly and speak because, "I'm a famous actor or writer and I want to share my opinion with you." But the people didn't let them. That was nice.

Alexandros, Zografou Assembly, Athens: Looking at the occupations of this summer, in Syntagma Square and in the neighborhoods of Athens, I think the foremost problem of direct democracy in this latest round of struggles was that it was kind of an abstract idea when we put it into practice. When people come together to discuss and decide about things horizontally, do not have anything else in common, do not share the same experiences in their everyday jobs, university, high school, or neighborhoods, even if there is a lot of enthusiasm for self-organization, they tend to reproduce the divisions from their everyday lives. How can an immigrant and a recently unemployed middle-class Greek come together, discuss together, and act together if not for a practical reason—to gain something practical, to bring results that will make their lives better? This created problems in the more politically experienced parts of this movement.

Fani, Ano Poli Assembly, Thessaloniki: People left their homes and sofas. They went to the squares, tried to communicate with each other and share their ideas, beliefs, etc. That is a big thing—you can't just ignore it. The negative aspect of it is that many political parties tried to co-opt this social dynamic. This was the main reason that the squares movement declined. People went there because they felt a freedom of communication, and when they saw the political parties gaining control of the assemblies for electoral purposes, they got disappointed.

Anestis, Peristeri Assembly, Athens: Over the summer a lot of participants thought of their participation as a way of building a directly democratic structure, and a way of opposing the austerity measures at the same time. We are struggling against something, and at the same time creating something new, with our ways of organizing, discussing, etc. Now we feel we are more against the austerity measures, and we do not have the time or opportunity to be more creative. Since participation has dropped, many of the participants see the assemblies as little centers of resistance. The increase of austerity measures had a big effect on how we saw our own assemblies. The participants see themselves becoming poorer and poorer every day. We don't see ourselves as representatives or the vanguard of the struggle. We are getting poorer, like anybody else.

Why is there less of a feeling of the creation of alternative structures? Is it due to the direction of our actions? Take the example of our local assembly. Last summer we had many discussions concerning how we are going to participate in a huge march in the center of Athens against austerity. At the same time we had discussions about how we are going to propose a new model of direct democracy to the whole of society, or how we are going to create structures that will begin to discuss new ways of relating and new forms of social relationships between us. After three months we abandoned this second sort of discussion, and our main conversations became the problems we have with the electricity cut-offs, with layoffs, and with a factory closing—but the way of making decisions stayed the same.

Theo, Micropolis, Thessaloniki: These values we have been raised with will not just go away immediately—especially those such as representation and maximization of benefit. We cannot expect them to just disappear, but at the same time we have to fight to establish new values. This is not an easy task, and it might take generations, but we have to always stick to these values. At the same time, we have to try and break with this attitude of representation, this attitude that I can't do anything with my life so someone else will speak for me, will protect my interest, etc. This is the creation of new values.

As social movements we have to be efficient—even if I don't like the term. We have to create structures that really work. And we have to overcome our ideological obstacles, as for example with the idea of horizontality as an absolute value and not as a means to an end. We know that the structures we know are hierarchical, so we have a fear of creating structures for the fear that they will oppress us. In this way, we are just giving an argument to our opponents. We have to create institutions that come from the assemblies and that have responsibilities and obligations and some sort of mild representation—we won't vote for a representative for four years and that is it, but we need to have people who are responsible for certain things, and these people have to be revocable at any moment. We have to build more specialized institutions in the assembly. For example, we cannot participate in an assembly for child care, for the library, for food—this is a misrepresentation of democracy. It means taking part in thousands of assemblies—this is a misrepresentation.

In the end, the assembly should be the instrument of deciding, not the organ carrying out all decisions—deciding how to do things, but not doing it themselves.

Electoral politics

Until the emergence of SYRIZA, most movement participants on the more autonomous left did not vote—or if they did it was not seen as an act of any political importance, but rather as a matter of choosing the lesser evil. As the below discussions reflect, this conversation has shifted a bit, though it is still contentious. On the one hand, many autonomous individuals and even anarchists voted for SYRIZA, while others saw them as no different from any other group-turned-party within the capitalist system of representative democracy.

Fani, Ano Poli Assembly, Thessaloniki: Voting is a hallucination of democratic action. People think that democracy is reaffirmed when they vote. I didn't vote. I wasn't supporting anyone, though it would be interesting to see SYRIZA win the election. Even if SYRIZA canceled all austerity measures, they would still face social discontent, and it would be interesting to see what the "left oppression" is going to be like. I think the social and political influence of the institutional left would diminish. People would realize that the left is unable to control this crisis situation. But I also think the elections showed us a shift toward non-representative organizational forms and a lack of trust in the traditional electoral behavior, and that's why SYRIZA got such a huge percentage. But the answers will be given anyway in the streets, not by the parliament.

Theo, Micropolis, Thessaloniki: A left government would mean less state repression, so we would be more free to campaign and do projects. This would be a positive thing.

As movements for social change, we are trying to defend commons. And the biggest threat to commons right now is neoliberalism, so an anti-neoliberal government would put a stop to this threat. So, for example, I participate in a movement against the privatization of water, which has its own proposal for the socialization of water. This means the users of water taking control of the company. For us, a great inspiration is the Coordinadora del Agua from Cochabamba, Bolivia, and Oscar Olivera, who was with us here a year ago. An anti-neoliberal government would be an ally in this first part, against the privatization—but then we would have to fight against this government for the second part, the socialization . . .

For example, stopping the gold mine that will destroy virgin forest and drive people from their ancestral land—stopping this is key, and if a government said they would oppose the mine I would support the government in that. These are examples of positive things a left government could do and be.

But then there are negative aspects. One is the instrumentalization of social movements by left governments in order to do social policies, and we have seen this a lot in Latin America. And this was part of the program of SYRIZA. They said, "We will try to support initiatives that come from society—what they are talking about is what we are doing: networks of solidarity, consumer cooperatives, organization in neighborhoods, etc." I think this would be detrimental to the social movements, because it is a different thing if these initiatives come from society or the government. If you take state power, you become the state—it does not matter how well-intentioned you are, you are the state. If you are the state, the state is a mechanism of exclusion or co-optation—there is no other language that the state can talk. The logic is: you are either with us or against us . . . There cannot be self-organization from above—it is a contradiction in terms. The state has its own logic. If these initiatives of society are subsumed into the state logic, they lose their dynamics and become instruments of the state. They get diluted, and they disassemble.

Another thread is demobilization, which would come from a government that would say, "You social movements, don't worry now, we will take care of things now. Thank you for what you have done. Go home—we are going to change the world now." We have seen this so many times, from here in the 1980s with PASOK demobilizing the unions and movements, and within five or six years they were the same right-wing government as others.

Anestis, Peristeri Assembly, Athens: If someone is active in the movement, and she or he is here every day together with us, it is not such a big deal to support with your vote someone who you think can be useful to the movement. So there was a big discussion within the movements about the elections. Not that they started believing in representative democracy—no, the question was: If we support SYRIZA, will it create a change that will be better for the movements or not? Some people in the movements said, "SYRIZA must be powerful, but if it comes first then we have a problem because"—and I think they are right—"after two or three months a government of the left will have to deal with capitalism."

SELF-ORGANIZATION IN WORKPLACES

There is a great deal of discussion about self-organization and workers' struggles, and while there is a long history of it in Greece, there are not yet that many workplaces or workers' organizations fighting for workers' control or self-organization. There are a number of examples, including the newspaper Eleftherotypia, *and despite skepticism, there is a growing movement toward workers' self-management and control. In 2011 the conversations with movement participants leaned toward the belief that self-management was nearly impossible, but only a year later a worker from a recuperated factory in Argentina was meeting with a group of workers in Thessaloniki. Five months after that, these workers occupied their abandoned workplace, and are currently running it. Things are moving rapidly in Greece.*

Grassroots unions

Anna, forty-two, works in a bookstore and is an active participant and organizer in the Union of Bookstore Workers and Publishing Houses and the Open Assembly of Workers and Unemployed—both horizontal and autonomous unions. She participated in students' collectives at university, and has worked in unions since the beginning of the 1990s.

Anna, Union of Bookstore Workers and Publishing Houses, Athens: We are a grassroots union. We organize with a council of representatives and hold elections every two years—though we have surpassed the institutional form that is necessary for a union to be recognized by the state. In our union there is no difference between a common member and a member of the council. Every Thursday there is an open assembly, called the Open Council, where anyone can participate. We talk about what is happening in the bookstores, discuss and coordinate our actions, etc. The people who participate in the Open Council are not always the same, but they form the core of the union. Each member of the union has a responsibility that the assembly is functioning—if they didn't, then there would be no assembly. The official assembly of the union is also open, and it takes place about every two months. In this assembly we make all important general decisions. Generally, we try to make decisions by consensus in the assembly—we don't vote. Before every official assembly we go to the bookstores, the publishing houses, and the book warehouses to inform the workers of the assembly and to explain why their participation is necessary.

We say that real participation and real action of the workers should be done by assemblies "from below." We support horizontal forms of organization. If we don't do that, if we work with representatives, we will end up in forms of organization that do not allow people to take their lives in their own hands, to be responsible, to make decisions and act by themselves. We want to feel as workers that we are active subjects and protagonists. We are against intermediation. We know it is difficult, but working in a horizontal way is an answer to the current situation that comes from the future. It is an answer that was given from the movements in Latin America, and especially from the Zapatistas. At this historical point, this is the best way to organize.

Workplace occupations and recuperations

Anestis, Peristeri Assembly, Athens: Here in western Athens we had two factory occupations over the winter. Not that they were closing, but they did not pay the workers for eight to twelve months. One was a metal factory (Loukissa) and the other a print shop (3E). There was also a small TV station in Peristeri that was occupied.

Because of the union's close relationship with the CP, things were difficult for us at the beginning. But after a few days, when the workers saw that our local assembly really meant to support them, they were willing to have a relationship with us.

The workers in the print shop already had a union, and they had participated in prior struggles—so they created an assembly, but the union was still directing it. In the TV station they had other sorts of problems, since they had an assembly but they did not exactly recuperate the workplace. You could turn on the TV channel and would see a black background with messages all day, like, "The boss has not paid us in eight months," "We would like your support"—or you saw programs about other struggles and those who had come to support them, or who the boss is and his illegal activities. We went there and spoke with the participants of the occupation. They said it was very helpful to see people from outside their workplace. But their assembly had many internal problems. The journalists and those who just work in the TV station, like cameramen, wanted different things—they saw themselves in a different position within the structure of the company, and this made unity really difficult.

There was also a very long strike in a big steel factory outside Athens (Elliniki Halivourgia), with many hundreds of workers. The union had agreed over the last two years to some reforms that were not favorable to the workers, like accepting layoffs and lower wages. So the bosses decided to push more, and demanded that the workers work five hours a day instead of eight hours, and that they accept a 40 percent salary cut, or else they would lay off half the workers. The union had an assembly, and since there was a lot of pressure from the workers, they occupied the workplace. After a few days, a big mobilization in solidarity with the steelworkers took place. People gathered food, money, and other things for them. There was also a solidarity committee in their area, which was especially strong. The majority of people living in their area helped them. But the main problem with that struggle was that the bosses can wait longer than you. In this case they transferred production to another workplace owned by them in Volos, where the workers did not strike or occupy.

What was really surprising, especially in the factories, was that people could not see the possibility of recuperating it from the boss. They saw their mobilization as a way of putting pressure on the bosses to get paid. Though the newspaper in Athens and the clinic in Thessaloniki are a different story—they recuperated in some ways.

I have read about Argentina and about Latin America, and I find it a very useful experience with interesting characteristics, but somehow in the past I felt that it could not be applied to Greece. My comrades and I used to argue against people who see the recuperation of the workplaces as a motor. Since last year, I think there are more possibilities because of the situation with so many workplaces where workers do not get paid.

But for recuperation there must be a certain level of identification with your workplace and what you do. What surprises me is that, whenever this is suggested, a lot of workers do not want to take the responsibility.

Eleftherotypia

Afrodite: We all worked at *Eleftherotypia* [lit: "freedom of the press"], the second-largest newspaper in Athens. It is a historical paper started after the junta in 1975. *Eleftherotypia* was a center-left newspaper, and it was supposed to be unaffiliated with any corporate interests, such as shipping and construction. The newspaper and the print shop all together had about 800 workers.

In July 2011 they stopped paying us, one month after Syntagma. We had many assemblies since August, and in the first assemblies most of the workers voted against going on strike. George, myself, and some other people said that we should stop working the moment they stopped paying us, but the majority said we should give the owner another chance, because she was supposed to get a loan from a bank. The most powerful argument in favor of being patient was that our paper was not like others, that it was against the austerity memorandum and the owner hadn't sacked anyone, so we should show good will. I was suspicious from the beginning and many others were, too, thinking that she was just taunting us. Finally, we started a strike around Christmas after all hope had vanished. We knew that she had already filed for protection under bankruptcy. So after five months the 800 workers were convinced that it's important to have a strike—it wasn't easy to convince them. And then it was really important and hard to convince them to print the strikers' papers.

Dina: In the beginning we were a group of ten meeting separately, and when we spoke to the assembly we were considered the "crazy ones." Every general assembly and assembly of the workers' committee for us was a fight. We are a minority in every way—because we are proposing a new way of doing syndicalism; a new way of printing newspapers, of producing newspapers; and finally, we are proposing different content for the newspaper. On December 15 we said, "OK, now we fifteen crazy people will stop working." A week later, after the boss didn't pay the extra money for Christmas, everybody got furious, and so they finally decided to go on strike. There was a proposal of self-management, of taking the newspaper into our own hands—but only twenty-one people out of 200 voted in favor of it.

George: That is not that bad . . . after that everybody started to use the word self-management, but actually they didn't know what it means to self-manage a newspaper like this. Everybody was using the word meaning something different. The strike became very famous, like the strike of the steelworkers. We were traveling around the country giving speeches with the steelworkers. It was the first time that journalists were saying, "We are workers, too." The people in the streets during the general strikes had big banners saying, "We support the steelworkers and the *Eleftherotypia* workers." There was a very big movement in support of the strike. People sent us food, and organized concerts.

Afrodite: The owner did not have a plan to face the crisis. So we planned a strikers' issue. That did not happen in the newspaper building, because the owner had locked us out. The system was shut down, the internet was shut down—we could not even look at our emails. She had locked all the computers, and of course the print shop was locked. So we had to print the strikers' issue in a different print shop, and pay for it. The first issue was published on February 15. We decided to print it in order to inform people about what was happening at *Eleftherotypia*. We called the paper *Ergazomenoi*—"Workers." For legal reasons, we could not use a name referring to *Eleftherotypia*. She took us to court anyway, in order to prohibit the second issue from being distributed, but the court decided in our favor.

George: We had to inform the readers. From the beginning there were different views among us. And the court was about to decide whether the newspaper would be under the protection of Article 99 (concerning pre-bankruptcy procedure) or not. Most of the workers did not want the legal protection, because it's common that entrepreneurs ask for it and then . . .

Afrodite: Then . . . they take from the business everything they can and transfer it overseas or to personal accounts. They leave the enterprise like an empty shell, and we are left with nothing.

The production of the strikers' issues was almost a clandestine exercise, because the owner had already taken us to court. We even received anonymous phone calls saying, "We'll fuck you up, you bastards—you took our computers"—which had not happened. We used a small office of a former left-wing magazine that was no longer publishing. The office still exists, and has some infrastructure. We borrowed some machines from friends and used USB sticks and emails to send our articles there.

Tasos: Guerrilla tactics in printing! Frankly, the moment we got the first issues from the print shop outside Athens, it was something like a revolution for us.

Afrodite: The atmosphere was joyous and festive, and we felt we were doing something. The union helped the first strikers' issue with a donation. But it has not been easy to get that money. The journalists' union has many tendencies inside, and many of them are in favor of the owners. It's not like a union controlled by the workers—it's mainly some kind of intermediary between owners and workers. Five of the eleven members of the council are openly in favor of the owners. There are also two Communists who are in favor of the workers, but they'll do what the Party says, so it's very difficult to reach a unanimous decision. It's half and half.

George: We produced two issues. We printed 50,000 and sold about 30,000 to 35,000 copies of each. That was very good for a newspaper—especially considering that it was not on Saturday or Sunday, but on a weekday.[12]

Tasos: There are some aspects of real democracy and equal participation in this process, but when it comes to who is going to do what and who is going to benefit from what, representation and hierarchy are still the strongest aspects—even when you are trying to do something different. There were signs of that even in the two first strikers' issues—beyond the

---

12   A few weeks after this interview, the workers published a third issue.

fact that we were against our boss, it was a newspaper like any other, only printed under very difficult conditions. We did not take the next step, which might have been to stop doing things like we used to, to eradicate every kind of hierarchy and division between us and between the readers and us. It might be a good step to really take it in our own hands and make something new . . . But now we are somewhere in between. Overall, I feel it as a great defeat—800 people were unpaid for one year, more than five months of a strike, and still no results in getting paid. And the people in favor of the boss now present themselves as the real strikers and as the real self-management process, but they have nothing to do with real self-management. At one of our last assemblies, I saw a person who was in favor of the boss saying, "Do you remember Argentina? We must do what they did in Argentina and take over the print shop!" The boss wants us to, because she wants to sell it. Nothing to do with self-management at all!

In March you would have seen that we shared a "semi-revolutionary" feeling, that we have won, we have published the issues. The pro-boss forces were defeated, and we were the temporary victors of the struggle. In October, when we lost the first assembly discussing the possibility of a strike, we were totally disappointed with our co-workers. Now we have again this feeling of defeat. Maybe in two months it will be different. I hope so.

Afrodite: Our mistake was not that we struggled. Our mistake was that we did not continue to do so. We reached a point when we said, "It's OK, we've published two strikers' issues. The court might be on our side. Now there is nothing else we can do apart from legal action." We did not communicate our struggle as much as we should have. We journalists think we are the center of the universe, while at the same time all of Greece was in turmoil. This is a big flaw of all workers' struggles here—each one is on its own, and it's very difficult to unite. We were also hooked on legality because we did not want to change the whole structure and content. We just wanted to print another paper. If we had managed to make this struggle first more known, and second more militant, more radical, the results would have been different—for example, if we had occupied the building when she locked us out. We made many mistakes, but mistakes are also part of the process. I would tell anyone that if you don't fight, you have no chance. If you fight you have a chance, which is better than nothing. And after one year of struggle we are different people. Our relationships with one another are different. We have struggled and we have lost, OK—but we can struggle again. We have realized that we are not so different from other people who are working or are unemployed. We have not been defeated inside.

Afrodite: *Eleftherotypia* finally shut down after a seven-month strike, in June 2012. It's now more than one year later, and we still haven't received a penny from the former owners. They owe us and the state insurance fund more than €20 million. The former workers are split into many factions, and involved in a time-consuming and tedious legal wrangle. After our "strikers' issues," three other issues were produced and published by workers. But they counted on the owners' permission, as a precursor to a new *Eleftherotypia*, owned by a new boss, with workers aligned with management. *Eleftherotypia* started again in January 2013, owned by a famous neoliberal lawyer. Around a hundred former employees, mostly journalists, are working there. None of them was compensated, and they work with individual contracts for less money. Right now their wages are at least three months overdue, and they are threatening to go on strike.

About a hundred of us who were involved in the strike formed a cooperative, and since November 2012 we have been producing a daily newspaper called *Efimerida ton Syntakton* ["Editors' Newspaper"]. The newspaper's politics are left of center, although our maxim is "Freedom of the press and information." The newspaper is strongly anti-racist and anti-fascist, and we publish many stories concerning labor rights, social issues, and job actions. We support self-management and cooperative projects, like Vio.Me in Thessaloniki, and have published many stories on the struggle of the people of Halkidiki against the gold mines. One of our biggest advantages is that we host the investigative journalism team of *Ios* ["Virus"]. They are probably the best researchers in Greece on the extreme right and neo-Nazis.

After almost one year I can say we have learned many lessons. The road to self-management is not paved with roses. It has been an interesting experiment for all of us, unprecedented in recent Greek history—at least at this scale (twenty workers are currently employed). We make decisions collectively in workers' assemblies, which abide by the cooperative's basic rule, which is "one member, one vote." All of us are getting paid the same—that is, when we are getting paid, which is not on a regular basis. There are also two elected bodies: one small board of directors of the anonymous company (similar to a public limited company) that issues the paper—and we are hired by the company, since journalists in Greece are not allowed to be publishers; and we have a board of directors for the cooperative. As usually happens with hierarchies, they have a tendency of acting independently and not feeling tied or controlled by the so-called "electoral body." Since all of us are former employees in media companies, we don't have much experience in making collective decisions, and are more familiar with the usual hierarchical structure of a newspaper— editor-in-chief, team editors, etc. Fortunately there is no censorship, or self-censorship, although we are often pressed by time and the newspaper format.

There are many contradictions in what we are doing. We also publish advertisements from banks and big corporations, and rely on them for our wages. Most see it as a way to survive economically—which so far we haven't quite succeeded in doing. But we are still struggling and doing better. We need more than 10,000 daily readers to sustain ourselves, and 15,000 read- ers on Saturday, and we are close to these numbers. Some see it as a chance to change what people think about Greek journalism, and to be truly inde- pendent and write for the people, rather than be hired puppets for the government and corporate interests. Some see it as a new *Eleftherotypia* that will gain the audience of the old one, and play a political role if and when SYRIZA becomes the new government. Some see it as a part of a new, not homogenous and quite controversial "self-management/cooperative/econ- omy of solidarity" movement. Personally I think we are affiliated a little too much with SYRIZA.

At least we have a job, and at the moment there isn't a big bad boss over our heads. It's a bit like having a small family business, when you bust your ass to get it off the ground and there is no one to complain when you are not getting paid since you are supposedly "your own boss"—a phrase I despise.

VIO.ME

Makis Anagnostou, Vio.Me, Thessaloniki: When the factory was abandoned by the owners, we first tried to negotiate with the politicians and the union bureaucracy. But we understood quickly that the only thing we were doing was wasting our time and slowing down the struggle. It was a difficult time, the crisis was showing sudden and intense effects. The suicide rate among workers in Greece rose a lot and we were worried that some of our fellow workers might commit suicide. Therefore we decided to open up our labor conflict to society as a whole and people became our allies. We discovered that the people we thought could not do anything in reality can do it all!

Many workers did not agree with us or did not continue the struggle for other reasons. Among those of us who took up the struggle, the common ground for our work is equality, participation, and trust. The goal of the Vio.Me workers is to create a European and international network with many more factories under workers' control, so that we can really say, "Factories into the hands of workers and wealth for those who produce it." Wealth is not coming from banks and the financial system, but from the efforts of the worker, the sweat of the peasant and the efforts of everyone struggling for their daily food.

Up until now we could not unite to strike back. But now we have the chance. We mean to be in the factories, occupy the means of production, and produce for society. We have proven with our actions that we can do it. We put society into the center of our production and orientate our production toward the needs of society.

We restarted production in February 2013. We are now producing organic cleaner, not the industrial glue we produced before. Distribution is informal. We ourselves sell our products at markets, fairs, and festivals, and a lot of products are distributed through the movements, social centers, and shops that are part of the movements. What we did during the last year is basically keep the factory active. We cannot say we have yet had a very positive outcome regarding production, distribution, and sales. Earnings are quite low and not enough to maintain all the workers. Therefore some workers have lost faith, or got tired and left Vio.Me.

Recently our assembly decided unanimously to legalize our status by building a cooperative. The decision again gave us an impulse to continue. We are twenty workers who signed the foundation act of the cooperative, but there are more waiting to see how things go. In the structure of the cooperative we also created the figure of "the one in solidarity," who is not a member of the cooperative as such, but supports the cooperative financially in exchange for our products, and participates in decision-making. They pay €3 a month and with that we pay the basic costs of the factory, like electricity and water. Having the society by our side through this construction we feel stronger.

We are happy that our initiative has encountered so much interest. But we do not want to present ourselves as some kind of vanguard, we do not want to march ahead of other struggles, we want to walk side by side. We do not tell other workers they should do the same as we have, but we tell them that they should gather in assemblies and make collective decisions together. Whatever they decide, we will support them in their struggles. We also have goals and one thing we want is that all self-administered and worker-controlled companies form a network and create a solidarity fund. Because we are not creditworthy, we cannot get any subsidies, we cannot hope to get any help from the state like the huge capitalist enterprises, therefore we need each other in order to support each other economically and through solidarity funds.

CHAPTER FOUR

Spain

The Spanish crisis began in 2008. Massive layoffs took place as a result of the implosion of the real estate bubble, which caused the subsequent collapse of the property and construction-related sectors. As people became more impoverished, the demand for goods and services dropped drastically, furthering the already negative consequences of the crisis. The possible rapid collapse of the world's thirteenth-largest economy frightened global financial actors and politicians. Harsh austerity measures were imposed by the EU, as well as by the social-democratic government of the Partido Socialista Obrero Español (PSOE), through to the end of 2011, when the newly elected right-wing government then made the consequences of the crisis even worse. After three years of austerity, national protests, which began on May 15, 2011 (15-M), seemed to come out of the blue. One week before local elections were to be held in Spain, over 100,000 people demonstrated in fifty-eight different cities under the banner of anti-austerity and "Real Democracy Now!" (¡Democracia Real Ya!, or DRY). While the media in Spain and around the world insisted on calling the movement *Indignados*,[1] the movement itself did not use this language, as had most traditional social movements of the past, but instead declared that it was for real democracy and inclusion,

---

1 Referring to Stéphane Hessel's book *Time for Outrage: Indignez-vous!* (New York: Twelve, 2011).

and against the false representation of the state. While it was later some-times referred to as the "Spanish Revolution," the participants themselves mainly refer to it by its date, 15-M, or as DRY.[2]

People came out into the streets and plazas because of their deteriorat-ing living conditions, and what seemed to be a total lack of prospects for their future. But as the main slogans of the movement point out, people mobilized because they felt that they had no influence at all on the deci-sions made regarding the crisis, nor any alternative choice. This impression was strengthened by the upcoming local elections. The mobilization consisted mainly of people with little or no prior experience in political activism or mobilization.[3] Like other recent movements around the globe, people were not mobilized by traditional political actors, such as unions or parties. The DRY platform appeared first on the internet, and spread through the dense network of radical groups and activists in social networks, blogs, and websites.[4] But this was not a "Facebook revolution." Gatherings, assemblies, and face-to-face contact were, and continue to be, crucial. In Spain the movement responded to the "Facebook revolution" myth with the slogan, "digital indignation—analog resistance."

The construction of encampments on central squares began in Puerta del Sol, in Madrid, on the night of the first mobilization on 15-M. After being evicted by the police on the first night, many more people took the square on the following day, and started building the camp that then evolved into the famous tent city seen in images around the world. "Real Democracy Now! existed before the 15-M," explains Amador, a partici-pant at Puerta del Sol from the very beginning:

> The gathering was called for in a very clever manner, using a language that communicates with many people. A very direct language—it has no ideo-logical rhetoric, and instead points out concrete issues that concern all of

---

2   Ernesto Castañeda, "The *Indignados* of Spain: A Precedent to Occupy Wall Street," *Social Movement Studies* 11: 3–4 (2012), pp. 309–19.

3   This phenomenon is central to the description of all participants interviewed. See also Mayo Fuster Morell, "The Free Culture and 15-M Movements in Spain: Composition, Social Networks and Synergies," *Social Movement Studies* 11: 3–4 (2012), pp. 386–92.

4   Neil Hughes, "Young People Took to the Streets and All of a Sudden All of the Political Parties Got Old: The 15-M Movement in Spain," *Social Movement Studies* 10: 4 (2011), pp. 407–13.

us. But Real Democracy Now! didn't call for the first night of encampments in Sol, the encampment, or what happened later. They evolved into
it there, participating together.[5]

During the following days the square encampment spread from Puerta del
Sol to the rest of the country. Many of the encampments were like little
cities—highly organized, even including urban planners. The encampments were an example of a decentralized and democratic alternative to
society in general—a glimpse of how society could be organized differently, a "now-time," as Walter Benjamin would have said, describing a time
that offers a different possible future. Throughout the day, various working
groups met in the squares, discussing issues ranging from education and
healthcare to alternative models of society, the internal security of the
square, and the organization of concrete initiatives and protest actions. At
night the squares usually held general assemblies. The camps in Puerta del
Sol, and in Barcelona's Plaça de Catalunya, became best known worldwide—but the movement could not be reduced to its best-known symbols.
People occupied squares in both large and small cities. Even in very small
towns people took over squares and held regular assemblies. The practices
favored by the 15-M mainly consisted of the encampment of public and
private spaces, including direct action in banks, demonstrations, and
public assemblies, and non-violent direct actions.

Some media and traditional leftists have accused the 15-M of being
responsible for the overwhelming victory of the right-wing Partido
Popular (PP) in the general elections of November 22, 2011. The 15-M is
blamed for not having taken a stand in favor of any leftist party, not
having engaged with electoral politics—having rejected them totally.
This accusation is wrong and misleading. The PP won only 550,000 votes
more than it had in the prior elections of March 2008. It only won the
election because the social democratic PSOE lost 4.3 million votes of the
11.3 million it had won in 2008. As it had been in government since 2004,
it is more likely that the reason for the defeat of the PSOE was rooted in

---

5 Amador Fernández Savater, thirty-eight—journalist, editor, philosopher, 15-M,
Madrid, author interview, January 9, 2012.

its politics, and was not precipitated by the 15-M.[6] The 15-M did not call for a boycott of the elections or for participation—it was generally indifferent. Beyond that, one of the main characteristics of the 15-M is its rejection of the logic of representation as non-democratic. The participants do not believe—or at least strongly doubt the claim—that change can be achieved through participation in institutionalized politics. They mistrust politicians and political parties, and think corruption in politics is growing—an opinion shared by more than two thirds of the Spanish population, with 95 percent saying that political parties protect people involved in corruption.[7]

Austerity for the people, money for the banks

In early 2010, the Zapatero government put into effect a three-year austerity program, consisting of €50 billion in cuts to public spending. A second austerity program, promising €15 billion in cuts by the end of 2011, was also approved at the end of May 2010. The sales tax rose from 16 percent to 18 percent, 13,000 civil servants were fired, and a hiring freeze was implemented. The PSOE government, under José Luis Rodríguez Zapatero, modified the layoff protection law, making dismissals easier and introducing the possibility for employers to reduce their employees' work hours and salary when facing economic difficulties (as in Germany). Cuts were also made to spending on home care for the elderly, and on child welfare. In 2011, the €2,500 support payment for newborn children was cancelled.[8] Regional governments were advised to cut their spending by €1.2 billion, resulting in more layoffs, cuts, and privatizations—of the hospitals, for example. One of the many actions taken by the 15-M was in Barcelona, when, on June 15, 2011, it mobilized and surrounded the regional Catalan parliament when it voted on

---

6   Miriam Calavia, "El PSOE pierde casi tantos votos como parados tiene España," *Cinco Días*, November 21, 2011.

7   Fernando Garea, "El 95% asegura que los partidos protegen y amparan a los acusados de corrupción," *El País*, January 12, 2013.

8   "Spanish PM Makes Debt Crisis U-Turn with Emergency Cuts," *Guardian*, May 12, 2010; "El Gobierno congela el salario de los funcionarios en 2012 y amplía su jornada laboral," *RTVE*, December 30, 2011.

regional cuts. People turned their backs on the parliament in their thousands, and organized real democratic assemblies.

Before the PP and its presidential candidate, Mariano Rajoy, experienced a landslide victory in the general election of November 20, 2011, they had promised to discontinue the strict austerity politics of the PSOE government. On December 30, 2011, ten days after having assumed control of the government, the PP announced €9 billion of cuts in public spending, extended the freeze on salaries and pensions until the end of 2012, and increased the working week for public servants from 35 to 37.5 hours. At the end of March 2012, Rajoy announced an additional €27 billion in cuts to public spending, and then, only nine days later, added another €10 billion in cuts to education (€3 billion) and healthcare (€7 billion).[9] Among other changes, a general co-payment for all medicine was introduced—even for pensioners.

In June 2012 the financial ministers of the Eurozone approved a loan of up to €100 billion in EU rescue funds, for a Spanish bank restructuring fund to recapitalize Spain's "bad banks"—mainly regional and savings banks. In order to meet conditions for the bailout, Spain's banks had to write off "hybrid capital instruments." While small investors have lost their money because of fraudulent investment plans and retirement packages full of cheap shares and bonds with almost no guarantees, the banks have been recapitalized. In July 2012, Rajoy presented a new austerity plan to parliament in order to save €65 billion in two years. Among other things, the austerity plan included a 10 percent reduction in unemployment pay after six months, an increase in the sales tax from 18 percent to 21 percent (a step Rajoy and the PP had rejected during their electoral campaign), and the cancellation of Christmas bonuses for public servants. In August, Rajoy increased the austerity cuts from €65 billion to €102 billion.

In only five years—from 2007 to 2012—3.2 million of the 20.5 million jobs in Spain were destroyed. This meant that 15 out of 100 employees lost their jobs, and 10 percent of all Spanish households, amounting to 380,000, did not have even one member working. Meanwhile, the drastic decline in salary for the working poor grew from 10.8 percent in 2007 to 12.7 percent in 2010. By January 2013, unemployment in Spain had risen

9   "Sanidad tendrá un recorte de 7.000 millones y Educación de 3.000," *El Mundo*, April 9, 2012.

to 26.2 percent, compared with 10.8 percent in the whole of the EU. Unemployment, reduced wages, cuts to social services, and so on, have led to a pauperization of the population. In the spring of 2013, more than 11 million of Spain's 46 million inhabitants already lived in poverty.[10]

From mobilization to self-organization

On May 27, 2011 "the Mossos"—the Catalonian police—made a brutal attempt to evict the occupied Plaça de Catalunya, in Barcelona. They used clubs and plastic bullets, causing more than 120 injuries among those in the plaza. Instead of crushing the movement, the state repression had the opposite effect—many more people poured onto the streets and plazas. In many cities, the occupied central plazas functioned as a sort of public arena for citizens' debates. In Barcelona, and particularly in Madrid, thousands of people gathered in the plazas every day, with the formation of hundreds of working and discussion groups. All of the plazas also saw regular public assemblies, where participants in the movement discussed and made decisions on various issues and actions.

As was true in Greece, a movement for change cannot be confined to a central square. After a few weeks in the plazas, participants in 15-M in the bigger cities began to organize in neighborhoods. The Puerta del Sol encampment was dissolved on June 12 by the full consensus General Assembly of the Plaza—an assembly that lasted all night. The decision was considered both the most likely to produce concrete outcomes, since the movement would be re-territorialized into neighborhoods and other locations, and the most democratic, in the sense that more people could participate. Barcelona and a few other smaller towns retained the plaza encampments for a little longer—and the more general re-territorialization did not entail a distancing from national or regional mobilizations. On June 19, 2011, demonstrations took place in more than eighty Spanish cities. Hundreds of thousands of people took to the streets of Madrid alone to protest the EU's economic and financial policies.

---

10   People are considered to be living in poverty in Spain when their income is lower than 60 percent of the average annual income. For a single adult, this means that the poverty level is an annual income of €7,300. Jaime Prats, "Más desigualdad, más miseria," *El País*, March 30, 2013.

Just as the media, in 2012, was beginning to declare the movements dead, as they had in the US and other parts of the world—not noticing the neighborhood construction, but only looking to the central plazas— there were again massive mobilizations. On February 19 more than a million people demonstrated in several cities against Rajoy's austerity program. On July 19, more than 4 million people again protested against the second austerity package of the PP government. Meanwhile the traditional unions also mobilized, and in the fall they called for a general strike. Instead of the movements being "dead," as so many were claiming, what was in fact happening was that they were reinventing themselves, and growing in depth and breadth—in a process that still continues.

Current mobilizations include the "siege of parliament" of September 25, 2012, as well as various new forms of action. Consistent in these formations is the continued practice within the squares of horizontal relationships, direct action, and self-organization. The pre-existing movement that probably grew most strongly as a consequence of the 15-M was the movement against foreclosure, the Plataforma de Afectedos por la Hipotéca (PAH). It is organized in chapters all over the country, and organizes concrete resistance to foreclosures—a trend that has involved hundreds of thousands of people since the crisis started— and also occupies empty buildings for homeless families. The PAH not only continues to grow throughout Spain, but also now offers an example to other movements throughout Europe and the US. Other examples of movements organizing in the wake of 15-M, and using similar methods—or the same "DNA" as many in the movements say—include the "green tide" (*marea verde*), the movement in defense of public education, and the "white tide" (*marea blanca*), the movement in defense of public healthcare. Far from being over, the 15-M is transforming into a way of organizing, and of pursuing politics, in a different way.

VOICES

Between December 2011 and December 2013, we conducted interviews with a dozen participants of the 15-M mobilizations, most of whom were interviewed several times over the course of those nineteen months. None belong to any political party. Most of the interviewees had studied at university, or were professionals, even if they did not have jobs in their professions. This corresponds to the general composition of the 15-M activists.

Crisis

When talking about crisis, people in the Spanish state mention the cuts in healthcare, education, pensions, and so on, as well as the lack of jobs and prospects, especially for young people. More than in other places, the responsibility for the crisis in Spain is attributed to the non-democratic system of representative democracy, in which two parties (the PP and the PSOE) have more or less shared power, and in which their representatives have used their political positions to enrich themselves. The rejection of institutionalized politics seems to be much stronger here than in other places, and is often the focus of conversations on the crisis. Politicians are generally considered corrupt, and, rather than being in-depth discussions of the crisis itself, the conversations we participated in tended both to reject representative democracy as it exists and, even more, to explore the new forms of democracy being developed by the movements.

Eva Fernández is a forty-two-year-old writer and novelist who works in the field of international labor cooperation and participates in the Cine sin Autor (cinema without an author) collective, which works in poor neighborhoods of Madrid and creates films collaboratively with the inhabitants.

Eva, Cine sin Autor, Madrid: The enchantment and inebriation ended— now they just plunder us. People say it's not a crisis, but a swindle. That's the cause of the indignation converging in the 15-M movement, and then the following "colors," green being the first, linked to the stand for a public, free, good-quality education. The "green tide" movement, the "white tide," with almost all professionals of the health sector mobilized, is very strong and has great approval in society. It tries to resist the aggressive policies of the present-day government to convert health services into private business, denouncing the balance of the national patrimony and political corruption, attacking on every flank all the parties that have achieved power with a vast majority, both PP and PSOE—parties that, in accordance with current electoral law, have alternated power between them until now.

Gerardo is forty-four, a filmmaker, multimedia designer, and scriptwriter. He is one of the founders of Cine sin Autor.

Gerardo, Cine sin Autor, Madrid: In Spain a brutal divide has emerged between political power/politicians and the people. There are chains of impressive corruption that have emerged: it is the monarchy that has been beaten already . . . and for the common people there are foreclosures, the millions of unemployed are ever increasing, and there are no prospects for a better future, so that an entire population will fall into poverty. It's a big division.

Aitor Tinoco I Girona, a twenty-eight-year-old participant in the Universidad Nomada, ¡Democracia Real Ya!, and in the 15-M in Barcelona, has prior organizing experience, from the movement against capitalist globalization to the EuroMayDay mobilizations.

Aitor, ¡Democracia Real Ya!, Barcelona: Cutbacks in pensions are handed out to the elderly—and more, the right of healthcare is also refused to them, and the right to education for their children and grandchildren too. They talk about cuts, but that's not what it is—it's privatization. For example, with the hospitals: they're making them private so that laboratories can come conduct research. We can see this process in all the common wealth we have generated as a territory, such as public education, hospitals, and beyond—and now they are privatizing. In Catalonia they told us we need to sell all public enterprises and that they are ready to sell them to their friends. Telefónica, for example, was a national enterprise, privatized by President Aznar, who sold it to his schoolmate, you see? The same will happen here. For example, we have a health minister who was former president of the Chamber of Hospitals of Catalonia—private hospitals, of course.

And why don't people have a right to bankruptcy? An enterprise that is a legal entity can declare itself bankrupt and all its debts disappear—if they don't have the money, they don't pay. So why must I keep paying my debts if I don't have the money? That's what happens with a lot of people who have been evicted. And, even worse, they're put on the lists of the indebted. And then, if they are lucky enough to find a job, all they earn will go to paying their debt. We need to give people the right to bankruptcy!

Ernest Marco, a thirty-four-year-old chemical engineering professor, and a participant in both the PAH and the 15-M, has prior organizing experience, from the movement against capitalist globalization to the EuroMayDay mobilizations.

Ernest, PAH, Barcelona: This is just the beginning. This crisis is not just economic and short-term, but will go on for a long period. I don't know what forms the movements will take. I have learned to be more humble. We've never been very ideological as groups. We have identified ourselves a bit with this Zapatista manner of doing politics: walking and asking.

No to representative democracy

Luis Moreno Caballud, thirty-seven, was active in both Barcelona and in the early days of Occupy before the occupation of Zuccotti Park, and had some prior movement experience. Together with a few other Latin Americans, he initiated Occupy en Español, a parallel Spanish-speaking assembly in New York.

Luis, 15-M, Madrid: In the surveys in which people are asked about the problems that most concern them, politicians are the third-biggest problem in Spain. People don't trust them—there were many cases of corruption, and people no longer trust representation. Another factor that has been crucial is that increasingly more decisions have been handed over to transnational institutions. Look at how fundamental the narrative of being part of the European Union has been for Spain. Neoliberalism was introduced in Spain in the form of becoming "modern" and admitted into Europe. And the figure that has most assumed the role of a "hidden power" is the market. Mass media repeat it all the time—markets this and markets that . . . markets have become a fundamental political factor for anyone that watches TV in Spain. It looks like a power in the shadows, to which, basically and constantly, political powers are responding.

Ana Méndez de Andés is an architect and urban planner, and has been a participant in the leftist autonomous research initiative, Observatorio Metropolitano, the blog Madrilonia, and the publishing house, bookstore, and café, Traficantes de Sueños.

Ana, Observatorio Metropolitano, Madrid: One of the ideas is that of democratic revolution. And this is in a certain way a surprise and a change for social movements. We had always thought what we lived in was a democracy, and that democracy had limits and was not enough, and we wanted something different. We wanted a revolution in which we will invent a new system that will take us to another place, and suddenly we realized that maybe revolution consists in asking for an authentic democracy. This is in a way a kind of shock for the people that come from a certain tradition of movements. At one point I found myself demanding something that would have to be surpassed.

This idea of "Real Democracy Now!" and that of "You Don't Represent Us" is the foundation of the 15-M movement. This is the most common feeling. It is authentic discomfort, because decisions are made over which we have no control at all. And how can we begin to win that control over our own lives through something that we call democracy?

The problem is "You don't represent us, this is not democracy"; but it's also the means and system of production of this financial capitalism that can't be democratic since, to work, it needs to create inequity. It's like if capitalism were the source of electricity and always needed positive and negative poles. It's not explicit, but there is a branch of the movement that is very clear that the struggle for democracy is an anti-capitalist struggle.

Ruptures and the Plaza Encampments

In Spain the conversation on rupture is linked to what happened in the plazas, particularly in Puerta del Sol and Plaça de Catalunya, and how that sparked the imagination of the population about other forms of organizing. Whereas in Greece and the US the plaza encampments themselves emerged out of an ever-growing rupture in society.

Aitor, ¡Democracia Real Ya! and Universidad Nómada, Barcelona: I knew "Real Democracy Now!" via Facebook, and because a friend told me a little while before about a mobilization that would take place on May 15, under the slogan, "We are not merchandise in the hands of politicians and bankers," which was something that sounded really new. It seemed like a really inclusive movement. The last meeting I attended was in February or March. It was a Friday and in a restaurant. There were thirty-five of us, but no one knew each other. I remember that there was an old man who worked as a security guard, and who didn't stop walking around the whole evening. I thought that he was the bar's security guard, because we were sitting down and nobody was consuming, and he was observing us. Then, when we decided to move to another place to hold the meeting, the old man followed us. When I approached him he told me that he was a security worker who also saw the call and came to join us. It was a real example of the variety and diversity of the people who took part in this from the beginning.

Ayelen Lozada is a thirty-one-year-old physiotherapist in Madrid, who was not politically active before the 15-M, although she had a marked political and social sensibility as the daughter of politically exiled Argentines.

Ayelen, 15-M, Madrid: The encampment was a fascinating experience, a mini-city in Puerta del Sol. Suddenly we were creating a new reality, something that we couldn't have imagined before. If they had said this would happen a week before, you would have said, "Impossible!"—and suddenly we made it possible. Breaking into the field of the impossible is great, because it made us think, "If this is possible, how many other things are too?" Then it links again with the need for people to ask themselves, "How many things happen to me that I am just reproducing blindly? And how many things am I not creating?" When the encampment shows as possible something we haven't imagined before, an infinite field opens for things to imagine and then, suddenly, you join with others to say: "And now what can we do?" This has imprinted itself a lot in people's daily lives.

I came to the square first when I heard about the repression—it was through Twitter and social networks, where we saw videos of the police repression, and so we went into the streets in response. May 17 is when the camp began to be built; it was on that day that Sol turned into an *agora*. I remember I began to imagine what a Greek *agora* might have been like. Then people there were talking, talking all the time, conversations, reflections . . . I walked alone through the square and saw lots of beautiful things happening. I stayed, talking with people for over an hour and a half, not even knowing their names. We all stayed and talked about things we had been thinking alone in our bedrooms, individually. It was hard to leave the square that day, and the next day I had to go to work early—yet it was three o'clock in the morning, and I couldn't tear myself away. I kept trying to leave the plaza, saying, "I need to go, I need to go," and something always happened that kept me there.

After the first night I went again every single day. The following day I was counting the seconds until work finished so I could go to Sol. When I arrived on Wednesday [May 18], I remember walking around and I saw a very young kid with a piece of cardboard with the word, "Reflection." I asked: "What's this?" "We are the reflection group," came the reply. And I said, "But what do you do?" "We have decided that we're going to think together about everything that is going on since it is so incredible." Then I said, "This is my place." And I turned to my friend and said, "I don't know about you, but I'm going to stay here." She went off to some other thing, and after that I started to collaborate with the reflection group.

In the first days we organized working groups to respond to basic needs, such as infrastructure, food, security, and legal advice. Then we started to organize things like a library, a school for children, translation, and the dynamics of assembly meetings—and from there we moved to organizing groups around spirituality, understanding, peace and love. In every group there was feminism, sexual diversity, and different abilities, so that everyone has a place, according to our principles of respect, horizontality, etc.

Hundreds of new things were being created and developed all the time! I remember one day I came and someone said, "We've made a vegetable patch!" and I said, "A vegetable patch? In the fountain?" Then suddenly there was a day-care center, a library . . . it was fascinating. There was a constructive atmosphere in which you could create things—creating, creating—and everything you wanted to do was possible. But we also felt the need to stop and say, "What is this?" And through the pathways, the streets of the mini-city, you hear that people are thinking, reflecting, and questioning: "And what is this?" "I don't know" . . . And so we created the intentional spaces for thought, to think about what this is and might mean.

Amador Fernández Savater, a thirty-eight-year-old journalist, editor, and philosopher, is a prominent movement participant in Madrid. His writings are followed by many in the movement. Ironically, he is the son of Fernando Savater, Spain's most prominent liberal philosopher, who publicly attacked both the 15-M and his own son.

Amador, 15-M, Madrid: The most important thing about what happened during the encampment is the creation of spaces for everyone—not for activists, not for radicals, not for anti-capitalists, but spaces where difference is respected. A common spirit prevailed in the fact that we all needed to not just take care of speech or organizational issues, but to make it a space that would be attractive to everyone. There was a children's daycare center, so that implied that we were expecting parents with children to come, or the elders. The moment they came, we gave them a chair so that they could attend the assembly and stay there for long periods of time; or people gave you sun block when it was needed. That is to say that democracy shouldn't just be something about the assembly, with formal things, with organizational issues, but is something in concrete space, and is a set of practices that maintain an open space for anyone—regardless of their physical condition or class origin—who, beyond ideology, could participate and [where] we could meet with each other.

Eva, Cine sin Autor, Madrid: I have a lot of friends who were close to politically involved people, but were not politically involved themselves. With the 15-M, they became politically radicalized. It comes to mind that many of those people—those who used to put up stupid things on Facebook—suddenly started to post political and economic opinions, things about the management of power . . . Another thing that probably will stay for good is that sensation that comes from being nobody, the person no one ever paid attention to, then becoming someone that has been listened to by 6,000 people—that you have had your opinion heard in front of 6,000 silent people. That sensation of empowerment will hardly go away. It was an experience lived by many people. Switching from absolute nothingness, from a feeling of powerlessness over one's own life, even day-to-day, to this sense of empowerment—I think it will remain with us.

FORMS OF DEMOCRACY

All over the world, where mass assemblies have been formed and direct democracy experimented with, movement participants are inventing ways for more people to participate, communicate, and create deeper forms of democracy together. In Spain, particularly in Puerta del Sol, this process was reflected on extensively, and attempts are regularly made to refine it.

General assemblies

Ayelen, 15-M, Madrid: I conceive of general assemblies as human places for encounter, debate, information, reflection, and decision-making. Depending on what is being discussed, mechanisms are defined promoting horizontality, where everybody has the same right to speak, and respect and tolerance are promoted. For an assembly along these lines to make sense, every difference must be welcome. I'm not afraid of conflict, discussion, or even disagreeing, as long as we are clear that what really matters is for us to disagree together. If that is clear, I will spend all the time necessary debating with you.

Collective thinking is not that everybody is thinking different things and we just join it all together. It must be something built together from the start, something that previously did not exist that has to be created. It doesn't consist in convincing, but building. It breaks down the concept of competition. It is very important to notice that maybe the person that says something similar to the final result contributes a lot, and so does another that says exactly the opposite, because it's their opinion that sparks your different idea.

We are reflecting all the time about how to improve our techniques, because an assembly in which everyone has the right to talk doesn't guarantee that everybody will feel free to talk. For example, affirmation is very influential, so it is the responsibility of the collective to give confidence to everyone, so that they feel encouraged to talk. It is important to notice how the collective reacts, and that has a direct influence on building true freedom of expression, freedom to speak. There are also group dynamics where implicit leaderships are generated. It's OK if the person that knows most about certain things can talk and say what they have to say, but it's also necessary that the rest can speak, too, in order to break the delegation of power that generates vertical structures. When we practice the horizontal power structure, we are all using our power, but internally there are still mechanisms of delegation—the idea that other people must know more than us, or that we are afraid of making some mistake, and that means I'm uncertain to talk about certain things. I'm in love with horizontality, but am also thinking about goals for improving it. What we saw in horizontality was that, if assembly meetings are fifteen hours long, one gets exhausted, decisions end up being taken by fatigue, and are taken by the ones that resisted until the end, and it becomes vertical again.

Comrades that were focused on resolving conflicts, or on being intermediaries with police or whatever, they weren't called "security"—they were called "respect." First they were called "defense," because it was necessary to defend us from police that came to attack us; then "security" because it should be necessary to take care of camp tents, computers; and then their name was changed on the third day into "respect."

The main issues in the general assembly were proposals by working groups, because there was an invitation to everyone who wanted to participate to find the right group. At the end of assemblies, there was always an open mic, and one could make a proposal, a new group, or raise a question for later.

In the beginning assemblies were attended by about 3,000 or 4,000 people. By the third day the assembly was organized with security pathways for people to walk on if they wanted, with intentionally made shade, with water being sprayed on us because it was hot, with people giving out sunscreen to protect us from the sun, every two or three hours distributing fruits or snacks for people to eat. And then there were all the dynamics teams and the sign language teams . . . In one of those assemblies, suddenly the assembly stops in a serious moment and someone says: "We have seen that there is a pregnant woman here, so we have a chair for her to sit down. Where is she?" In the middle of 3,000 people everything stops for one person to take care of her. Those that took charge of infrastructure were there, waiting on whatever might be needed.

Hand signals

Ana, Observatorio Metropolitano, Madrid: Hand signals are used in almost the same way in the encampments and occupations around the world, but there is one we use in Spain that I don't think others use, which is also very useful, which is, "I don't see it, but I don't block it." That is one where you put your hands in front of your eyes . . . it's different from "I disagree"—the one of crossing hands, that is for blocking ideas. But "I don't see it, but I don't block it," means that I'm not convinced but I won't say no or try and stop the process either.

Pablo García, twenty-nine, is a PhD student in ecology. Pablo participated in the 15-M in Madrid, moved to the US for a semester, participated in Occupy Mount Desert Island in Maine, and then continued his studies at the University of Thessaloniki in Greece, taking part in the local movements there.

Pablo, 15-M, Madrid: In the first days of the mass assemblies, the open mic technique was used, and people just let go and talked and talked. It's necessary to understand that people needed to talk, but at the same time we saw the need to structure things. This is done through facilitation. For example, facilitators can help gather together various ideas, sometimes putting people together with similar ideas so they can structure their ideas, and then those ideas could be collectively improved on, and then brought back even more clearly to the collective. It's very effective, and I've seen it in Sol, I've seen it in Occupy Wall Street, and in Mount Desert Island—the same method and process, with the same effect on people, and how those people fall in love with it.

Consensus

Amador, 15-M, Madrid: Rejection of the majority–minority game often took us to unanimous consensus, which neither seems to me to be the most efficient nor smartest approach. Unanimous consensus allowed a single person to block agreements. That seems excessive to me. It's one thing to incorporate dissenting voices, and another to give one person a right to block everything, because that could easily become manipulation. But the most important thing is to refuse the majority–minority game—the idea that when you vote there are others who are more right because there are more of them than you.

Ayelen, 15-M, Madrid: From the beginning, unanimous consensus was instituted in a natural, spontaneous form, and we couldn't depart from that unanimous consensus because we had the assembly working in that way, and we couldn't find a way or process to break the unanimous consensus. One example of how it was a challenge was with a proposal put forward by the education working group. They suggested we agree that education should be public, free, of good quality, and secular. Almost everybody said yes with their hands [twinkling] except for just one person, who vetoed the proposal that it should be secular. So, that proposal was vetoed. Consensus is a beautiful idea, but up to what point can it be sustained and allow that a democracy can be at the same time something agile, dynamic, flexible, and not an endless, clumsy bureaucracy that doesn't move forward and doesn't make decisions.

There were tons of working groups that proposed other mechanisms. Then came the quality-consensus . . . The idea was we collect all dissent, we add them to the act, and state that the consensus be by an 80 percent and the other 20 percent has been thinking about this. But that was impossible to pass because, in the end, what we were proposing was to break the unanimous consensus—and since we were working by unanimous consensus, there was always someone who disagreed. That paralyzed us so much, weakened us, and it taught us a lot—but we couldn't resolve it.

The composition of 15-M

The composition of the 15-M was something the media continually attempted to caricature, depicting it as either a bunch of lost young people or a pre-organized group on the left. What the participants stress is that it was neither only young people nor only older people, neither left nor right, but was instead a coming together of a diverse group of people without predetermined ideologies, inventing something new. There were many challenges with regard to participation and diversity, such as the participation of immigrants, as discussed at the end of this section.

Aitor, ¡Democracia Real Ya!, Barcelona: In the beginning they were saying about us, "It's a movement of young people"—but that's wrong. Our movement has always incorporated youth, middle-aged people, young families, etc. This movement is totally trans-generational, because all are hit by the crisis.

The driving force of this is what the movement says about itself: inclusion, respect, horizontality, etc. There were also some people who had their convictions, their minds armored against any novelty that this movement could bring. I remember an assembly in which there was a group that pushed hard for the banner that we were going to take to the rally to carry the slogan "Down with Capitalism!" I might be against capitalism, but to me that banner was a big mistake. That couldn't be our identity in the beginning. Concrete issues needed to be specified, and then we had to build concrete practices that went beyond capitalism, to build other ways of life, but not announce them rhetorically, because this would only cause divisions.

Ayelen, 15-M, Madrid: For many years I didn't attend rallies because I didn't believe in the traditional way of rallying. I felt that it was an escape valve for us to calm our conscience and for the pressure cooker not to explode. But 15-M attracted me with the slogan "Real Democracy Now!" because it was the first time that I had heard anyone question democracy. In Spain the "No War!" movement occurred, and was a big, big mobilization, but it never questioned structural issues. When I see that slogan "Real Democracy Now!" I feel that it's questioning something that was institutionally deeply rooted. This is what attracted me to go to the 15-M mobilization. I said, "This is different." And when I arrived at the plaza it was shocking, because it was a different environment indeed—a lot of different people, very diverse, and a way of speaking that I was able to identify with.

Amador, 15-M, Madrid: The assembly form in [Puerta del] Sol used a unanimous consensus form of decision-making. It was an impossible miracle—a very nice thing that showed that we could come together. The power is that we can be together, and not let ourselves get divided into factions. The aim is for us to be an unrecognizable movement, so that they cannot say: "There are the leftist ones, or the radicals, or those anti-systemic ones, or the punk-occupy ones." Here we are the people, a little bit of everything, and that's the force it has had, and the joy of finding all kinds of people. The space is opened, but not in just any manner: the space is open under certain slogans. 15-M's force, in general, is that it communicates universal messages, so that many people can relate to it. The Slogans are: "Real Democracy Now!"; "You don't represent us"; "You call it democracy and [it] is not"; and "We won't pay for this crisis." Everyone can feel involved through these slogans. First, it is a rejection of what democracy is or looks like. There were a lot of people, and many supporters, and many provided meals, but it was not all the people of Madrid here. The only ones helping were those who felt attracted by these slogans, though we didn't know exactly what they meant. These were open questions.

Migrant participation in the movement

Aitor, ¡Democracia Real Ya!, Barcelona: One of our weak points is the question of immigrants. This is a "white" revolution: we haven't been able to integrate immigrants very well. The [PAH] is different, however. Why? Because, in the end, immigrants have been the people most affected— often they have been tricked into bad mortgages, and now they are the first to lose their homes. Immigrants have to fight for recognition of their rights as citizens, and direct participation—things that the current political status quo rejects. We haven't been able to create that shared imaginary with them, no matter how much our convictions might be shared.

Ayelen, 15-M, Madrid: There were immigrants who participated. But there's the question of legal fear. We were all identified by the police, we were all very visible, and immigrants were obviously afraid of repression. I've seen many Argentines, but for sure, Argentines are more integrated into Spanish culture, and they also tend to be more secure in their legal status. Immigrants have been treated so badly here, so to ask them to identify with the Spanish people is like a bad joke. We had to demonstrate that we were practicing a different type of Spanish citizenship. In Sol there was a working group on immigration, and in a week it was able to bring together more than a hundred immigrants' associations from Madrid, but that is not the same as direct participation in Sol.

What inclusive meant in practice was hard sometimes. For example, on the first day of the encampment, feminists hung up a banner that in my personal opinion was a little provocative: "Revolution will be feminist, or won't happen." That is not inclusive. You are throwing out the person who by consciousness or by ignorance does not identify with that. These people didn't stay silent, and I think it's wonderful because, taking into account that movements and rallies have always been full of the most familiar discourse, the general anonymous voice had never really appeared. First we tried to negotiate with the women who hung up the banner, and proposed adding the word "also," so it became "Revolution will *also* be feminist or won't happen." They didn't accept it, so it was removed.

From encampments to neighborhood and village self-organization

A conscious decision was made in Madrid to no longer occupy Puerta del Sol, and instead re-territorialize to the neighborhoods. As in Greece, the movement found that more concrete work could be done from the areas where people lived, worked, studied, and built their everyday relationships. This phenomenon of neighborhood assemblies had already developed in dozens of towns and villages throughout the country, inspired by Puerta del Sol and Plaça de Catalunya.

Luis, 15-M, Madrid: For the movement to be real-life, and everyday life to be the movement, it has to intersect with people's lives. The problem with activism is that it puts on social events and people don't go. The issue is to understand that the movement could be of the people and our quotidian life, then to turn politics into something that is very important in terms of friendship, affinity, family—things that in Spain are extremely important—to politicize those relationships, and to learn that this is politics, too.

One important path for getting here has been to move from the plazas to the neighborhoods. In some neighborhoods it has worked pretty well, and in others it has not. I don't know if the neighborhood assembly is too artificial a structure. Surely the big movement assemblies are, since they are not able to bring the movement into everyday life. In the neighborhoods I think it works better, because there is a base with what people have in common, and it is on the micro-level with everyday life; we can put more issues on the table, like jobs, housing. The big 15-M assemblies are more like ceremonies, to be together for a period of time, but they do not have influence on the reality of things we need in the day-to-day.

Begonia, 15-M, Madrid: One cultural element in Spanish life that has been helpful for the movement is that the plazas worked well because in the squares it's easy to integrate everything into everyday life. The elderly have walks in the afternoons, they cross through the squares—and the youth are there, too. For the Spanish it's a really important meeting and social place—its spontaneous, a place where you don't need to have an appointment, where networks are built.

Elena, a university student in her early twenties, had no prior activism, and got involved with the 15-M in the main Plaza of Sol. She is now active in the Austrias neighborhood assembly in the La Latina neighborhood of Madrid.

Elena, 15-M, Madrid: In Sol, when the encampment was still there, a list was hung up that specified in which square of every neighborhood the assemblies would take place, and from there people began to go to their area's plaza.

I think that has been very important, because the social fabric in the neighborhoods was totally destroyed. For example, during the 1970s neighborhood associations were very important in Madrid, but then they were all defeated, absorbed by political parties, and within the neighborhoods it was not very organized. For sure in neighborhoods such as la Latina, basically a nightlife neighborhood, the situation was different, and then, suddenly, they started to join us in the square every Saturday, talking about politics with people of all ages who did not know one another, and that is amazing.

I have learned a lot about how beautiful it is to learn together, and from everyone, especially other generations, those who participated in older struggles, who tell you about their experiences, or how they are taking all this newness in, how they view the movement and what they think is most important. These relationships to me are an amazing advance.

On a more practical level, what was done from the beginning was to organize in working groups. The weekly assembly is for everyone, and then during the week the working groups meet and each person decides what group they want to be a part of in a sort of day-to-day way. It started in Sol with 25,000 working groups for everything, from education, feminism, the environment, road infrastructure—every single kind of working group. And well, all that has become less important, and in our case, in our neighborhood, there are two groups that are especially strong—politics and economy, and arts and culture. These are the two groups with most people, that every week do things and formulate proposals for activities.

At the first neighborhood assemblies I counted 150 people, maybe even 200. There were some, in the more politically involved neighborhoods like Vallecas, that had lots of people, and still have, but in general the number has fallen. For us during the winter and on any Saturday of the year, it is normal for assemblies to be attended by thirty to thirty-five people. What happens is that, if there is not a specific activity being discussed, not everything happens at only the assembly meetings, because people are in touch through email lists, Facebook, and Twitter. There you can organize, keep informed about what assemblies are doing. Resolutions and agreements that have been reached are posted, and you can also stay in touch with the surrounding neighborhoods' assemblies this way. The idea is to work in the neighborhood, to make things better in it, and to create a neighbors' network.

Ayelen, 15-M, Madrid: In Madrid alone, there were more than a hundred neighborhood assemblies. I don't know how many are still there. Some have disappeared, and clearly the number of people actively participating has decreased, but there are things that emerged from the neighborhoods that still remain—occupy actions, vegetable gardens, time banks—and importantly stronger relationships among neighbors. It has been a kind of explosion or rediscovery of what participation can be.

Some neighborhood assemblies were absorbed by traditional movements, and got bureaucratized. In other neighborhoods there was a true development and explosion of leadership, with many people creating things. There are neighborhoods that have fomented affinity groups, and some that are really humanizing their surroundings, meaning people have become more social, more human with one another, doing things like greeting one another on the street when they didn't before, or having beer together.

One of the typical criticisms made of the neighborhood assemblies is that they are focusing too much on the local scene. They are very neighborhood-centered, and lose a global perspective. I think both things are necessary. It's great to have people doing things at a local level, recovering the relationships in the neighborhood, but it's necessary not to lose the global view of what we have in common.

The anti-foreclosure movement

One of the strongest and most generalized of the movements to deepen due to the 15-M was the anti-foreclosure movement. Since 2011, the number of participants has increased exponentially, and the contagion effect has been tremendous—both in Spain and around the world, with movement participants from the US, Greece, and other parts of Europe coming to learn directly from the PAH as well as Skyping and corresponding to learn tactics and share lessons.

Ernest, PAH, Barcelona: The Platform started three years ago, and it was in part a collective venture between people from a previous network who used to work in social rights offices with immigrants from the social center Ateneo Candela—people who had labor problems and problems with housing rights. At the end of 2008, many unemployed people who couldn't keep up with their mortgage payments began to come. Interest rates started to rise. People started to see that what they had signed up for was crazy, and began to realize that they had been swindled in many situations. Given that context, it was something new for us, who in Barcelona started to dialogue with people of the V [*Vivienda*, or "Living"] movement.

We began to discuss the situation, together with lawyers, to figure out what the situation was and how we could socially intervene. And the Platform for those Affected by Mortgages was born in February 2009. The Platform is a pre-15-M movement, but it was given impetus by the 15-M. It is one of the suggestions for organizing for many neighborhood assemblies, and encampments of the 15-M movement. After they left the squares they didn't have a clear idea of where to go. Before the 15-M there was an assembly of the Barcelona Platform, and another in Terraza, and after the 15-M, in just a short period of time, forty-four

Platforms were created across Spain.[11] In addition to this, we need to take into account the fact that there are many city-based assemblies that don't call themselves "affected by mortgages," but that are fighting foreclosures in the same way, and are also dedicated to blocking eviction attempts for some families. In other words, there are forty-four Platforms, plus other neighborhood assemblies, that have the same action guidelines. They give them some kind of counseling or they bring them to the Platform, but above all, when there are announcements of foreclosures like this next Monday in their neighborhood, they get active and call the neighborhood together so that they can all go to prevent it, knocking on doors to mobilize people to prevent the foreclosure from occurring . . .

According to the available data for the second trimester of 2012, issued by the General Council of Judicial Power (CGPJ), the number of foreclosures in Spain has increased, and has now reached an average of 532 per day. Nevertheless, what we observe is that families that take part in the PAHs are organized, with more experience, and now there's more PAHs in the territory—more than seventy. For instance, many banks are giving up because of the pressure put on them by many families, and accepting restructuring or forgiving of debts. As a result, what we can see is that, from data from the CGPJ, now we have to stop much fewer evictions than in the past year, because we are achieving more victories, with regard to the families that take part in the PAH, and starting new negotiations. With respect to us, we have started to negotiate collectively—not individually, as in the past—with banks' central headquarters, instead of local branches, since directors of branches don't have enough real power when managing these types of situations, and linking families to the bank in which they have their mortgages, to pressure them more.

The methodology and organizing structures of anti-foreclosure

Ernest, PAH, Barcelona: What we do is divide families into two groups. One is for the people that come for the first time, that don't know anything about

---

11   By the November 2013 Malaga gathering of PAH groups across Spain, this number was 150.

the Platform. In this group of people we give an introduction to the main activities of the Platform—what we can do and what we cannot do, to inform them a bit, not to create false expectations, nor to allow them to believe that we will ask them for money, because there has been a lot of fraud with this issue. People are desperate, and there are lots of lawyers taking advantage of that and defrauding them, so it's difficult to gain people's trust. Our activity is prominently political, and besides, it is the only way for them to get something. And then there is the second group, for whom this is the second assembly they attend, in which they fill in a kind of survey we have designed, and with that survey they can locate easily on a map at what point of the foreclosure process they are. Because then you can carry out different activities designed to pressure the bank, the administration, social services, the judge, etc. Then they locate the point they are [at], and decide what action to take. And then there's the issue of the community, saying, "Well, I want to do this, I want to go to the bank to deliver this letter, I want you to come help me." And there is also a theater company that offers to put on shows to pressure institutions to receive people. Then they carry out some activities specially designed according to the person's situation, and then the last link of the chain, in case we didn't achieve anything from this, takes place the day of the eviction. This is the most media-covered moment, but is also true that for many families it doesn't come to this, because many victories are won—many people, with the help of social pressure, get a re-evaluation of their financial obligations. That's our main demand—it consists of the bank accepting their rights to the property and cancelling the debt. Assemblies last long enough—around four hours. We provide tools and counseling about what to do, and, above all, turn individual cases into something more collective.

Christina, a forty-eight-year-old single mother, first became active with the 15-M encampment in Lanzarote, Canary Islands. She was evicted for not being able to pay her mortgage and is now occupying a home with her daughter. She is one of the founders of the PAH Lanzarote.

Christina, PAH, Lanzarote: There are no hierarchies. They don't exist. But it is not that they don't exist because someone suggested it, but because it is a space where each person becomes the owner of their life and everyone has every opportunity. If we are all in control of our lives and we have all the opportunities, there is no desire for someone to come and tell you what to do. The objective is that you have all the tools, all the capacity and opportunity to seek freedom and the freedom of all—so of course, hierarchy does not fit, and we don't feel it, or want it ever.

The importance of victories

Ernest, PAH, Barcelona: We need to be capable of winning, because if not, people will believe that mobilizations in themselves do not resolve anything. Now, with the 15-M, this is the big challenge. In that sense, with the example of the Platform of those Affected by Mortgages, for example, it has that virtue of having two levels of struggle: one, in the short term, which has weekly victories, since every week there are evictions of people of the Platform, and people organize in the neighborhoods in a peaceful way, but convincingly enough they confront police and the bank officers, allowing the family to keep on living there; but on the other hand there's a more long-term objective, harder to achieve, which is a change of the current mortgage law, and [a fight] for some specific rights for the home occupier in these cases. To win something every week or every fortnight gives people hope, and a reason to participate.

The anti-foreclosure movement and 15-M

Ernest, PAH, Barcelona: With the Platform, what we focused on first was to visualize forms of resistance—to preview, in a moment of economic crisis, that families could guarantee housing rights, that they remained housed—because the problem in Spain is not one of supply. There are around 5 million empty properties; it's a problem of housing access.

The mortgage issue is very public. People see it in the press, then come with enough force to fight. Before the 15-M we often formed assemblies of just three or four people, and now we are more or less fifty families. Lots of people stayed at the entrance of the social center and didn't enter, because they were ashamed to recognize they suffer this problem. It was very socially stigmatized. And also in those spaces there are bio-political elements of the people that are crying with shame when they enter, that find it difficult to talk. In that way they receive support from the people who empower them, and they leave the assemblies with enough force, energy, and dignity to go to the bank and say to the director what they want to say, to organize actions like being at the entrance of the bank premises every single day, telling other clients what the bank is doing, etc., so that they can get their first payment.

Thus, at that point there wasn't any social debate about this issue—it was just like a drama of what happened in Spain, which in fact is very important, because from 2007, when the housing bubble burst, until now, according to data from the Judicial Power General Council, a sort of official database, there have been more than 314,000 foreclosures, and if in every [one] of those foreclosures there's a family, we're talking about millions of people that are now out on the streets, dispossessed and with a lifetime of debt.

Christina, PAH, Lanzarote: I was born in the 15-M. My daughter and I were part of the encampment here, and for me there was a before and an after. And yes, I fight now for my house and the issue of housing because I had participated in the 15-M, clearly. It was because of this I fought and knew to call the PAH and see how to set up a group here in Lanzarote. When we first started organizing, people in the town came up to me all the time and said, "we don't do that here, we don't protest" and, well, now we do.

Women and immigrants' participation

Ernest, PAH, Barcelona: The Platform is also a very mixed space—a major part of the movement is made up of women. There are many immigrant women, and the other half are native. There are more women because, while the economic crisis has affected men and men's salaries most, what happened was that most of them got depressed or became alcoholic, and are too ashamed to declare their problems publicly. This is a situation in which women take control and fight day and night, taking care of children and participating in the assemblies. The large amount of immigrant participation has many explanations. Ten years ago in Spain there was a lot of credit available for buying property—there were fiscal obligations. In Spain leases are expensive, scarce, and poor quality. In addition, you would always worry about if something went wrong, you could lose your property, and that the house will always increase in price. When the housing bubble burst, many native families, instead of organizing and struggling to change their situation, what they did is ask for family savings, family, networks of friends who might be willing to lend them money, or house them in their homes. Immigrants, on the other hand, are alone. For that reason the only choice they have is to fight.

From the Platform we always speak about Real Democracy Now! The people from the Platform go to their assembly meetings, to help provide solutions to their problems, and fight for other people in the same situation, too. In the 1990s we would talk about trying to create a kind of umbrella that might group together both immigrants and natives, to find common causes both could fight for. But now that is taken more or less as read, and native people, even some that are racists, who have troubles with their mortgages, they go to all the evictions of immigrants, creating a kind of novel relationship. Suddenly people don't talk about if you're foreign or a native, but they talk about the problem, and counsel and help each other . . .

The incredible and exciting thing is the solidarity among people. In Catalonia, for example, there are around seventeen or eighteen Platforms, and the entire state is . . . the community with the most Platforms. And when there's a foreclosure here in Barcelona, people come from cities 200 to 250 kilometers away—they come at 7 a.m. to support their comrades, including people with their problems already resolved, families that are in the housing problem and neighbors' associations. That is something in which we work. We have a girl who is a lawyer that has taught us within the Platform about this issue, and who is in charge of going to different neighbors' associations of Barcelona, to put on instructional workshops for the neighbors and also provide counseling to people in their neighborhoods.

One year later

Ana, Observatorio Metropolitano, Madrid: It's necessary that this atmosphere we created of "this is not democracy" focus on more concrete actions. We don't know for certain up to what point the assemblies can really be the thing to channel that, or whether it should be all these diffuse satellite groups.

In contrast to the media reporting the end of the movement every few weeks, the participants on the ground are convinced that the huge mobilizations were just the beginning of much bigger movements to come. Gerardo, who works constantly in close contact with working-class people in popular neighborhoods of Madrid, is convinced that now the social fabric that was totally broken is starting to be fixed, to create a real organization, and to have power that transforms it. I think we are preparing for a long period, though at the same time things look like they could move quickly. Sometimes I think that a big move of social uprising could happen, greater than the one that already happened.

Two years later

Luis, 15-M, Madrid: People have said many times that the 15-M was dead, but there are always things going on.

The squares had the quality of being a small place of commons, organizing resources in common. It had the idea of autonomy—a little island in which we would try out how we want to live in common. But that can happen only for some time. So in Spain the move to the neighborhoods happened. But people saw also that it is very difficult to work in the neighborhoods. Now the big thing in Spain is mainly to recuperate the institutions of the welfare state, the public institutions, schools, and hospitals. These are very interesting movements now. They are called "tides"—the green tide is about education, the white tide is around health, and there are many others, but these two are the most important. It is very interesting, because these movements somehow have the DNA of the 15-M but are a different thing. They could not have happened that way without the 15-M. They are not 15-M, not the squares—they are new, but have the flavor and the characteristics of 15-M, like horizontality, working in networks, not necessarily having the same ideology but being very practical . . .

Sometimes it is difficult to point at concrete results, but there are effects. We have a specific political climate. There is still a big feeling of opportunity and openness—everything could happen. The institutions are falling apart. The political climate is characterized by the terms the 15-M put forward. Because, alternatively we could have a mood of resignation, like, "Well, there will be other governments and they will be corrupt again . . ."

CHAPTER FIVE

Occupy! (US)

Dating the beginning of Occupy is not as easy as it might seem. Many use September 17, 2011—the day of actions and assemblies that ended with the first night of the occupation of Zuccotti Park. We agree with this, but also see the need to place it in the context of the preceding weeks, as well as the history of movements in the US. Since one of the authors was a participant in Occupy—as well as in the assemblies and organizing leading up to it in the New York General Assembly—what follows is based on recollections and contemporaneous notes.

Adbusters, a Canada-based culture-jamming media group, made the first call to "Occupy Wall Street" in July 2011. In response, people got together to discuss the call and what sort of mobilization might take place in response. After a few gatherings—one in which people who had prior political experience in more horizontal groups won the argument for an assembly and not a traditional rally or speak-out—it was agreed that there would be an attempt to "Occupy Wall Street," and decide what that might mean. From there began the first assemblies of what became the New York City General Assembly (NYCGA). Each week the general assembly would meet, usually in the Lower East Side of Manhattan's Tompkins Square Park. There were generally a few dozen people participating in the assemblies, with facilitation initially provided by a few people who had some prior organizing experience in more horizontal, consensus-oriented groups. Soon there were facilitation training sessions, and an attempt was made to train others in the facilitation process. Since there were only a few dozen people, and since many had no prior political experience or experience with the consensus process, there was a sufficient base of agreement to determine that decisions would be made with consensus, striving for a full consensus minus one block—or, failing that, a 90 percent vote. This form of decision-making carried over into Zuccotti Park, with none of the initial participants ever imagining that, only weeks after the initial assemblies, the New York City General Assembly would become Occupy, with thousands sometimes participating and attempting to make decisions together. There was a great deal of criticism of this approach, as described in Chapter 2, but little could be done to depart from it once thousands had been involved in making the decision.

The early NYCGA rapidly organized working groups and a training structure that was then easily adaptable as the early framework of Occupy—specifically, in August and early September. Of course, while the NYCGA had around a dozen working groups, covering legal, medical, food, art, media facilitation, and so on, Occupy had hundreds by early October. They covered issues like mediation, library services, structure, kitchen services, people of color, Occupy en Español, as well as including a variety of women's and queer groups.[1] This prior organizing structure, though little known, helped a great deal in establishing a mood of trust and consensus-seeking. This was evident the day of September 17, which was organized as both a day of action and a day of assemblies—though the second of these was little known. The Tactical Working Group was to decide what park or plaza we would occupy and inform people on the day. We had already trained teams from the NYCGA to facilitate smaller group discussions. The questions that were initially proposed for discussion, as agreed at an assembly in early September, were, first: What is the crisis, and how do people experience it? And, second: What can we do about it? Many of the dozens of assemblies that gathered in Zuccotti on September 17 did address these questions, but most, if not all, eventually moved the discussion to the question of occupation and what it would mean.

---

1 For a full list, see www.nycga.net.

REALLY? WE WILL OCCUPY?

Those people who were involved before September 17 often joke with one another about how we were the only people not to bring sleeping bags with us that day. While we did want to occupy, we were so focused on that day and night, and honestly many of us thought we would be repressed by the police, as is the history and custom in New York City, that we did not believe it would happen—much less last as long as it did. Thus, we were not totally prepared for almost 3,000 people who participated in the evening general assembly and wanted to occupy. The facilitation team for the night assembly on September 17 comprised NYCGA facilitators, armed with a few bull-horns. Soon after the facilitation began, however, the police made it clear they would not permit the "amplified sound," and a quick decision was made. It was also not very effective to speak to almost three thousand people only with bullhorns. In a facilitation training session only the night before, one of the many role-playing exercises that was conducted addressed how to communicate on the street with many people if your communication systems (phones, radios, and so on) went down. We practiced the "People's Mic"—something that had been used on the streets of Seattle during the anti-WTO protests to communicate which blockades needed support. In Seattle, phrases were shouted and then echoed by people farther down a block, and then the next one, and the next, forming a massive human chain of communication. In the same spirit, we decided while facilitating to try to use the power of our voices in repetition to amplify one another. It worked, and became a powerful tool not only for communicating with large groups, but also as a way to encourage active listening, with each person repeating what they heard. The use of the People's Mic took off not only in New York, but later around the US, and even in other parts of the world. Together with "twinkles" or "jazz hands"—the American Sign Language sign for applause, it became emblematic of the global movements for real democracy.

Almost everyone who participated in the assembly of the evening of September 17 recalls it with a sort of wonder, and speaks of having chills at the time. The assembly went on for hours that night, with the main focus being whether there would be an occupation. The vast majority of the people there did want to occupy, but there was not yet a full consensus when the police announced that the park was to be closed. It was ultimately decided that we would occupy, but that all decisions that were to pertain to the occupation would be made by those people who were staying to carry it out. Later that night, the first assembly of the occupation was held.

ECONOMIC CRISIS AND PRECONDITIONS OF OCCUPY

Much has been written about the economic conditions that precipitated Occupy, but these have not been discussed to quite the same extent as in Greece, Spain, and other parts of Europe. It is true that the crisis was felt more severely in other parts of the world, but there are other reasons for this—including the culture of individualism and pride in boot-strapping one's way out of all predicaments, which can prevent people from even acknowledging that they have a problem, much less seeking help. For example, it is uncommon for people to reach out to one another when they lose their jobs; in fact, it is more common for someone to pretend it is temporary, or even lie outright about it and take out loans to survive. The same is true of losing one's house, trying to repay student loans, or paying for medical care.

Occupy turned this on its head. Beginning by putting into the public conversation the 99 percent and the 1 percent, in a country that has not talked about class in any substantive way—much less a confrontational way—for decades. It is now commonplace for people to talk about those with economic power and wealth and those without them. This empowering shift has resulted in increased sense of dignity in many realms of society. No longer is it an individual's fault if her job has been cut and she loses her home—there is another explanation. Thus, instead of feeling guilty, hiding the facts, moving into a car or van, and feeling unworthy, people have begun to organize and fight back. This can be seen most powerfully in the Occupy Homes movement that began almost immediately after Occupy, and continues all over the US to this day. It is also growing with the Strike Debt movement, with increasing numbers of people discussing how debt is acquired, and beginning a movement to refuse to pay it, as well as collectively working to support people who are losing their homes due to debt.

The crisis

Upon examining the distribution of wealth in the US, it becomes clear that Occupy was quite close to reality with its slogan: "We are the 99 percent." In 2010, the top 1 percent had a 35.4 percent share of all privately held wealth, and the next 4 percent had a share of 27.7 percent. The top 20 percent owned 88.9 percent of the wealth. The crisis exacerbated this inequality, reducing the share of the bottom 80 percent from 15 percent in 2007 to 11.1 percent in 2010. The percentage of households with no marketable assets at all rose in the same period from 18.6 percent to 22.5 percent. In total, official US Census data for 2012 lists 46 million Americans—15 percent of the population—as poor,[2] and the number of US residents depending on food stamps rose from 26.3 million in 2007 to 47 million in 2013.

Crisis and economic restructuring has destroyed $19.2 trillion in household wealth, according to the US Treasury Department, with noticeable differences along race lines. The median white household's net worth in 2007 was $151,000, while the median black household's net worth was $9,700, and the figure for Latinos stood at $9,600. By 2010, the median white household's net worth was down one third, at $97,000, with the figures for blacks and Latinos standing at $4,900 and $1,300— representing respective declines of 50 percent and 80 percent.[3]

It is on the topic of debt that Occupy was really able to shift mainstream debate. The US is a nation of debtors. In 2011, 69 percent of US households were in debt. That share had dropped from 74 percent in 2000, but the average debt rose from $50,971 (inflation-adjusted) to $70,000.[4] While in the early 1980s the average household debt was equal to 60 percent of the average annual income, by the time of the 2008 financial crisis, that share had "grown to exceed 100 percent."[5]

---

2 Peter Edelmann, "Poverty in America: Why Can't We End It?," *New York Times*, July 28, 2012.

3 Edward N. Wolff, "The Asset Price Meltdown and the Wealth of the Middle Class," New York University, August 26, 2012, appam.confex.com.

4 Tim Mullaney, "More Americans Debt-Free, but the Rest Owe More," *USA Today*, March 21, 2013.

5 *Strike Debt! The Debt Resistors' Operations Manual*, Strike Debt!/Occupy Wall Street, 2012, p. 21.

Households of thirty-five-to-forty-four-year-olds saw the biggest increase in debt, with an average of $108,000. The crisis has also hit seniors hard. Their median debt doubled to $26,000, and the share of seniors owing money grew from 41 percent in 2000 to 44 percent in 2011.[6] This meant that people could not maintain a decent standard of living based on work and income, but had to acquire debt. Increasingly, pensions do not provide enough income to meet basic needs, as retired people were forced to live with family and other elderly people, go back to work, acquire more debt, and sometimes go without basic services such as medicine or heating.

The figures are even more alarming if concrete debt is considered. The Federal Reserve reported in the first quarter of 2013 an outstanding mortgage debt of nearly $13.1 trillion, of which $9.86 trillion was on one to four family residences; outstanding student loan debt totaled $1.2 trillion in the US,[7] with 40 million US residents are affected; and the average student loan debt for those who graduated in 2013 was $31,509.[8] Meanwhile, credit card debt volume was slowly shrinking,[9] but this was due to credit card companies writing off increasing amounts of debt as uncollectable.

It is no wonder, then, that out of Occupy grew Strike Debt. It is now operating in a number of cities and towns around the US, and is incredibly popular with almost anyone who hears about its mission and politics. While Occupy made inequality and class issues to be discussed, and poverty something to be angry about rather than ashamed of, Strike Debt has increasingly changed the conversation on debt. Through material such as the *Debt Resistors' Manual* and other forms of popular education, as well as workshops and actions including burning student debt forms and organizing public testimonials on personal debt, the conversation has moved from one around guilt and individual blame to one that points to the banks and the system of lending as unfair and predatory.

With the official number of homeless people in the US in 2012

---

6   Mullaney, "More Americans Debt-Free."
7   Institute for College Access and Success, "Average Student Debt Climbs to $26,600 for Class of 2011," ticas.org.
8   Tim Chen, "American Household Credit Card Debt Statistics: 2013," nerdwallet.com.
9   Federal Reserve, "G-19 Consumer Credit Report July 2013," September 9, 2013, federalreserve.gov.

reaching 633,782, approximately 38 percent (243,627) of whom were unsheltered,[10] it is also no wonder that every Occupy encampment had homeless people coming for shelter and food. In some cities, such as Philadelphia, there were often hundreds of homeless people, mainly women, at any given time.[11] This large number of homeless people—often not in the encampments for the same political reasons as other occupiers, but rather for reasons of survival—created various challenges, and sometimes conflicts. With the foreclosure crisis prior to Occupy, it is no wonder that Occupy Homes became a central part of the movement.

We conducted fifteen interviews in the US with participants in Occupy and the various Occupy-inspired groups that existed at the time of writing, such as Occupy Homes and Strike Debt. One of the authors was also an active participant in Occupy Wall Street in New York, and therefore the relationships with the interviewees in New York, as well as some of the individuals in California, has been ongoing and often quite close. We decided to select only a few cities for our interviews, to be consistent with our investigations of Greece and Spain, though Occupy was and remains in many hundreds of locations, and perhaps more than a thousand at its peak. Having traveled to many locations throughout the US in 2011 and 2012, often sharing experiences from Occupy as well as the new movements globally, we were struck by the sheer number of Occupy and anti-foreclosure groups in existence. Almost every town or city had one.

VOICES

The majority of the people interviewed were non-white, coming from various backgrounds—Palestinian, Bolivian, African-American, and Indian—and half were women. Three were union workers, and half come from a working-class background, while one was formally homeless and incarcerated. Seven individuals did not have regular work, and could be identified

---

10   National Alliance to End Homelessness, "The State of Homelessness in America 2013," April 2013, endhomelessness.org.

11   "Occupy Philly Draws Hundreds of Homeless," *Real Change* 18:43, November 9, 2011, realchangenews.org.

as precarious workers, while eleven had university degrees. This demographic might not be fully reflective of that of Occupy—but we selected interviewees based only on our relationship to them and their leadership in the movement. It is also important to note that New York and the Bay Area of California are much more diverse than many other parts of the US. All of the people interviewed had some prior political experience. A few had experience in horizontal organizing, such as in the Global Justice Movement and the new Students for a Democratic Society.

Plaza and occupation descriptions

New York's Zuccotti Park remains the main reference point in discussions about Occupy in the US. But the phenomena of occupation and directly democratic assemblies took place in more than a thousand towns and cities around the country. The descriptions below are from New York, but people everywhere have stories of empowerment and transformed subjectivity due to their participation in real democracy.

Matt Presto, twenty-five, is an elementary school math teacher, and was part of the safer spaces and conflict resolution/mediation working groups, New York.

Matt, OWS, New York: I think a lot of people who recount the evening of September 17 attribute this mystical quality to it all. That it just was this otherworldly experience. When I look back I certainly feel that way. I remember first arriving there. I had also gotten to the park earlier, before everyone else had, and wasn't sure what was going to happen next—if people were gonna stay, if this was something that would be engaging enough for people. And then . . . people came and some of us spoke up and encouraged people to form these breakout groups and talk about what they identified as problems right now, and it just happened. People formed these breakout groups with complete strangers and had these amazing conversations. I remember just being on the periphery, walking from one place to the next and listening to people speaking, and it was amazing to see people take ownership and self-organize. And that evening we had the massive general assembly, which presented its own series of problems. But it was the beginning of this incredible experiment.

Marisa Holmes, twenty-six, is a filmmaker, and was in the structure and facilitation working groups of OWS, New York City.

Marisa, OWS, New York: We didn't anticipate it at all—that we'd go down and that we'd actually even occupy. I thought, "Of course the police were going to disperse us, right?" but that didn't happen, so we just kept going. And there was this problem with the megaphone. It was this sort of makeshift rig, so we started using the "people's mic." And it just kind of happened organically. I don't remember having a conversation with all of you where we decided to use the people's mic—it was just something that made sense intuitively. So we tried to communicate to the crowd, but we were in the middle and surrounded by this circle, so most people couldn't hear us—we'd have to sort of repeat it from one side to the next. So logistically it was hard. But we got through this conversation about whether or not to occupy the space. There were legal questions raised, and then, in the end, most people seemed to not care about the legal questions and wanted to stay. Because they came to occupy, right? And so we decided to stay, just stay in the park.

And then, throughout the night, there was music, dancing . . . People were reading poetry, and just connecting with each other. It really was this kind of mind-meld experiment. And it felt really safe, despite the fact that we were surrounded by cops—it felt really, really safe to be there . . .

The night before I felt isolated, afraid, and just on edge, anticipating the power of the state. And then, the night of the occupation, I felt completely at ease, and at home. Even with people that I'd never met before. That was an amazing shift.

Gopal Dayaneni, forty-three, is a member of activist collective Movement Generation: Justice and Ecology Project, a trainer and board member of the Ruckus Society and the Center for Story-Based Strategy (formerly smart-Meme), and an advisory board member of the International Accountability Project, and Catalyst Project.

Gopal, Occupy Farms, Berkeley: There's three aspects of the occupations: one is the political space it creates for people to gather, come together, plug in, and organize, and all of that—which I think is really important.

And that's typified by the general assemblies, the workgroups, the organizing that comes out of it—the marches, the demonstrations, all of that, the general strike. So that's one piece of it and that's absolutely essential. And having a base to work out of is critical. And I think that's one of the huge values of the Occupy encampments.

A second aspect of occupations is the prefigurative politics of it. Occupy Library, Occupy Kitchen, Occupy Gardens, Occupy Clinic. And it's the idea that we are going to model a better way to be in the world—we're going to meet our needs better together. And I think those were hit-and-miss, and they were different in different places, with some aspects being better than others. The Occupy medics and Occupy clinics have been some of the most successful, because people with real skills set up shop. There was Occupy Social Workers, and things like that, trying [to] meet people's needs. Occupy Library was also a piece that was very popular, because anybody could come and give books, anybody could figure out how to organize it, so it was a model.

Those aspects of it were very interesting, but again, that is one of the places where the self-governance challenge comes, or our ability to do anything at scale becomes a problem. So, born out of that idea is some of the kinds of things that I think are the new face of Occupy, like Occupy the Farm. People who were in the Occupy Gardens take the three to six months it takes to find that destructive development project happening in your community on arable land, and do it at scale. Occupy at scale. Plazas are pathetic—we should be occupying at scale. What's that vacant building? What's that bank that closed and that building's still vacant? Occupy it and start something at scale, that models the democratic process, the horizontal structures, the participatory nature of it. All of that. So that was the second aspect.

And then the third aspect, and I think the most vulnerable aspect, was the encampments. The failure of the encampments are about scale, about people not understanding the scale of human activity, and what it takes to create a high-density environment in a small space. I think folks, especially folks in the city, who have no idea what it takes to grow food for people, and no idea what it takes to provide water for people, and no idea how much human waste is produced in a single day, could not self-govern these encampments effectively. What happens when you create an environment with a high concentration of people, many of whom will have special needs, where the tyranny of the eccentric, and infiltration, and toxic group processes can quickly train-wreck your self-governance?

The encampments create the double bind of "We can govern better than you." That is the action logic of the encampment—we can meet our needs better than you are meeting our needs. And the moment we don't do that, we eliminate the decision dilemma for them. The moment somebody gets hurt in the encampment, we have proved that we "cannot provide safety as good as they can." Obviously it's not true—they cannot provide safety through policing either, in fact it's worse—but that's not the popular narrative of safety and security: people assume the police can keep you safe. So unless we create a situation that clearly disrupts the assumption, and that creates a vision that's better, then they don't have a dilemma.

So Occupy the Farm, for us, was: What does it mean to do it at scale? What does it mean to address some of the issues around the self-governance questions around the encampment, but still use the Occupy tactic and strategies around this idea of urban land reform? What does an urban land reform movement look like in the United States? That's the question this collective here has been asking itself for four years. What does an urban land reform movement look like in the United States, one that's based on agro-ecology and principles of ecological resilience and all of that? What does that look like? So this was an opportunity for us to engage in that.

Everyone we spoke with, from the occupations in the US to those in other countries around the world, talked about how incredible it was to have so many people living and making decisions together in the park, and shared some of the same challenges. One of the most prominent of these was internal conflicts that arose without any definite method of conflict-resolution. In the most severe cases, this took the form of physical violence, from sexual assault to physical harassment. In Spain a security team was set up, later called "respect," and in the US there was Safer Spaces, as well as mediation and sometimes conflict resolution. All participants agreed that this was one of the weakest areas of the encampments and one of the most open to infiltration and political police disruption.

Matt, OWS, New York: A lot of people ask about early on why we didn't have some kind of accountability, or some kind of community agreements, or some of these other things that seemed kind of logical. We just hadn't anticipated actually staying in a park for more than an afternoon or evening. So once it became clear that this was going to be more long-term, we had to address the inevitable problems of a large number of strangers sharing a space together. And from fairly early on, people—particularly women and queer and trans folks—were expressing that they didn't feel safe sleeping in a park at night. There was a lot of rampant misogyny and heterosexism going on. So out of that came Safer Spaces, to address that issue, but also broader issues of oppression that manifested within the park.

Safer Spaces was initially concerned with designating safer sleeping spaces for people, where within that particular space there would be a group of people who would take shifts overnight to just keep an eye on things, as well as have clearly stated intentions on a sign of what that space was about—that it was queer/trans-friendly, and feminist, among various other things. The group also helped develop a community agreement, the intention of which would be a list of ideas from the entire community of what would make them feel safer in Zuccotti, and then synthesize information into a document that once consented upon, everyone entering that space would have to agree to—certain principles about respecting boundaries, basically.

Unfortunately, that didn't get finalized until after the eviction. But we were also doing what was called Community Watch, so we were working with this mediation group that had been formed, with a de-escalation group, as well as with the medics and the mental health support people, to just keep an eye on things at night, and to de-escalate situations when they arose—and, once the instances of sexual assault happened, figuring out approaches to preventing certain people from coming back into the park. The very difficult question was how to do that, and respecting the wishes of the person who had been harmed, and not bringing the police in, which would exacerbate the situation and put other people at risk.

Zuccotti in many respects is this microcosm for society, both current society and an experiment for the society we'd like it to become. And the notion of prefigurative politics is very important to us, and thinking very deeply about how our principles could be consistent with our actions. So if the world we want to see is one without police, without these punitive measures, and without the prison-industrial complex, then how are we going to resolve issues in a way that is directly democratic and horizontal and all these other things? And I think for us it wasn't about arriving at definite answers, or having a blueprint of how to approach these issues, but an ongoing experiment to see what works and what doesn't, and how to constantly adapt to changing circumstances.

Forms of democracy

While forms of direct democracy and the use of consensus are not without precedent in the US, and in fact were widespread within the global justice movement in the early 2000s, the use of assemblies rather than meetings, and face-to-face discussions of all people involved rather than delegation or representation, is new—especially in terms of its reach, with hundreds of thousands of people around the United States being involved, most of whom had little or no prior political experience. In many ways, the use of assemblies and direct democracy was a reflex, and not a political decision.

Matt, OWS, New York: On August 2, initially, when I arrived, there was a group of people speechifying and it just seemed very much like the kind of traditional politics I was getting tired of—having people talk at me, and then going on a march for an hour or two, and then going home and feeling good about ourselves for having done nothing. And so once people started to call for something different, to have this horizontal assembly, to organize for Occupy Wall Street in a directly democratic fashion, it seemed much more enticing to me, and slowly but surely other people began to join this circle. What that signified for me was that I think there was a much larger disillusionment with politics as usual. That people were looking for a break from this framework of politics solely within this electoral framework, within parties. And they wanted to take control of their own lives—they wanted to organize without trying to relegitimize these existing power structures, but rather to disrupt them.

On August 2, as soon as we began this horizontal meeting, breakout groups were formed, and we thought very consciously about the decision-making process, and more broadly how we would operate—if we'd empower working groups to operate in this decentralized fashion, if we'd use consensus and take into account, using progressive stack. The emphasis from the start was on being horizontal and directly democratic. A lot of the early language was very specific about that.

Marisa, OWS, New York: At the second meeting, after August 2, we finalized this modified consensus model. So there is a sort of conflation of direct democracy with consensus. Consensus I think is a form of direct democracy. People wanted to engage with each other directly outside existing social and political institutions, because those institutions had become illegitimate—not only the government, also the social left had become illegitimate. So it was sort of a break with both of those trajectories.

Matt, OWS, New York: Since the crash of 2008, there were numerous attempts to organize some sort of movement or series of actions against Wall Street, and they'd all been very top-down, and controlled by various political parties, or some of the institutional left. And all these efforts had largely failed, up to and including Bloombergville. And so I think people were ready to try something refreshing. And what we were seeing happening in Greece and Spain and elsewhere was an inspiration for us for a different way of organizing.

At the first meeting there were members of left parties there, but they were simply outnumbered. There were more people interested in a horizontal way that came early on, so people who had been working under a different framework had to adjust to the zeitgeist. I guess it was surprising because there's usually this dominance of the old left, and very hierarchical ways of working. And usually anarchists are the ones pushing against that, in the margins. In this instance, it seemed like the right moment—anarchist and autonomous ways of doing things were part of the zeitgeist, and people had to just accept it.

Gopal, Occupy Farms, Berkeley: It was hard, and it was never totally perfect. There were a couple of things that happened. One thing is that we made a proposal around decision-making, and that took several meetings to land. And the thing that was truly transformative about the farm was there were a lot of people, a lot of *young* people, from Occupy Oakland. They'd found their place, and there was something about it that wasn't really right, and they didn't know what it was. And the farm answered that question, which was a purposeful productive activity and a goal—a real outcome, that you could imagine winning, as opposed to an oppositional framework. Very, very few people who were involved in Occupy Oakland and Fuck the Police protests imagine that they're going to dismantle the state through Occupy Oakland's confrontations with the cops. I do not believe that the vast majority of them deep down believe that that was the way forward. But it was the first place to offer the political space to have a robust analysis and a broader critique, and to offer this sort of idea of democracy, that there's more to democracy than voting and shopping. That idea was exciting for folks . . .

There are a lot of folks here who have never been part of a direct action spokescouncil. Their idea of direct democracy is this idea of everybody sits in some massive circle and twinkles their fingers. Folks have not been engaged in scaled interventions of thousands of people organizing mass mobilizations, let alone long-term governance structures, like Direct Action to Stop the War in San Francisco. We ran that for years on the spokescouncil model. And it dissolved after a point, but the idea that it could grow and contract, and it was scalable, and all that . . . people just don't know the history. I'm forty-three—I'm one of the oldest people involved in the project. And people think of me as a liberal, 'cause I'm trying to think about strategy, as opposed to just like, let's fight with the cops.

Sandra (Sandy) Nurse, twenty-nine, is a political scientist and was in the Direct Action working group of OWS. She now runs a youth empowerment project, BK ROT (a compost collection service in Bushwick), New York.

Sandy, OWS, New York: It's really strange how we organize—at least, it's something I've never experienced before, coming from a big institutional background. I think the way we organized, at least in the first week, was like, "Who's gonna do the food?" And we were like, "Somebody needs to get together and organize for food," and so people were like, "I know how to do that" or "I'm interested in it." Then they started working together—people were like, "We need to go disrupt what's going on down on Wall

Street," "I want to do that." So we got together, and now we have an action committee. So it is kind of like needs- and issues-based, and people coming together based on what they like to talk about, and what they want to organize for, and maybe what kind of skill sets they already have, and what skill sets they'd like to learn . . .

In this situation here, you can find someone who has been homeless, who maybe doesn't have any strong formal education, can come off the streets, step into a space, and suddenly become involved in something that really impacts a lot of people. I find that to be the most creative and meaningful way of organizing and working, and it's been the most inspiring thing to see so many people that have found meaning in doing work. It's pretty wild, actually.

I don't know what this process should be called. There are a lot of words, from being a student of history and political science. People can call it direct, people can call it liberal, people can call it electoral. This is not electoral—it's not institutional. I think it's . . . I don't know, it's just like, my voice is heard, everyone's voice is heard, and we come together and we decide what to do with that. I don't even know what that is actually termed. It just is something that's powerful—if it's direct democracy, if it's localized democracy, localized direct democracy. I'm not really sure. I think what's happening is something completely different.

Anthony Leviege, in his thirties, is a dockworker and member of the International Longshore and Warehouse Union in Oakland, CA.

Anthony, ILWU, Oakland: I think that everyone should have a say in society. That would be a more fair system—that society should be run to meet the needs of the people, and not profit. My idea is that society should be here to take care of Mother Earth, all of our home. No borders, so some people can control that.

Nobody really cares about American Airlines, United Airlines, you can just have one airline, then people would say, "It wouldn't be fair competition." Well, shit, I always say, the flight's still the same, even though it's competition, but they spend so much money on advertisement, and competing with each other for the market, that it's ridiculous.

I just think that workers and people must have way more control and we need a system where we produce for what we need, instead of profit. That would be something that I'm for.

I've been on both sides. I grew up in the ghettos, and struggled, and went to jail, and gang-banged, and all that stuff, and now I make a decent life. I married my wife, and I get to travel and all that, so I get to see both perspectives. But I understand that it was luck that happened to me. And a lot of people think it's hard work, because of what we see on TV, and "If you work hard . . ."; but the reality is that for some people it's like Vegas—yeah, some people are gonna win, but the majority of them are going to lose. And, just me personally, I realize that now. I was lucky—my mom lived out here, so I was able to get out of LA, and get a different start. And then some people didn't have that.

Why not representative democracy?

For many in the Occupy movement, the rejection of representative democracy, similar to the use of direct democracy, came as a sort of reflex or reaction. People often saw the "system" as the problem, and tied in with that was the use of representation. Person after person would tell us how they wanted to speak for themselves, that there was no way that any politician could represent them—and that, even if they could, they want to speak and be heard directly.

Amin Husain, thirty-six, is a Palestinian-American lawyer-turned-artist, involved in Occupy Wall Street Direct Action working group and Facilitation, New York, and is the co-founder of Tidal: Occupy Theory *journal.*

Amin, OWS, New York: People don't want to be represented. People don't want to have someone tell them what is and what isn't. That's the time we're in.

I don't understand why we can get to the moon thirty years ago but we can't have a democracy yet. This isn't a democracy. We don't live in a democracy. We live in a republic. And it's been proven for over 200 years that this myth is just that—a myth. We're yet to have a democracy. That's what I would like to see.

Marisa, OWS, New York: People do not trust representation. I was part of the Structure Working Group, and when we tried to move toward the use of the spokescouncil there were all sorts of criticisms as it being this representative body, which of course it isn't. That was not the intention. But people have this idea as a result of Occupy, which is they have this great healthy distrust of representatives, and of any kind of authority figure. So I witnessed that firsthand. On a more broad level, representatives haven't actually helped serve the basic needs of people, and there are so many glaring contradictions of bourgeois representative democracy that people are now experiencing firsthand in ways that maybe they didn't before. Especially the middle class in America is facing these contradictions like they've never faced before. So I think there is a critique of that. In the last three to four decades there's been a steady erosion of trust in government and elected officials, and Occupy is coming at the tail end of that.

Bhawin Suchak, in his thirties, is a teacher active in Occupy Albany–Housing Action Group in Albany, NY.

Bhawin, Occupy Albany, Albany: There's no democracy here in the United States. It's never been a democracy. From day one the power was white male landowners—women and people of color, especially African-American people, people of African descent, had no power, had no voice. Native indigenous folks were killed off, massacred, were moved off, penned into reservations. I feel like this idea of democracy is mythology—it's a story. And I think that myths are more powerful than truth, and that's a fundamental part of the United States. The United States was built on a lot of myths. As a teacher I understand my role in the perpetuation of mythologies to children. Because children learn these things at a young age: the founding fathers, the constitution, all these kinds of things. And it feels like they are not changeable. You can't touch them, you don't feel it, you don't feel democracy in your daily life. You don't have power. We try to be different in the place where I work—the Free School, it's called Democratic School. The kids have a vote—the kids have a say in how things are done. They decide the rules themselves. We don't decide for them. We tell them all the time, "You actually outnumber the adults in this space." We hold them accountable, and we make sure they understand the responsibility to the community, but we tell them, "You guys have power, you need to find your voice."

And I think that's the thing about this country right now, is that people are starting to realize that this idea of democracy is a sham. We need to find our voice. We've got an election coming up. It's like bad theater to watch this stuff. You got Obama just parroting the same old lines about jobs and the economy, and you've got these Republicans talking about values, while they're out there getting caught stealing and scamming and having affairs and all this kinda stuff. To me it's actually shocking that there hasn't been a fucking uprising in this country before! It's crazy. This is overdue.

Beth Stephens, fifty, is a professor at UC Santa Cruz and artist active in Occupy Homes Bernal, Bernal Heights, San Francisco, CA.

Beth, Occupy Homes Bernal, San Francisco: Driving to school today, I was listening to Democracy Now!, and they were talking about Julian Assange, and that he's probably going to be extradited to Sweden so that the United States can then grab him, and bring him over here and execute him or whatever they're going to do—and I was just thinking: What a fucking lie! There was something about how the judicial system is really set up to serve the interests of institutions. And it struck me—this is where I'm thinking about the power of metaphor, too, because the metaphor of democracy and the story that's woven around it is I think a very beautiful thing, but it never has been put in effect. It's really been used as a kind of decoy to keep people's attention and their fury away from the injustices that happen around democracy.

And, at the same time, democracy has always been linked with capitalism, and so you have people who are in power, that are also getting completely rich and wealthy and dispossessing other people, and of course making their wealth on the backs of other people. I just find that very, very difficult to stomach. And I always have—it's just that now I have sort of this pace in my life where I can become more active, and I'm doing that. My way of engaging activism is through art. I think democracy is really a beautiful utopian vision that we've never been able to engage. I'm always just amazed at how neoliberalism can take a term like, say, "multiculturalism," and just turn it on its head, and use it to oppress people of color, or different genders or sexualities. Democracy has that same power, where you track this word out there, and you track these beautiful shining ideals out there, and then it's used to extradite some guy who's telling the truth about US military engagements.

Then you have someone like George Bush, who's the leader of the democratic world, and he's just such a liar, murderer, and cheat, and all he does is get richer and richer. And I find the kind of irony involved in that horrific—it's a nightmare. It's infuriating, because democracy is really used to enslave many, many people. And I'm dedicated to trying to attain some other kind of democracy.

Shanna Goldman, thirty-three, is a former non-profit worker. She is active in Occupy Albany–Housing Action Group, Albany, NY.

Shanna, Occupy Troy, Albany, NY: The way I was trained in what activism is, where you go straight to the legislators and have an "ask"—you always have an ask—and you make sure there is a decision-maker who can give you what you need. And what really excited me immediately about Occupy was the fact that it was like, "Screw the decision-makers—they're not doing their job," so we're just going to protest, and there was no ask. And I think there didn't needed to be an ask, because it was just about letting people know it's OK to protest, it's OK to be angry. And so I just thought it was brilliant that they went straight to Wall Street, and skipped City Hall and skipped the Capitol.

Influence of OWS democratic forms

Below is one of many examples of how the use of assemblies and direct democracy permeated other groups and movements. Many, like John, refer to it as "Occupy style." Others who use forms from Occupy might not refer to the movement directly, but the similarities are clear—as for example when the Walmart workers began their job actions in 2012 and mic-checked managers and bosses; or, in many cities, from New York to Oakland, where more traditional groups, such as trade unions and human rights organizations, came together with Occupy and used the assembly form to decide how to work together, from May Day actions to anti–police brutality struggles.

John Cronin, Jr, twenty-nine, is an organizer with the Restaurant Opportunities Center of New York and OWS–Immigrant Worker Justice working group.

John, OWS/Immigrant Worker Justice, New York: Fast-forward a few months from the beginning of Occupy in September to February. We had a membership meeting called the Roccupy membership meeting. (ROC is the Restaurant Opportunities Center.[12]) So the whole membership meeting, we did it in an Occupy Wall Street–style of meeting—which means, you know, with all the hand signals, the kind of consensus thingy, which I think some of it is pretty goofy but . . . it made the conversation different. And we made sure that we sat in a circle, which sometimes doesn't happen just based on space, but we made sure we had some space. We had a big round table in a conference room where we sat. And we had some people from Occupy come and sit with our Immigrant Worker Justice Group, and also some of our members. And we just opened up a conversation of what people's thoughts were on it. One member had a son. She said, "My son's an Occupier"—she is a woman of color. Some of the stuff the media was saying—"Yeah, they're just a bunch of white hippies"; and our people said, "No, I've been down there," and there was a real conversation about it. That's another thing about Occupy—it's about throwing out some of the otherization that can happen, where you can't say, "Oh, *those* people," because a lot of people are participating, so it's not just those people, it's my cousin . . . And I've found that when I go home—I'm from Providence, Rhode Island, the white, blue-collar section of that town—and people go like, "Oh!"—they ask me questions, and they know, "John's down there, I know he's normal." So I think that's been one of the breakthroughs, too.

---

12   *John:* "Now, some of our workers have been involved in the workplace justice campaign now we have organized workers at the Capital Grille and against another workplace. It's weird. So we do the workplace justice organizing, but we also do the job training, and honestly right now the majority of our membership comes from people going through the job training. So you have to become a member to take the training—it's free—but you have to go through orientation classes and Team Meeting, which is about organizing workers' rights—there's two political education classes. So people come in looking for jobs, but there are also people who are the affected groups who should be the agents of change. So they catch on to the politics that we have, and come in. So technically, on paper, we have 5,000 members; the active membership probably will be different than that."

So back to the ROC thing, we had a meeting, run Occupy-style, talked about what their thoughts are, then said, "Well, how does the 1 percent/99 percent fit into the restaurant worker narrative?" We had a really great discussion on it.

Direct action and not representation

Matt, OWS, New York: I guess, for me, I am a firm believer in the power of direct action and basically creating conditions where one would force the state to come to the negotiating table—and consequently making these changes, rather than the framework of demands, which is perhaps a slightly less passive form of begging or petitioning, which I think often re-legitimizes the power of the state. It is obviously a very difficult question of how you address some of the very immediate suffering without giving power to the state. And for me, I think, at least part of that answer is in the direction of direct action.

Marisa, OWS, New York: Demands are limitations, right? You can go out and take a street corner and put up a soap box, and then the police will come and attack you, and you are negotiating in that moment because they confronted you—they came to you and forced a negotiation. But a demand is going to them and recognizing their power. And I wanted to avoid that with Occupy—I wanted to avoid making demands altogether. And we had that discussion over and over again early on before September 17. And it was tabled every time—people just were not really interested in pursuing demands.

Matt, OWS, New York: The question we get asked constantly: "What do you want?" And our answer is that you have nothing that we want. What we want is from one another as people. So we were having a conversation a while ago about the case of ACT UP!, which did direct action but also it did issue very specific demands, which was access to HIV and AIDS medication, which in that particular case does make sense because these companies do have something that they need to survive, and in that very immediacy it makes sense. I think when we are talking about the context of capitalism we can't demand an end to capitalism, for example.

Challenges with direct democracy

Considering the plazas and assemblies were mass experiments with direct democracy, there were relatively few challenges in the beginning. As the experiences progressed and the months passed, these challenges deepened. To a large extent, the challenges that arose were a natural part of the growing pains of the movement, and the forms of democracy used were seen as flexible and in need of change as the movement changed. In New York this became a tension, with those wanting to shift to a spokescouncil model, as had been used in the global justice movement and in Occupy San Francisco, and those who wanted to maintain the mass-consensus-based assemblies. In other areas, such as Occupy Farms in Berkeley, they modified their democracy, still adhering to direct democracy, but at the same time taking up the issue of disruptors and what is referred to as the tyranny of the eccentric. While not resolved, the tension reflects the depth of the experiment with democracy.

Marisa, OWS, New York: In direct democracy, everyone's a leader—everyone's empowered to make decisions about what affects them. The problem is the ossification of leadership and the form of institutional structure—so, having any kind of permanent position and/or executive ability to make decisions. So what we try to do is "step up, step back" rotation of leadership, so that people can take on specific tasks and if they have particular skills, and they can bring those forward, and they also share those skills, and bring new people in—and I think that's how you maintain a horizontal movement.

The problem is with the institutionalization of leadership, and permanent leadership—[whereas] in representation, that's what you have, representatives. But there are all sorts of informal social relations that result in some people having more influence than others, and so I think we always have to be critical of that, recognize it, and try to have a dialogue about it, change it. So it's not a matter of just letting everything be structureless and organic—then, of course, you tend to replicate the patterns of the existing society. You're coming from the society, so of course you're going to replicate these patterns. So we tried to address this in dialogues over the summer, and it's an ongoing process. It's not so much that we're leaderless—I like the "leaderful" framework. Also, of course, we have informal leadership, and we need to be critical of that.

Bhawin, Occupy Albany, NY: When you bring different groups of people together, there's a lot of challenging conversations that in my opinion have to happen, and have been happening, and to me are just slow, but part of a process. I feel it's really hard when you step into a space with predominantly white middle-class people, and also young middle-class people, who feel that they are this vanguard of some kind of revolution, without taking a step back and seeing their place in perpetuating the system actually, and how their voices that are constantly at the forefront need to step back, and we need to hear different voices. And that has been really frustrating . . . as a person of color organizing mainly in communities where there are people who have historically been marginalized, have not been noticed. So I think that's been a push and pull—that's been a struggle here in Albany, [and] I think with a lot of Occupys too. It started with a lot of homeless folks coming to the encampment. And I think it was great—it posed a direct challenge, and I think that the movement as a whole failed to really address that adequately and deal with it. They sort of shooed it around and avoided it. But I also think these are all good things. And I think if this movement's going to keep going, it's going to have to address these things.

Gopal, Occupy Farms, Berkeley: So this gets into the horizontalism for me. Tyranny of the eccentric and toxic group processes are the two things that crash our truly democratic-left processes—and it's because of different trends within our movement, one of which is the thing that people are now calling the tyranny of structurelessness, or the idea that "autonomy" means lack of organization, or that "anarchist" means that we don't believe in structure. Those of us who come out of the movement—the left direct-democracy movement—believe very much in structure and process; but if democracy isn't structured in, then power dynamics in our society play out, and two of the worst are tyranny of the eccentric, and then the left is just prone to toxic group processes: processing the process. As soon as somebody becomes uncertain about the agenda, then we spend three hours on actually hacking the agenda, instead of trusting the facilitators to just guide us though the process.

Self-organization and direct action in neighborhoods and workplaces

As the Occupy movement moved away from the plazas, often due to eviction, the assembly form, together with direct action, continued, often in neighborhood assemblies and workplaces. Much of the neighborhood work has focused on anti-foreclosure and eviction-defense organizing, as in Spain, while the workplace actions tend toward supporting campaigns underway, using direct action tactics to support organizing efforts. In many cities and towns, as the example of Occupy Farms in Berkeley reflects, the assembly form with direct action permeated organizational forms. Beginning in New York, Occupy was the catalyst for anti-debt organizing, as well as hurricane relief and mutual aid work. The anti-debt organizing has now taken off in numerous cities, and the model of mutual aid with relief work has also spread to cities where natural disasters have hit.

Housing

Molly Martin, sixty-two, is an electrician. She is active in Occupy Homes Bernal. Molly was involved in the anti-war movement in the 1960s, and has been an activist ever since.

Molly, Occupy Homes Bernal, San Francisco: All of us in Occupy, we all felt like we were part of Occupy—were saying to each other, "What do we do? What do we do? What's the next thing we do?" And I somehow got invited to go to a home defense in the Bayview neighborhood, which is just south of us. It's the poorest neighborhood in the city, and it's the neighborhood where most black people live. It was put on by ACCE—it used to be ACORN, it's a community organizing organization—and they held (it was at Thanksgiving I remember) a community lunch—they had turkey and food out on the sidewalk, on this block in Bayview, where there were eleven homes in foreclosure, on the same block. And these people who were in foreclosure were there—they were all organized, and they were handing out the leaflets. I was terribly impressed. So I met another neighbor there, and he said, "What's going on in our neighborhood? Are people getting foreclosed on in Bernal?"

So then I started talking to friends in my neighborhood, and we said, "Let's see if we can find out what's going on here." So we managed to get a list of foreclosures in the neighborhood. There were eighty-eight homes in foreclosure in this neighborhood at that time.

We learned a lot by knocking on doors. We put a group together and we'd go out, mostly on Sundays, and knock on doors, and find out who these people were. And the stories varied. But for sure there's a lot of shame people have to overcome. Some people we had to go back and talk to many times. We didn't push people. We just said, "Look, if you feel like you need help, we're your neighbors and we're here to help you, and we have some ideas about what we can do to keep you from losing your home." That's what we would do.

And we worked with them, and we found partners to work with, because most of us didn't know anything about foreclosures. What happens? We didn't know. You get foreclosed on, and you get evicted, and your home is sold at auction. And the auctions take place on the steps of City Hall. I didn't know that. Every day they're auctioning off people's homes on the steps of City Hall.

So now we've stopped a lot of auctions—that's kind of a last-ditch effort, once the home is getting auctioned off. We're trying to stop the foreclosures before that. And now we're starting to think about what we need to talk to people about before they even get into foreclosure, because the more time we have the better it is, if we're really trying to save people's homes.

A lot of people were skeptical at first, but there are people who've gotten their loans modified through work that we've done—their home would have been auctioned off, they would have been evicted. We feel like we're doing something for our neighbors, at least.

And one thing that I found out, once we started looking at who was in foreclosure—we found out who they were: they were almost all people of color. This is a very diverse neighborhood, but I would say most of the people who live here were white people, so that people of color were the ones who the bank targeted for these bad loans. So it feels to me like— this is the main reason that I'm active in this—that the face of my neighborhood is getting changed every day by the banks, these big banks that made fraudulent loans to my neighbors. I'm just outraged. I'm outraged all the time anyway, but this is really outrageous.

Beth, Occupy Homes Bernal, San Francisco: I wasn't the first to organize the housing group, but I helped fire the first shot. I called David Solnit, a longtime direct action organizer from the Bay area, about a neighbor of mine down the street who was being foreclosed upon. And this is an elderly African-American man—we've lived down the street from each other for about seventeen years, and so I'm very fond of this person. He's someone who served in the navy as a young man, and then he worked at the US Mint in San Francisco making money, literally making money— he was a dye operator for his working adult life. And he is one of the few African-American men in San Francisco who managed to buy his home. And so he bought his house—you know, he worked really hard, he did everything right, and . . . it's doubly difficult for African-American men. So he purchased his house, and he's lived in that house, and in that neighborhood, since the '70s. But he had a series of misfortunes happen, one of which was a fire. And when he got his insurance payment to repair the house after the fire, the money wasn't enough money to do that, because the city came in and demanded that he bring the house up to code. And so he didn't have enough money to do that, so he took out a home equity loan—or some kind of loan, I'm not 100 percent sure what that loan was, but it was a predatory loan . . . There was no way in hell that Thomas could have ever paid the loan that he has. And so it was obviously a predatory loan. And I found this very upsetting, because here was a man who worked hard all his life, and he just got screwed.

Strike Debt—You are not a loan

> Strike Debt is building a debt resistance movement. We believe that most individual debt is illegitimate and unjust. Most of us fall into debt because we are increasingly deprived of the means to acquire the basic necessities of life: education, healthcare, and housing. Because we are forced to go into debt simply in order to live, we think it is right and moral to resist it.[13]

---

13   Strike Debt, "Principles of Solidarity," July 1, 2013, strikedebt.org.

Leina Bocar, thirty-two, is an OWS artist, a participant in the Sunset Park Assembly and Strike Debt, Brooklyn, NY.

Leina, OWS/Sunset Park Assembly/Strike Debt, New York: Strike Debt is helping people escape from predatory debt collectors, working on abolishing and resisting debt and easing the burden of debt in very concrete ways. We raised $500,000 for the Rolling Jubilee, and have been able to buy approximately $9 million in distressed medical debt with that amount. The fundraising far exceeded our original goal of raising $50,000. This proves that the idea of mutual aid is alive and well in the greater population, and not merely a fringe, leftist ideal. Most of us come from Occupy Wall Street or older anti-capitalist and anti-globalization traditions. I'm thrilled that our idea of Debt Resistance is becoming more mainstream and accessible. No one should be denied medical care or face financial ruin or harassment due to unpaid debts.

Pamela Brown is in her forties. She is active in Strike Debt, OWS, and Occupy Sandy, New York City.

Pamela, OWS/Strike Debt/Occupy Sandy, New York: An inherent contradiction of the all-consuming capitalist economy we are living in is that even in the acts we take to "strike" it, we end up as participants. With the Rolling Jubilee we understood this contradiction, yet weighed the benefit of opening the conversation about debt—particularly what is legitimate debt—to a new audience more heavily. The Rolling Jubilee was never meant as a way to alter the debt economy. It was never a solution. It was a way to shine a spotlight on a predatory system, where some people profit from the misery of others—where people lose their homes and go bankrupt in order to save their lives because of our inhumane system. It was also a way to alleviate the true suffering that being hounded by a debt collector causes. And it also was a way to deprive the system of some money—since no profit can be made off the defaulted debt we purchase, and collecting on defaulted debt is a very profitable industry.

Hurricane Sandy to Occupy Sandy

Diego Ibañez, in his twenties, is active in OWS and Occupy Sandy. He is originally from Bolivia.

Diego, OWS, Occupy Sandy: From day one, crisis mode seemed unreal—as if the shock was just settling in for the community. Slowly, people's food in their fridge began to rot. The wet surfaces began to must [a stage before mold], and the silence of no electricity moved people into the streets looking for something—looking for anything. There was a self-imposed curfew, the community told us. Even worse than people breaking into your homes was the police, who were getting more aggressive by the hour, distrusting every person of color. They even tried to kick me out once. The first night I slept on the moldy floor of our distribution site, called YANA [You Are Never Alone], I knew that this was going to be something different. People looked at us with fear and distrust, thinking we were the government. I looked at every person in the eye, and could feel their struggle. This was more than providing food, water, and blankets—this was about providing humanity, dignity, and respect. This was about showing that community came from the heart, and about showing that power already existed amongst the people. The community soon caught on. I began thinking big. We needed an office—we asked them, and they gave us a house. We wanted a community clinic—we asked them, and they gave us a storefront to clean, doctors and prescriptions filling it the next day. Everything we envisioned was created. We expanded farther down, looking for churches, gyms, and schools. We opened huge distribution sites feeding thousands, but even better empowering the community members to run it themselves.

For over two weeks, while the electricity was out, we had the eyes and ears of the people. For over two weeks people had no choice but to plug into the community for real power. However, when the electricity came on, I could feel how some of the community disengaged from that energy, plugged back into the system and turned on their TVs. That was a hard day for me, because even though we were happy, the system was now providing comfort. But the hardest work was yet to come. Now we were moving from recovery to rebuilding, and aiming toward resistance.

For many, the loyalty toward unity was still there. They saw the inequities of the system when their streets had no lights, but in the rich areas Chase Bank was installing ATMs. They saw how the Red Cross, FEMA, and the National Guard were only interested in moving supplies. They saw that the only people who could help them were themselves. On a corner of a street read a sign: "The hippies took over my town, and brought it back to life."

Occupy Farms—Berkeley CA

Gopal, Occupy Farms, Berkeley: With the farm, we took over this big Gill tract, which was originally 104 acres; it's now 13 acres. We occupied the part that has the last best agricultural soil in the urbanized East Bay. And it is public land governed under the University of California, Berkeley. So we took that land and we started a farm, right away—and with 200 people, on day one, we managed to put in about forty French intensive rows as a direct action, because it was easy for anyone to plug into, as opposed to permaculture, or some other form of sustainable agro-ecology. My kids, family, and whole household were there—this was an all-inclusive direct action, and the direct action logic was farming, and the slogan was "Farmland is for Farming."

We could have been fighting to get the University of California to put an urban agriculture farm and center there. But we are not fighting to change what the University of California does on that land—we are fighting to take the land away from the University of California, and put it in a commons. And the closest thing we have to a commons under law in the State of California is a conservation easement. An agricultural conservation easement is the only in-perpetuity easement you can get in California. There's a very big difference between a campaign to change practice and a campaign to change power dynamics.

So with the Take Back the Land housing fights, right now housing is understood as, "There's private property, and there's public housing. There's private land, and there's public land." And the idea is to construct that third space of the people's. So that right now it's public and private, and we need the people's. And that's where we're trying to create common-centered housing. How do we leverage the land trust model in a way that de-speculates the soil, that takes land off the market? That's where it becomes about contesting for power. And there are lots of ways to do land trusts that don't contest for power—like buying the land and then putting it into a land trust. So then it's a one-time purchase, now it's de-speculated ideally, but it doesn't actually change power relationships and power dynamics, and how property is held.

So Occupy for us—just getting back to that—for us it's this very exciting moment of, Wow! Goals without demands. I can imagine all kinds of goals without demands that are truly transformative.

Oakland general strike and port shutdown

Anthony, ILWU, Oakland: The first shutdown, there was a lot of talk about shutting the ports down, a lot of communication, a lot of meetings going on. It actually wasn't a port shutdown—the idea was more of a general strike. For Longview, everybody had a different reason for what it was called, but it was called by Occupy, and there were a lot of different reasons—the longshoremen of Longview [were] definitely one of the reasons. At the beginning of the day, the day shift worked. And so early with the general strike you got maybe 10,000, a good amount of people came out—it didn't end up as a general strike, but a good amount of people came out. There were a lot of positive things—banks were forced to shut down. It was like people said, "You're closing your doors today." And it was beautiful, because it wasn't a permitted thing—people did what they wanted to do that day, and so there was a lot of success. But then that evening, I mean, you know, thousands of people came out, after work, and then that led to the first port shutdown. Obama himself couldn't have stopped that without bloodshed. You had like 40,000 people approaching the port, where you have to go over this ramp. And longshoremen were dispatched that day for jobs; but they told the longshoremen to go to a certain area, and at the terminals they pretty much said, "We can't work—you can't even get back there." There was so many people—it was a huge success,

The second time the port got shut down, it was more planned, and it was going to be done all day, along with up and down the coast. At first it was just an Oakland thing, but this time it was going to be coordinated up and down the coast and in other cities all over by the Occupys. That's when we really had a stronger tie—a few longshoremen, the union and Occupy—to make this happen.

When you think of Occupy, it's the community of Oakland. It's just a title that they got because of the tents, but to me it's nothing more than the community. It's different people—it's the unions, the homeless people, working people, black, white, green, it's just a whole multitude of people. Occupy met here in West Oakland—like I said, union people, workers, retired people, things like that—and to my surprise we got 2,000 people that morning, at five-thirty in the morning. And we took buses and shuttles, and we marched down to the port.

We didn't know what to expect. We were a little nervous: Were the police going block it? The port is down this way [points], so there's one main entrance. Were they going to block the main entrance, or what were they going to do? Were we going to have to make alternative plans? What was going to happen? Then there was a light drizzle. But you got about 2,000 people. I'm still talking about five-thirty in the morning. But, as time went, more people started to come. But the workers were aware of this, so not that many terminals were working. Only two shifts were in, so those got completely shut down, so the ports were shut down that day. And I think this had more to do with the longshoremen than the first.

And then that night you've probably got about 15,000 to 20,000 people, again, that came to shut the ports down that night. But the ports tried to be slick, and do like a 3 a.m. shift. So usually it's an 8 a.m. shift, then the 7 p.m. shift, and then we also have a 3 a.m. shift.

I was out there all day—from five-thirty in the morning all the way to three o'clock in the morning, playing a buffer between my brothers . . . And because you have, like, white people, young white college students, and you had a lot of . . . predominantly black longshoremen, with this beef, "They just out here, this ain't about us, this ain't about that" . . . so I wanted to make sure that I was there to say, "No, this is about us." Even if you don't agree with it, let the company deal with that. Don't you take on yourself to go and deal with it, and move them out the way—let the company deal with you getting a safe way into the port. It's not your job; it's not safe for you to go to work. So I was glad I was there, and I was there all morning.

CHAPTER SIX

Argentina

How to understand what happened on [19 and 20 December 2001]? Was it a failed outburst of the slogan, "They all must go," that was never concretized? A problem only of the savers? Or is it a point of inflection in history, in the political culture of the country, and with crucial scope for all of what has happened in this decade that is now ending, and in so much of what is continuing to occur?[1]

This passage, by writer and movement actor Raúl Zibechi, on the tenth anniversary of the popular rebellion in Argentina, encapsulates not only the central questions of the importance and longevity of the horizontal organizing after the popular rebellion, but also suggests larger questions of how one thinks about social movements, societies in movement, the meaning of success, and revolutionary change. These are some of the very same questions that are today posed to the new wave of movements; many of the lessons learned in Argentina are relevant to those new movements as they take their next steps.

The movement in Argentina precedes these movements by a decade. On December 19, 2001, something broke. After a decade of ever-increasing financial crisis, growing poverty, unemployment, structural adjustment policies, and the response of the government freezing all bank accounts

---

1   Raúl Zibechi, "19 y 20: los días que parieron und década," Lavaca.org, April 10, 2013.

indefinitely, the people of Argentina said *¡Ya Basta!* It began with a few hundred individuals going out into the street, banging on pots and pans—*cacerolando*—and then the hundreds turned into thousands, and then hundreds of thousands. There were no political parties, banners, or slogans on placards—people self-organized and mobilized day after day. Within two weeks, four governments had resigned, the minister of the economy being the first to flee, on December 19, with the president following the next day. Despite the state of siege being declared on December 19, even more people came into the streets, breaking with a past full of fear. And then the sound of the *cacerolazo* found a voice, a song. It was a shout of rejection, and a song of affirmation. *¡Que Se Vayan Todos!* was sung throughout the streets, spreading everywhere.

Ten years later, the movement continues, and has struggled a great deal with the question of how to maintain horizontal relationships and autonomy in an ever-changing political climate—and in particular how to relate to the state when the desire is to construct outside of it. The movements are of course different, and many of the formations are not in existence any longer, but that does mean the movement stopped existing. Just as, in Spain, people refer to the continued organizing as having the DNA of the 15-M, in Argentina they speak of being *hijos* ("children") of December 19 and 20, 2001. Hopefully these reflections will give some glimpses of what is possible for organizing today, as well as perhaps help avoid some of the pitfalls the movements faced in Argentina.

THE MOVEMENTS

The movement of 2001 was as diverse as its many participants. Many projects were born of the rebellion of December 19 and 20—neighborhood assemblies, art and media collectives, collective kitchens—while others existed previously, in incipient forms, and blossomed after the rebellions, such as the recuperated workplaces, and indigenous and unemployed movements.

The neighborhood assemblies are in many ways the most similar to those of Occupy and the similar movements of the squares around the world—especially in the first months of the occupations of plazas and town centers.

People in the neighborhood assemblies first met to explore new ways of supporting one another and meeting their basic needs. People in the streets began talking to one another, saw the need to gather, and began to do so—street corner by street corner, park by park, intersection by intersection. Everyone I met reflected on this experience as something totally new and spontaneous. "This did not obey an ideological decision. People simply met on a street corner in their neighborhood, with other neighbors who had participated in the *cacerolazos*," explained Pablo, a participant in the neighborhood assembly of Colegiales in Buenos Aires.

> In my assembly, in the neighborhood of Colegiales—and I know many other cases—someone simply wrote on the sidewalk, in chalk, "Neighbors let's meet here Thursday night," period. Who wrote this, no one knows. In the first meeting there were maybe fifteen people, and by the next week it was triple. Why did it increase in this way? It was not an ideological decision, or an intellectual, academic, or political one. It is like asking why did the people go out to *cacerolas*. It was the most spontaneous and elemental thing, to go out in the street and meet others on the corner.[2]

In each neighborhood the assemblies worked, and many continue to work, on a variety of projects, including helping to facilitate barter networks, creating popular kitchens, providing alternative medicine, planting organic gardens, and sometimes taking over buildings—including the highly symbolic creation of community centers in the shells of abandoned banks. These occupied spaces house kitchens, small print shops, day-care areas, after-school help for children, libraries, micro-enterprises, and free internet access and computer usage; one even has a small movie theater.

Hundreds of neighborhood assemblies emerged in the first year after the rebellion, each comprising anywhere from 100 to 300 participants. There are currently a few dozen assemblies, but nothing like the numbers in the first years after the rebellion. There are many reasons for this decline, but the fact that the number of assemblies has fallen does not

---

2   Marina Sitrin, *Horizontalism: Voices of Popular Power in Argentina* (Oakland, CA: AK Press, 2006), p. 41.

mean that the form of horizontal organizing has changed—it is just in different locations now.

There was also the *piquetero*, or Unemployed Workers Movement (Movimiento de Trabajadores Desocupados, or, MTD), which arose in the north and south of the country in the 1990s, when unemployed workers, as well as broader-based popular movements, in the context of a growing economic crisis, organized against local governments and corporations. Generally led by women, unemployed workers in the provinces of Salta, Jujuy, and Neuquén took to the streets in their thousands, blocking major transport arteries to demand subsidies from the government. In a decisive break with the past, this organizing was not done by or through elected leaders, but directly by those in the streets, who decided from moment to moment what to do next. In some places neighbors came together first, tried to discover what needs existed in the neighborhood, and from there decided to use the tactic of blockading roads, using *piquetes*. Many of the neighborhoods in which the MTDs are now located are on the outskirts of cities, in areas that some might refer to as slums. These are neighborhoods that often lack paved roads, and sometimes have no electricity or water connected to the homes. They suffer unemployment not so much as an episode of bad luck as a state of being. You are likely to be regularly unemployed, and your children face similar prospects. Not having a place of work, the traditional means of protest for a worker—a strike or industrial action—was unavailable. Thus, the *piquete* was created. Many talk about the *piquete* as not only being the space of protest, but of what opens up when the road is shut down. Movement participants sometimes refer to this as "free territory." It is in this freed space that forms of *horizontalidad* and new subjectivities have emerged.

From the *piquete*, which forced the government to give the first (small) unemployment subsidies in the history of Latin America, many groups became movements—expanding their operations, and creating autonomous areas upon which they have built housing and gardens, raised livestock, created alternative education and healthcare, among many other subsistence projects. These autonomous projects are organized geographically—MTDs emerging with neighbors in different neighborhoods, many of whom work together in network formations. As for the assembly movement, there has been a decline in the number of participants in the autonomous MTDs.

Finally, Argentina's recuperated workplace movement is perhaps the most influential in form, tactics, and strategy around the world. Workers from Argentina have been invited to speak with other workers and movement participants all over the world—most recently in Greece where their influence directly inspired workers in Vio.Me to take over their workplace. This movement is also one that continues to grow numerically, as well as in its depth of organization.

The dozen or so factory occupations that existed at the start of the 2001 rebellion grew in only two years to include hundreds of workplaces taken over and run by workers, without bosses or hierarchy. Almost every workplace sees itself as an integral part of the community, and the community sees the workplace in the same way. As the workers of the Zanon ceramic factory in the south of Argentina say, "Zanon is of the people." Zanon is now called FaSinPat—Fábrica Sin Patrón ("Factory Without a Boss").

Workplaces range from printing presses, metal shops, and medical clinics to cookie, shoe, and balloon factories, as well as a four-star hotel, schools, grocery stores, and a daily newspaper. Participants in the recuperated workplaces explain everywhere they go that what they are doing is not very complicated, with the exception of the financial challenges, and quote the slogan they have borrowed from the Landless Workers' Movement in Brazil: "Occupy, Resist, Produce." *Autogestión* is how most of the recuperated movements describe what they are creating. The vast majority of workplaces have equal pay, and use *horizontalidad* as a way of making decisions together. The few workplaces that have variations in pay and use representational forms of decision-making are almost always the newer recuperations, with workers who have not had as many years together in the workplace, and have generally not had to resist government repression to defend their recuperation. This reflects deep connections with levels of militancy, trust, and radical democracy.

The recuperated workplace movement continues to grow and gather support throughout Argentina, despite threats of eviction by the state and political and physical intimidation by the previous owners. So far, each threat has been met with mobilization by neighbors, and by various collectives and assemblies organized to thwart the government's efforts. In the case of Chilavert, a printing press, the elderly from the retirement home across the street came out, and not only defended the factory from the police but insisted on being on the front line of its defense. The recuperations are hugely popular, and many outside the movements explain them quite simply, saying that there is a lack of work, and these people want to work.

Over time, recuperated workplaces have begun to link with one another, creating barter relationships for their products. For example, a medical clinic will service members of a printing factory in exchange for the free printing of its material. Some of the workplaces have organized community centers in spaces that are not being used, or when the factory is closed. There are workplaces that have space that alternative video collectives can use, where political prisoner support groups meet, or where there is internet access; some host social events in the evenings such as art classes, salsa lessons, concerts, and tango nights.

These movements will continue to take over buildings, land, and factories. Part of what is so unique about the movements in Argentina is the methods they have used. As in many of the new movements we have described, the language of subjectivity and protagonism have been used in Argentina to explain what is happening. People feel like actors in their lives—and not just because they are now running their workplaces, but because they are doing it together, basing their actions in love and trust.

Horizontalidad is a word that formerly had no political meaning. Its political usage emerged from a new practice, and came to characterize the new social relationships forged by Argentina's middle class in assemblies, by the unemployed in neighborhoods, by workers taking back their workplaces, and by all sorts of art and media collectives that emerged in the wake of the crisis. It continues to characterize the way in which most people organize now when coming together for any reason.

The social movements in Argentina also described themselves as autonomous—a term used to reflect politics of self-organization, *autogestión*, direct participation, and a rejection of power as something wielded over someone else. In fact, the way in which anarchists worldwide have historically spoken of self-management comes closest to its current use in Argentina's autonomous movements. Projects in autonomous spaces, for example, are *autogestionada*, in the sense that they are self-created and self-managed. In the unemployed movement's neighborhood bakeries, organic farms, popular schools, and clinics are all *autogestionada*. They are run collectively, directly democratically, and horizontally, often using decision-making processes based on consensus.

A friend from Chilavert, an occupied printing press, once rejected a conversational description of him as "political," explaining that he was not "political," but rather "an actor and protagonist" in his life. Chilavert, like hundreds of other recuperated workplaces, uses *horizontalidad* as a tool for making decisions collectively—decisions that range from whether or not all workers, despite different hours and tasks, should be paid the same, to questions about what and how much to produce. Many in the autonomous movements do not call themselves activists, but rather "protagonists and subjects."

As with the newer movements, the emergence of these new approaches was linked to a politics of affection (a love- and trust-based politics), and the practice of collective reflection. A few months after the rebellion, participants from numerous autonomous movements— from assemblies, MTDs, recuperated workplaces, and various art, media, and culture collectives—began gathering on Saturdays to reflect together on what they were creating, what they were breaking from, and the obstacles faced. In all of my years of militancy, I, Marina, have never experienced such a high level of theoretical discussion, all based in the day-to-day experiences of the social movements. I remember that the whole of one Saturday was dedicated to a discussion of the meaning of autonomy, based on each group's experience. This collective reflection, as well as the reflection that takes place in each movement, is fundamental for the continuation of the autonomous movements.

I had never heard so many people speak of "waking up" before my time living in Argentina after the rebellion—until, that is, the new movements that are taking their next steps forward today.

THE AUTONOMOUS MOVEMENTS OVER TIME

One of the things that occurs in these moments of rupture is that forms of institutional power, for various reasons, are no longer in the foreground. We relate to one another for a time without immediate interference from the state, or other forms of dominating or hierarchical power. But when these forms of power wake up to a society moving ahead without them, those of us creating vast landscapes in the spaces left face some of the most serious challenges to our creation. It is in these moments that movements and freed communities are most often defeated. Inherent in the role of the state is its inability to allow people to organize outside it—just as corporations cannot allow people to run parallel economies, and political parties, on the left or the right, over time are rendered obsolete when people organize independently. These groups and institutions fight to destroy the movements, whether through direct repression, co-optation, or some combination of the two. This is what continues to be attempted in Argentina. Fortunately, there is a growing resistance to this, and alternative approaches continue to proliferate.

The years after the rebellion have witnessed a significant decline in the vibrancy of neighborhood assemblies and autonomous unemployed workers' movements. While the recuperated workplace movement continues to broaden, it is not without its problems, many of which are similar to those faced by other autonomous movements. There are numerous reasons for the change in the movements' form and size, and it is from exploring some of these that we will be better able to think about a longer-lasting revolution.

Repression

The government has found thousands of overt and covert ways of repressing the movements. Movement participants have been killed, sometimes while in the act of rebellion, as in the state-sponsored murder of Darío Santillán and Maxi Kosteki on a *piquete* in 2002. Evictions are attempted, often violently, against groups occupying buildings and land. When the full force of the state and police is employed, these evictions often succeed—though, depending on the level of resistance, sometimes the government backs down for fear of losing further legitimacy in the face of such popular power. This has been consistent in almost every case of an attempted eviction of an occupied workplace. But in some cases the state has not been able to dislodge the workers when the community has supported them. In Corrientes, in the north of the country, multinational companies, with state support, are attempting to exploit the earth with mines and water projects; but the people have organized horizontally, and despite state-sponsored violence, the corporations have had to back down.

Co-optation

In the early part of the 2000s, especially 2003–2005, one of the biggest challenges that participants in the autonomous unemployed workers' movements faced was that of attempts by the state to co-opt people through the use of Peronist political parties. Offers of cash, sometimes a great deal of it, have been used to encourage people to leave the movement. The crisis this has created for the movement is not only in the fact that participants leave, reducing both numbers and morale, but that it becomes a topic of conversation that occupies a great deal of time—not only when a person leaves the movement, but also when they want to come back, often within a matter of months. What should the movement do in such circumstances?

Another frequent form of attempted co-optation, and one that has increased in the past few years, is the offering of goods and services to autonomous neighborhood groups and movements. This has been particularly common for the unemployed movements. In itself, this might not sound like much of a challenge, but various issues have emerged. One is that the question of whether to accept state help has become such a contentious debate in the movement that it distracts from the discussion of all of the projects the movement is organizing around. Another is that, when goods have been accepted, movements have sometimes stopped producing those goods themselves, and have become dependent on the state. In the most extreme cases, which have most commonly affected the unemployed movements, accepting help from the state has made the movement materially, and thus politically, dependent on the state. It is from such a situation that the *piqueteros* K emerged— "K" standing for the Kirchners, both Néstor and Christina, who have held the presidency in Argentina since 2002. Alternatively, the government has offered premises to many of the neighborhood assemblies. Not only has this created a time-consuming debate, but those assemblies that have accepted such offers have later found themselves to be in legal agreements—not only signing leases, but even agreeing to pay rent for some period into the future.

The question of how to relate to the state while also maintaining autonomy is the most challenging yet, and is one that has caused great confusion within the movements. John Holloway argues that we need to be "in, against and beyond the state," and that we need to make our own time.[3] Some in the movements—especially the unemployed movements—seem to be organizing along these lines. It is not easy, however, and the numbers of movement participants who leave out of a very real fear repression, or who join a Peronist Party—even temporarily, so as to receive gifts and money—has not been insignificant.

Resisting the state agenda

The struggle to remain autonomous is common to all the movements. Since 2009, however, most of even the more autonomous movements have begun to shift their positions, and decided to relate to the state—though on their own terms. The MTD Chipoletti in Patagonia, for example, first decides what it needs—a building or foodstuffs—and then takes the necessary materials from the state. Receiving raw material is necessary to build the buildings, but is not the same as the state giving you housing; receiving ingredients to cook collectively is not the same as being dependent for your bread each day. Then the movement, organized in various working groups, uses these raw supplies to create what it needs. The idea is that, if the supplies do not arrive, they are not without food or housing—and, most importantly, what they receive is based on what they decide they need.

The MTD Solano began a process with a very similar approach to that of Chipoletti in late 2009. It subsequently entered another transition, finding ways to build autonomously while taking some things from the state. Initially, the MTD Solano attempted to break from all formal economic relationships with the state, beginning in 2005, mostly not going out into the street in *piquetes* to demand the small monthly subsidy. Its collective opinion was that a constant *piquete* created a dynamic of perpetual supplication to the state, and that it detracted from autonomous creation in the neighborhood. In subsequent reflections on why it stopped taking subsidies, it highlighted their effect on internal relationships within the movement.

---

3   Marina Sitrin, interview with John Holloway, "Against and Beyond the State," *Upping the Anti*, no. 4, 2007.

Political party disruption

After the first months of the neighborhood assemblies' self-organizing, a number of political parties saw an opportunity for recruitment and potential domination. They actively "entered" assemblies in an attempt to control them. When domination proved elusive, as it almost always did, they then created what has been called a disruption campaign, which caused many participants to leave assemblies out of frustration. The campaign adopted various faces, from groups that created false neighborhood assemblies so as to intervene in the discussions at the times of the *interbarrial*—the gathering of all neighborhood assemblies in parks to make coordinated decisions—which was intended to enable them to win the microphone and push their agenda, which often had nothing to do with the neighborhoods, consisting instead of proclamations and global statements such as the call for the end to imperialism, capitalism, and war. In these situations, the speakers so often ignored the facilitator that participants in other assemblies ended up leaving out of frustration. Similar tactics were used within the assemblies, where political party members would attempt to dominate the agenda, ignoring the facilitator until the other participants had left, not wanting to fight with them any more. The lesson of how to resist political party domination has been mostly learned, and parties ostracized.

The Zapatistas say, "Walking, we ask questions" and "We walk slowly since we are going far." The walk toward autonomous creation continues in Argentina despite the massive challenges posed by the state and political parties. But progress is slower and more uneven. Lessons are being learned in many movements, while in others the state is much more successful, and the lessons have yet to be internalized. Some of the challenges that have appeared were foreseen by movement participants. Some people even reflected early on that some of the structures of organization might disappear—though, were that to happen, it could be withstood since people had been so fundamentally transformed. The argument was that the movements would continue if people's subjectivity had changed, individually and collectively. Many today are confident that this is the case.

The resilience of the movements in Argentina can be explained in many ways. While the crisis of 2001 created a rupture that caused people to take to the streets and meet one another, it was the new politics of *horizontalidad, autogestión,* "other power," and *politica afectiva,* that kept people organizing. Without the various forms of collective organization that emerged to facilitate an analysis of power, which in turn created changes in subjectivity, the movements in Argentina might easily have gone the way of their counterparts in many other parts of the world when crises developed.

VOICES

The interviews and conversations included in this chapter took place between 2002 and 2013. Marina lived in Argentina where she collaborated with the autonomous movements and compiled an oral history, Horizontalism: Voices of Popular Power in Argentina.

Movements whose experiences are reflected here include neighborhood assemblies, recuperated workplaces, unemployed movements, alternative media groups, and, most recently, an anti-extraction environmental group that includes many towns and villages in the north of the country, in Corrientes. The majority of the interviews took place in Buenos Aires and the surrounding area, including some neighboring towns and cities, but there are also a number of interviews from the far south in Patagonia, including the occupied factory of Zanon and unemployed the movements in that region. Some of the movements have changed their names—in particular, the unemployed movements that no longer want to identify with the status of unemployment. The ages of the participants at the time ranged from seventeen to fifty-five.

Claudia was in her mid-forties at the first interview, and is now in her mid-fifties. She was active against the dictatorship as a teenager in human rights organizations, and cofounded a number of alternative media projects and collective publications, including Lavaca and MU.

Claudia, Lavaca.org, Buenos Aires: I believe if we pay attention, and people are left to their own devices, you will notice that people naturally organize horizontally, and the rest is a process to unlearn hierarchy. Children are a good example of this. We can observe how they naturally organize, come to agreements, divide roles, and generally come together as a group. It is not that they immediately elect a leader and other children have to talk to him to play in the group. This sort of natural coming together appeared in Argentina when everything else disappeared. Everything in Argentina disappeared—money disappeared, the institutions disappeared, and trust in leaders and government disappeared. The system had been becoming increasingly decadent, and then it was left naked. And in response, but naturally, people began to organize in this way, horizontally.

Alberto was in his early fifties at the time of the first interview, and is now in his early sixties.

Alberto, Recuperated Clinic Medrano, Buenos Aires: There are a ton of factories that are not in any formal grouping. In this clinic we are also politically independent. Our politics are as a cooperative, where everything is resolved in assemblies, from the most minimal individual questions including, for example, a change of hours. These types of things might not seem necessary to decide in assemblies, but for us, we want to be careful not to have only a few individuals making the decisions, and so we discuss among all of us and make all decisions together. We feel that, the more people that participate in the decision, the less likely we are to make mistakes. With this idea in mind, we meet about practical issues related to the functioning of the clinic—things like equipment questions, relationships with doctors, travel allowances; more than just the work in itself—all that is institutional. We also meet to talk about all types of internal organizing, from shift schedules [to] how to organize shifts, etc. All of this is not to say that we do not make mistakes, because to have an assembly is not to say that all of our decisions are written in stone—there is always space for error.

Paula and Gonzalo were in their twenties at the time of the interview. They are both in HIJOS (Hijos e Hijas por la Identidad y la Justicia contra el Olvido y el Silencio—For Identity and Justice and Against Forgetting and Silence) a group first comprised of children of the disappeared.
Paula and Gonzalo, HIJOS: In HIJOS we always try and reach consensus. We vote when it seems necessary, but most often, based on the level of agreement we generally have, it does not seem necessary. When we are

discussing something that is really complicated we may decide to have a go around, where each person in the group shares his or her position. Sometimes people get frustrated or angry, but that is usually because we have been discussing the same thing for two hours or more. Clearly, at four in the morning we might decide, OK let's vote—but that is not the most common outcome. Almost always there is an agreement.

Carina was in her late twenties at the time of the interview. She had not been active beforehand, but is now involved in alternative media and film work.

Carina, Argentina Arde, Buenos Aires: I think all of this is a process that requires a lot of time and patience. For example, there are people who go to an assembly and speak for the first time in their life—people who have never spoken in public, and really just generally stay in their house. I think people are so much more engaged and excited about being involved in things, because now they have the space to express themselves. There are moments when you don't speak, because you do not have anything to say—and other moments you are dying to speak, and you are not able to say the things you want. I am talking about myself here. At first I did not speak, and I waited for someone to tell me what I should do. This happened in almost all groups. Later, when all of the idols and leaders began to fall, and I saw young women with really clear things to say saying them, well, I noticed that . . . yes, yes, I can.

Neka was in her late thirties at the time of the first interview, but is now in her late forties. She is unemployed, and one of the first people to bring together MTD Solano—now a network of collectives. She works in the alternative health project, as well as in the women's group.

Neka, MTD Solano, Greater Buenos Aires: First we began learning something together. It was a sort of waking up to a knowledge that was collective, and this had to do with a collective self-awareness of what was taking place within all of us. First we began by asking one another and ourselves questions, and from there we began to resolve things together. Each day we continue discovering and constructing while walking. It is like each day is a horizon that opens before us, and this horizon does not have any recipe or program—we begin here, without what was in the past. What we had was life, our life each day, our difficulties, problems, crises, and what we had in our hands at the time was what we used to go looking for solutions with. The beginning of the practice of *horizontalidad* can be seen in this process. It is the walk, the process of questioning as we walk, that enriched our growth, and helped us discover that strength is different when we are side by side, when there is no one to tell us what we have to do, but rather when we decide who we are. I do not believe there is a definition for what we are doing—we know how it is done, but we are not going to come across any definition. In this way it is similar to *horizontalidad*. More than an easy answer, it is an everyday practice.

Carlos, and Julian, are all in their thirties. They are active in Zanon, Neuquen Patagonia, and were not active before recuperating the factory.

Carlos: Here we try and make decisions using consensus. In the assemblies we try and create a space where each person and position is heard, so that whatever decision we make is ultimately based on all of our opinions, or at least the majority. Here in the plant we are organized into different sectors based in areas of work. Every day each sector has a meeting. The meetings of all sectors of the plant take place on Wednesday, where each sector shares equally what they are doing. It is in this space where we decide things—like, for example, to pay all people the same 800-peso salary.

Julian: Something we have observed is that each assembly is increasingly participatory. Through this we have been able to see a sort of waking-up process of all the *compañeros*, really all of the *compañeros*, and that it is not just talk, but everyone is putting their all into this. In this waking process new critiques are constantly developing, and in a way that is a part of always moving this conflict forward, toward the north. It is from there that we put aside our differences and try to get to this north, the solution to this conflict. This is how we organize ourselves.

There are so many discussions in every assembly that it feels like they happen while flying—for example, one person presents an idea, and *pa! pim! pum!* we explode talking, and it all goes great. Despite everything, we are always full of unity, and unity about everything. It is more than that. For example, in the first assemblies we had to vote on unity and the commitment to unity, and now, day-by-day, it is so much more than a vote—we are living it and applying it.

With the factory, before we took it over, the only thing we had to do was work, and did not worry about much more. But now, with this . . . conflict, we have to move forward, and the company is not going to solve any of our problems. This is also not what we want—in no way do we want this; it is like an older *compañero* said, "It is not for us to wait for them to solve things for us—those that treated us only as numbers and tortured us." Now we are all clear on this.

New social relationships

Carina, in her early forties, was active as a university student before the rebellion and is active in the World Social Forum Argentina.

Carina, World Social Forum, Argentina: I changed. For me it wasn't a political awakening, because from a practical and theoretical point of view I was always involved. But what I did have was a really skeptical attitude—a typical sociological point of view. For me, there was hope after [December 19 and 20]—although it was difficult economically, I didn't have this hope before. What I had before was lousy. It made me sad to feel like the only person who was going to save me was myself . . .

Two years ago I thought about applying to a European or Yankee University, and going to do research, because I thought I would like reading and researching in another place. And now I want to stay, and this is important. I'm from the class of people who can choose to leave. We can choose another type of life abroad, and have better economic opportunities. If the country doesn't offer me anything, then I can read and research, because as a last resort these are noble things. So, given that I can't do them here, what part of the world should I do them in? . . . Now I feel like this is a place to stay and work. In spite of the problems—not just economic, but everything else that I told you about, because of the old politics that are kept in practice, there will always be favoritism and there will always be problems. But, in light of all of this, Argentina is a place where I want to stay and continue being involved.

Candido, in his fifties at the time of the interview but now in his sixties, worked at the Chilavert recuperated workplace. He was still active at the factory, though retired. He had been active on union issues only, but is now active in city-wide organizing in recuperated factories.

Candido, recuperated printing press, Chilavert, Buenos Aires: I am Candido Gonzalez, member of Chilavert, a workplace that was reclaimed by the workers. Our print shop was not only retaken by the eight workers on the inside, but by an entire society committed to us—one that has grown tired of our governing body's inefficiency, and tired of waiting for change to come from the top. So, together we have begun to change from the bottom.

I am a printer with more responsibilities than I had before we took over the factory—not just responsibilities with regard to the print shop, where we all assume additional responsibilities, but now we have more moral duties to assist other *compañeros* to take over their own factories. This is a chain, the movement of recovered factories. It's a chain to which we add new links all the time. The last link added is always a little wobbly, or unstable, and that link needs and receives reinforcement through the unconditional support of other recovered factories—whatever help they need, including resisting the police if necessary. If there's one thing that all the recovered factories agree on, it's that we are not alone, that we are together. It is about all of us, really all of society, other recovered factories, and everyone. Once you feel and receive this commitment, it's as if it is engraved on you by fire—you feel you have more power than money.

Neka, MTD Solano, Buenos Aires: This experience brings you in and makes you commit right from the start. Something that made a profound impression on me related to the idea of affective politics was listening to Luís Mattini speak on his participation in the struggles in the 1970s. He was giving a self-critique, and said something like: "We have fought against and attacked the capitalists, but we did not know how to combat capitalism. We can annihilate all the institutions of capitalism, or of any other system of domination. We can annihilate private enterprise and the corporations that symbolize all of that. But, if we don't combat our way of relating, which reproduces all these things, it seems as if we are fighting an empty battle."

Sergio was in his late forties at the time of the interview, and is now in his late fifties. He is the author of a number of political and historical books.

Sergio, Lavaca.org, Buenos Aires: If an earthquake struck and we became uncertain as to what rules should guide us, I can let the rules of affect guide me. If I like someone, I get the feeling that something can work, and this sentiment generates action. Moreover, what I think has changed, in terms of the new autonomy that is growing, is that previously the person was obliged to relinquish the self. The self was dissolved in the massive collective of the traditional political parties of the left or the right. The person had to cease their existence. It seems to me that what we have going now is something akin to a recovery of the self.

Trust is one of the most complex subjects for all of humanity, because no one really knows how it is generated or how it is destroyed.

Challenges with horizontalidad

Paula and Gonzalo, HIJOS, Buenos Aires: We aspire to achieve horizontal relationships, while at the same time we are conscious that true *horizontalidad*, with true equality of conditions, does not exist. For example, we have *compañeros* who have ten years' experience in the movements and *compañeros* who have two months. We all come from different places and experiences, and one of the things we try and do is bring everyone to the same level, as much as possible. This is not to say that difference does not exist—it does, and we still need to appreciate this difference. Knowledge is always power, and in many cases we are able to use this power in ways that are good in an assembly; but it can also have another manifestation, which is bad, when someone uses this ability, whether language or knowledge of history, to manipulate other *compañeros*. We try not to abuse knowledge ourselves, and also try and not permit others do it . . . we construct together.

Martin K., from Buenos Aires, was thirty-three at the time of the interview. He is a psychologist who became active after December 19 and 20, 2001 in his neighborhood assembly of Colegiales, as well as in regional discussions and in organizing on the issue of autonomy.

Martin K., Assembly Colegiales, Buenos Aires: Something really powerful I remember from when we first came together in the assemblies was that we were everyone—from housewives, students, and retired people to professionals and *cartoneros* [cardboard collectors], there on the corner, talking, and there was no difference between us, and our sharing, it was crazy and really fun. And this is a part of what *horizontalidad* is and allows. I say we are equal, but we did have a hard time finding a way of speaking a common language, and we have had to work this out in different circumstances; but still, the main principle that allowed us to organize was *horizontalidad*, with each voice being valued as equal.

Urgent situations come up all the time in the assembly, and it is a real challenge to use direct democracy under conditions where you have to respond quickly all the time. Not having sufficient time to make decisions can complicate the democratic process. It is as if, once again, the enemy is able to force you into a time paradigm that is not yours, and one that does not permit you the most minimal conditions to put your process into action. Direct democracy in this way can represent the tension with representative democracy, which, through delegation to something or someone, can seem more expedient.

It is really difficult to sustain all of this in practice, from *horizontalidad* and direct democracy to autonomy. These are all ideas and ways of being and reorganizing society that are very much against the established logic under which we live—we do not live in a horizontal society. One can be really horizontal in the assembly, but maybe in your daily work environment you are in a situation of subordination, and are forced to participate in games that are not at all horizontal. This contradiction is really difficult—one cannot live in two worlds and say, OK, I am changing worlds now: "click." It does not work like that.

Natalia is from Lomas de Zamora, part of La Toma—an occupied building with three assemblies. She was a student in her early twenties at the time of the interview.

Natalia, La Toma, Lomas de Zamora: In our assemblies and activities, sometimes we observe that what we want to do and what we are doing are not the same. For example, we recently saw this with something that happened in the *merendero*—the popular lunches we organize for many children—with the issue of yogurt distribution. Yogurt is really expensive, though we were able to get some donated for our *merendero*. It happened that many people began to approach those of us who volunteer in the *merendero* to ask for yogurt. It was then up to us to decide who got or did not get the yogurt. We observed that what we were doing, in making the decisions, was also reproducing a power relationship. And then the question became, What do we do with this? How do we resolve this? And so we began to have assemblies to discuss these things collectively with those people who worked in the *merendero*, who are not necessarily the same as those in the assembly of *La Toma*.

Some of the questions we discussed in this assembly were how to distribute yogurt and food generally, as well as who we are in relationship to others in the community, the assembly, and the *merendero*. We also asked ourselves if the fact that we were the ones getting the yogurt from donors gave us the power to decide who gets yogurt and who does not, or if we should give it all out in one day, leaving none for the following day. One of the proposals we came up with, in light of these questions, was that those who eat at the *merendero* also come with us when we ask people to donate yogurt and other food. So we decided that we would all go collectively to ask for food, both children and adults. This was especially important for us, because it reflected that we are not the owners of the food, or in charge of the process of getting food.

I guess this is just one example of power relationships that are developing and how we are learning to think about them. It is all a real process, and one that is created as we go. It takes time, and we are changing both the process and ourselves along the way.

Autonomy, the state, and resisting co-optation

Claudia: One of the problems we are facing as a movement is the issue of how to articulate what we are as a movement. Any attempt at articulation was a frustrating experience, because in one way or another articulation would amount to reification of a particular social order or ideology.

Neka: I believe that the purpose of articulating what we are as a movement is fundamentally not about building a hegemony or unified movement, but rather it is precisely a step toward creating diversity. This is where articulating what we are as a movement becomes interesting.

Claudia: Yes. The thing is that we must figure out how to promote respect for differences. No movement is the same as any other. No experience is the same as any other. No situation is the same as any other. And, that does not mean these things cannot be explained accordingly.
Neka: It is precisely those definitions that are rigid, closed, and structured that limit us, that limit our ability to be free. As we discussed previously in the workshop, once you taste freedom, you will forever fight to remain free. Then, when the set of criteria that at one time functioned as an agreement and served as a basis for organizing instead begins to operate as dogma, or law, I believe that is when movements naturally begin to seek ways to combat that which might ultimately become normative, or status quo.

Emilio, from Corrientes, was seventeen at the time of the first interview, and is now twenty-nine. He was a participant in the neighborhood assembly Tierra del Sur, located in an abandoned bank in Buenos Aires. He now works in Corrientes with anti-mining struggles, helping organize autonomous projects.

Emilio, Tierra del Sur, Buenos Aires: We don't need anyone to impose on us a new *Communist Manifesto*, and throw us into that camp like a bunch of fools. After I abandoned that form of a communist idea, I said to myself, "What is it that we want? What is our project?" The good thing is we have no program. We are creating tools of freedom. First is the obvious—to meet our basic needs. But the process of finding solutions to

204 THEY CAN'T REPRESENT US!

meet our basic needs leads us to develop tools that make us free. And, for me, that is the meaning of "autonomy." Because, if you begin to take note of what concepts constitute autonomy, and you then start to discuss the notions of *autogestión*, self-sufficiency, web, and network-like articulations, non-commercial exchange of goods, horizontal organizing, and direct democracy, you eventually end up asking yourself, "Well, if we achieve all these things, will we then be autonomous?" Autonomous from what? No. If one day we achieve true autonomy, we will not be autonomists, or autonomous—we shall in fact be free.

And yes, we will reach that state, by all means. If I did not believe it were possible to end capitalism I would not be attempting it. The notion that autonomy can exist within the capitalist system is something that often becomes a stumbling block. The idea that we can be non-capitalistic within a capitalist system is a fallacy, because capitalism intersects our lives all the time and everywhere. What we can do, however, is build and create different things without following the logic of the capitalist system. We can attempt to create the revolution in our day-to-day living. The day when all these things succeed, when we truly succeed in all these things, we will have arrived. We will in fact be free, rather than autonomous. Autonomy is a bubble that exists within the larger system. Autonomy is not in itself a system of governance. Autonomy is a tool for gaining our freedom.

Toto helped to initiate the MTD la Plata and was in his twenties at the time of this interview.

Toto, MTD la Plata, la Plata: If you were to walk into any neighborhood and walk up to anybody and ask, "Are you people autonomists?" of course the general response by the majority might be, "I don't know." On the other hand, if you were to ask, "How do you relate to the other movements, or to the government?" then I can assure you the response would be, "No, we will not allow others to impose foreign interests on us, or to make decisions for us." The same would certainly apply to *horizontalidad* if you were to ask any *compañero*, "Are you a horizontal or vertical group?" On the other hand, if anyone were to ask them, "How do you people make decisions?" Well, surely anyone of the *compañeros* would mention the process where some of us get together and hold weekly meetings, make decisions together, all participating, etc. This is why I say that the issue of attaching a label to certain ideas is something that comes from the outside. We talk about this more in terms of how we do things, as opposed to what to call the things we do. Because what might happen is that we would constantly refer to ourselves as "horizontal," and then end up forgetting what that means, and act in some other way. In other words, to me it seems much more important to remain attached to certain ways of doing things than to start attaching labels that ultimately contradict what we do in practice.

The state

Ezequiel is active in an assembly located in an abandoned bank. He was in his late twenties at the time of the first interview and now is in his thirties, working as a university professor and writer on politics and history.

Ezequiel, Assembly Cid Campeador, Buenos Aires: From the very beginning, the assembly took a very clear stance against having any links with the state and government. For example, my assembly's meeting place is located very close to one of those City of Buenos Aires government administration and participation centers. In theory, these centers are intended to decentralize government action and to encourage local civic participation. We always flat-out rejected having anything to do with that center—even to the point of absurdity. For example, even though this center allows anyone to walk in and make free photocopies, we would prefer to pay for photocopies rather than enter that place for free copies. In this respect, our intention was always to remain on the margins of the state, but not out of the belief that we were creating an autonomous space. Rather, it seems to me that, at least initially, we were manifesting our rejection of representative government—our rejection of politicians in general. I believe our de-linking from the state came from this place.

As an assembly, we have always been somewhat schizophrenic with respect to the state. On one hand, we have been vehemently opposed to having any links with the government. But, on the other hand, there have been cases when in fact we have accepted and received state support. For example, the city government started giving us bags of food some months back. These we did accept, and used to start a popular kitchen, and so on.

In this respect, these things soon result in a de facto link to the state, though we don't accept it as such. We do not want to view this as a link to the state. In assembly jargon, we refer to this as something we snatch away from the state, as opposed to something we ask from them, or something we give to them. Therefore, at the very least, our distance from the state is kept alive in our discourse.

Alberto S, from Solano, was in his late thirties at the time of the first interview, but is now in his late forties. He was practicing as a priest when the MTD Solano movement began, and was one of its founders. He left the priesthood, and is now working on land occupation, crop cultivation, and animal husbandry in order to sustain the movement.

Alberto, MTD Solano, Greater Buenos Aires: We believe that the tension continues, even though Kirchnerismo has tried all things it can to make it go away—like all power sectors will do to be able to regain governability without a crisis, this government was born in the middle of a very profound crisis, so its project was to return the institutions to normality. Then they took all these symbols, such as human rights and wealth distribution, which generated an illusion in some militant sectors, many of which went to work directly with the government. We remained in a critical position—critical in the sense that we did not believe in their discourse, we do not believe there will be a transformation. So we do not believe in their very pretty speeches that are not translated into practice.

And we persevere in this critical time without subordinating our logic, believing that the hope in Argentina is the movements, with their work half hidden at times, working and weaving the network that will permit a profound transformation. We are careful not to antagonize those who in the past we were together with, and who now we believe will have to learn in practice—though many of these movements have gone into the logic of senators and deputies, and have paid a high price.

Neka: It seems to me, at this point in the game, that the discussion is, if you take things from the state, the state is generating conditions for you. The thing is, today, to live is necessarily to live through money, so the question is how to start thinking about experiences that go around, overcoming this subjectivity—that is, taking things that are necessary to live without getting trapped in these things. I think that's the challenge. How to get things from the state in everyday life is another story. How do we build anti-capitalist spaces and break up the market logic? This is the strongest challenge.

There are small openings. For example, we occupy this land in the countryside, here in Varela, and we can consume eggs, vegetables, etc., without buying them—things we produce ourselves; and that's a beautiful experience. There is no relationship with money, and we even produce the seeds. This is an experience where we have all the knowledge and skills. We have self-management of some other things, like health, for example, preventive work, the recovery of natural medicine, a lot of things—creating opportunities for group reflection to heal some things. So there are openings outside market relations—there are these cracks we talked about today. We are poking holes in the system, in capitalism, but they are cracks, and we need to enlarge them. I believe the biggest question is what we want for our lives—not what the government can do for us, but what we want and how we are going to strengthen this desire from this experience. That is the hardest for us.

El Vasco, in his fifties at the time of the interview and is now in his sixties, was imprisoned during the dictatorship. He is a trained optometrist, and helped begin the MTD Chipoletti and Allen, now working with the MSD (Movimiento Social Dignidad)—standing for Movement for Dignity in Chipoletti. In particular, he works with young people in the movement.

El Vasco, MTD Chipolletti, Patagonia: I believe that relations with the state have always been complicated. To put forward autonomy necessarily implies not to get caught up in the state agenda, but to look for ways to meet your concrete needs that you have, and take them from the state—and to do it in a way that does not harm our sovereign space most of all . . .

It is a difficult relationship, but there are issues that we are clear about in this regard: from the state we will take what we can get, and will not let the state condition our own practices or constructions. If it seems like that is happening, we have a sort of red light or alarm that goes off, and we all run fast the other way. But we start from the premise that everything the state has is ours, so then what we are doing is taking back what is ours, and always serving in the construction of an autonomous area . . . This does not mean that the state is not constantly attempting to co-opt what we are trying to do. But we don't take it. We won't accept it.

Placido was in his mid-forties at the time of the interview, and is now in his mid-fifties. He was active in his local community before taking over the print shop.

Placido, recuperated printing press, Chilavert, Buenos Aires: The state is encouraging all workers to come together and form cooperatives, like the MTD Solano is doing, though without any initial capital, and then the state proposes that it will support this project with initial capital. This is a good program to help alleviate unemployment, but for us this does not help, since we need someone to sell to on the market. We are trying to continue to exchange things with other recuperated workplaces, and when this begins to go well [the state] is then there, always putting obstacles in our way—like inspections, permits—and right when you are going to get back to work, there is another bureaucratic obstacle that takes all your time, and you end up doing nothing.

Claudia, lavaca.org, MU and MU Punto de Encuentro, Buenos Aires: I find that there are those who say, "It's all co-opted, all useless." And then, when you get directly involved, it's the opposite, and you say, "This is full of life." In other words, between the discourse and practice there is a great divorce. I think it will take many years of thinking to figure out how to conceptualize or theorize about what is happening now—it is quite challenging . . . So, the intellectual, logically, what he does is defend his position and hold his ground, because otherwise this process undermines him.

Emilio, Ibera Guardians, Corrientes: With respect to what we talked about and what I understand of autonomy and horizontalism, clearly this is a process that began in Argentina on December 19 and 20, 2001, with experiences that can be seen in direct-democracy roadblocks, the assemblies of the movements of unemployed workers, etc. It was developed in a process years before [then], but the social explosion was generated from [that point], so everything that had been brewing came to light and was magnified, became much larger and more diverse. All the energy that was released on December 19 and 20, and all that happened again in 2002, 2003, and later did not slow down in Argentina. That is, there was an epochal change. It has been more than ten years already—[there has been] a change in the government, and we have a government that already has a long continuum of Kirchnerismo, and the changes in Latin America. But the important energy is citizen participation, to join a meeting to discuss problems, listen, create tools through direct action, struggle with roadblocks, demonstrations. That is not stopping, but the opposite—something that was spread by new movements and movements that already existed.

So yes, sure, one can go to Buenos Aires today and not find a neighborhood assembly in every neighborhood, on every corner, as it was in 2002. But it is no less true that today, if you went around the whole country to all the provinces, in many you would find horizontal assemblies of territorial defense, fighting unions, endless struggles taking place in the form of direct meetings with strong horizontalism, and where the discussion of the role of the state or unions or institutions is strong and permanent—that is, the discussion about the autonomy of these experiences is permanent.

Ibera Guardians was born in April 2011, during a direct action we did in a town called Colonia Carlos Pellegrini on the banks of Lake Ibera, and we were repressed and some members of the organization were detained by the police. In all the confusion that was generated then, in the various groups and assemblies they began to talk about Ibera Guardians as an organization. That was what we were discussing when it was born. And today the Ibera Guardians is composed of the towns of the valley where the group Alma Fuerte operates, in Chavarria.

We understand the need to finance our productive projects, and we can use state funding as initial investment on all of our projects—realizing that the money has come from the workers, and the workers can use that money as seed capital to generate our own projects to be autonomous and independent from governments and private employers. It is a way to recover rent that comes from the status of workers—to use that money to build our self-productiveness. In the other cases where the national government intervenes to enforce national laws, which are exploited by private companies in Corrientes, we understand that as part of our demands and part of our struggle, and to the extent that our demands are met they will be welcome.

Yes, our vision of autonomy is based on the strong territorial presence and strong political independence of the organization, in the sense that the sovereignty of our decisions is the people in each village assembly. We will not allow the state or political parties or businesses—no one, neither the church nor anyone—to violate the political sovereignty of our assemblies, and therefore of our organization. Now, that does not mean we cannot have a dialogue or relationship with the church or the state—because they exist, they are real, because they interfere in our lives, and so we can set up specific issues. And in the case of the state, the state exists and captures the workers' money, so I do not think there is any contradiction in obtaining financing for our projects, provided they do not violate our policy decisions.

CHAPTER SEVEN

Venezuela

When analyzing the changes in Venezuela, most journalists, historians, and social scientists concentrate on the prominent figure of Hugo Chávez, and give a somewhat "institutional" account of the transformation process called the "Bolivarian Revolution."[1] However, the leftist government that has held power in Venezuela since 1999 is without doubt the result of strong grassroots movements, as is the fact that it has survived several attempts to topple it. When the right-wing opposition and high-ranking military, with the connivance of the employers' association, staged a coup in April 2002 to oust Chávez, millions of Venezuelans took to the streets and forced the self-declared government under the leadership of the employers' association's president to resign and flee. The overarching role of the popular movements was demonstrated by the mobilizations organized from below opposing the "business strike" in 2002–2003, and in several other destabilization attempts by the opposition since then.

---

1 There are a small number of books that take a clear movement perspective: Dario Azzellini, *Venezuela bolivariana: Revolution des 21: Jahrhunderts?* (Cologne: Neuer ISP Verlag, 2007); Dario Azzellini, *Partizipation, Arbeiterkontrolle und die Commune: Bewegungen und soziale Transformation am Beispiel Venezuela* (Hamburg: VSA, 2010); George Ciccarello-Maher, *We Created Chávez: A People's History of the Venezuelan Revolution* (Durham, NC: Duke University Press, 2013); Roland Denis, *Los fabricantes de la rebelión* (Caracas: Primera Linea, 2001); Roland Denis, *Rebelión en Proceso* (Caracas: Nuestra América Rebelde, 2005); Sujatha Fernandes, *Who Can Stop the Drums?: Urban Social Movements in Chávez's Venezuela* (Durham, NC: Duke University Press, 2010).

Venezuela represents the most far-reaching process of social transformation of the twenty-first century so far. Massive self-organization and the recognition of the movements' central role in social transformation are at the core of the Bolivarian process.[2] The process of social transformation arose under circumstances that have a lot of similarities with many of the new movements we have seen in the last few years. Venezuela allows us also to glimpse the specific situation of a transformation "from two sides": from both state-centered and autonomous approaches. We can learn from the rich expressions of self-organization, from the experiences with formal state institutions, and the difficulties and achievements of pursuing a society based on solidarity, not profit.

Starting in the early 1980s, Venezuela faced a serious economic and social crisis that became a systemic political crisis. It was precisely the failure of the liberal-democratic model to satisfy the basic needs of the population, or to guarantee political participation, that led people in Venezuela to roundly reject the logic of representative democracy, and instead demand direct democracy—a desire that is expressed in the new 1999 Constitution as "participatory and protagonist democracy."

Among the mainstream scholars of the social sciences, Venezuela was considered a model democracy in Latin America, at least until the Caracazo—the popular revolt against the neoliberal structural readjustment program in 1989 (see Chapter 1). In the 1990s researchers noted an important loss of legitimacy on the part of the Venezuelan political system and traditional parties, resulting in a crisis of representation. Nevertheless, several liberal authors continued to praise Venezuela's two-party system as an outstanding example of stability[3]—even though the loss of legitimacy was widespread, resulting in the collapse of the country's party system only a few years later.

Growing social polarization and the breakdown of the existing representative framework contributed to the December 1998 election of Hugo Chávez, who had led a leftist civilian-military revolt on February 4, 1992. Chávez's candidacy was supported by numerous leftist parties,

---

2   A reference to Simón Bolívar.

3   Miriam Kornblith and Daniel H. Levine, "Venezuela: The Life and Times of the Party System," Kellogg Institute Working Paper No. 97 (Notre Dame, IN: Kellogg Institute, 1993).

organizations, and individuals. Following the elections, a National Constituent Assembly was elected, and a new Constitution was drafted sanctioning considerable direct popular participation, and was accepted by referendum in December 1999. The Constitution seeks a "protagonist and participatory democracy" based on a far-reaching idea of participation that, in addition to redefining political participation, includes social, economic, and cultural rights, as well as collective rights for specific groups.

During the first years, the notion of participation was consistent with a democratic discourse in search of a "third way," beyond capitalism and socialism. Starting in 2005, the emphasis of the discussion and the mechanisms of participation has been on popular power, revolutionary democracy, socialism, and councilism. The envisioned goal is "Socialism of the Twenty-First Century" to distinguish it from the state socialisms of the past. István Mészáros, who traced his basic ideas for a transition to socialism in his book *Beyond Capital*, has become an important theoretical reference in Venezuela, as he proposes a "communal system" involving communal production and consumption cycles.[4]

Councilist structures in various sectors of society, cooperating and confederating at higher levels, would form the basis of Venezuelan socialism, and in the longer term replace the bourgeois state with a communal state. The new participatory instruments being experimented with include various councils (communal councils, workers' councils, student councils, land workers' councils, women's councils, and so on), the democratic administration of socially owned businesses, by their workers, and many other communal and collective institutions. As philosopher and educator Simón Rodríguez—Simón Bolívar's teacher and a central reference in Bolivarianism—affirmed in the nineteenth century: "Where can we find models or templates? Because Hispanic America is something original. Its institutions and its government have to be original. And the means of establishing both must be original. Either we invent or we fail."[5]

---

4 Istvan Mészáros, *Beyond Capital: Towards a Theory of Transition* (London: Merlin Press, 1995), pp. 759–70.

5 Rodríguez cited in Enrique Contreras Ramírez, *Educación para la nueva República* (Caracas: Fundación Editorial Fabricio Ojeda, 1999), p. 112.

THE APPROACH FROM TWO SIDES

The transformative "approach from two sides" in Venezuela is forging a new path that is unique among struggles and strategies of social transformation. Blending strategies from above and below, it is pursuing an anti-imperialist politics of national sovereignty. The state and institutions are reinforced, and pursue a strategy of active economic regulation, in a mixed (capitalist) economy. However, according to the normative orientation of the Bolivarian process, the popular movements must assume a central role in the development of change, and at the same time remain autonomous with respect to the state. Various popular organizations, such as the trade union federation UNT (National Workers' Union), founded in 2004, the National Campesino Front Ezequiel Zamora (FNCEZ), the National Communards Network (RNC), and the Urban Land Committees (CTU), among many others have, despite their support for the government, repeatedly assumed positions in opposition to it. The approach from below is reflected by self-administration structures and the decentralization of state decision-making processes. These initiatives from below are an active part of the construction of a new state and a new society that seeks to eliminate the division between political society and civil society. The Venezuelan process takes into account the fundamental opposition of the state and its institutions to emancipation and the construction of a socialist society.

The "two-sides" approach is driving social antagonism toward the state's core. New institutions are arising that have been re-tasked with assisting and supporting the grassroots and movements in building structures intended to replace the state and its institutions. At the same time, there is institutional and organizational resistance to that construction within the state. These tensions are intensified by the central role played by petroleum in the Venezuelan economy—a circumstance that encourages and strengthens statism, centralization of power, and vertical structures.[6] This economic distortion also gives rise to another Venezuelan

---

6   Fernando Coronil, *The Magical State: Nature, Money and Modernity in Venezuela* (Chicago: University of Chicago Press, 1997).

peculiarity: the rentier economy[7] has shifted the locus of class struggle so that it operates within the state; in other words, it revolves around access to administrative resources, on the assumption that it is the state that redistributes social wealth.

The Venezuelan transformation process is practically re-signifying the state and society as a result of the interaction of forces from above and below, creating the possibility of overcoming capitalist relations. The main challenge is keeping this process open, and developing a modus operandi from above that supports, accompanies, and reinforces the energies emerging from below, but without co-opting or limiting them. At the same time, this is a question of developing strategies from below that would enable active participation in the construction of the new without being absorbed into the structures of the state.

The danger persists of reproducing the logic of constituted power and traditional approaches—hierarchies; representative mechanisms; division between those who govern and those who are governed, leaders and those they lead; bureaucratization. Clearly, power asymmetry between state and self-organization can easily lead to the initiatives from below being influenced by the state, and not the other way around. Initiatives from below would no longer be the seedbed of the coming society, but rather an appendage of constituted power. For that reason, the defenders of popular power emphasize the centrality of autonomy and the importance of critical debate from below.

PARTICIPATORY AND PROTAGONISTIC DEMOCRACY

In its 1999 Constitution, Venezuela is defined as a "participatory and protagonist democracy." Its point of departure is its criticism of representative democracy as non-democracy. This criticism refers not only to processes and mechanisms, but also to political culture,[8] given that

---

7   An economy that sustains itself primarily through income from resources and capital, rather than productive activity.

8   Carlos Lanz Rodríguez, *La revolución es cultural o reproducirá la dominación* (Caracas: Gato Negro; 2004); Carlos Lanz Rodríguez, "La vigencia del marxismos crítico en la costrucción socialista", *aporrea*, July 26, 2007, aporrea.org; MinCI (Ministerio del Poder

Venezuelan culture is still very much marked by a paternalistic state and a strong patronage system.[9]

Participatory and protagonistic democracy is an incomplete and constantly evolving concept. It is influenced by discussions about radical and direct democracy, and particularly by concrete practices developed in Latin America and guided by historical experiences based on the concepts of autonomy and popular power.

The demand for participation in Venezuela first arose in the 1980s. The concept of participatory and protagonist democracy reached widespread popularity with Chávez's 1997 presidential campaign, which took up this demand and translated it into a new form. The basis for overcoming inequality and marginalization is that the poor and marginalized are no longer statistical objects, but agents of strategies for attaining equality and justice in diverse social fields. The 1999 Constitution extended political rights that had previously been limited to parties, linking the economic, the social, and the political. Social and collective rights must be understood as a necessary part of participation more broadly—without these rights, social and political participation, particularly for the poor, becomes difficult or impossible.[10] In other words, if someone has no access to education or does not have other basic needs covered, it is unlikely that political participation under conditions of real equality can exist.

Without question, the material situation of the general population improved a great deal under the leftist government. Poverty in Venezuela fell from 50.4 percent of the population at the end of 1998 to 19.6 percent at the end of 2013, and extreme poverty fell from 20.3 percent at the end of 1998 to 5.5 percent at the end of 2013.[11] From 2011, Venezuela trans-

---

Popular para la Comunicación y la Información), *Líneas generales del Plan de Desarrollo Económico y Social de la Nación 2007–2013* (Caracas: MinCI, 2007).

9 Coronil, *The Magical State*; Dick Parker, "¿De qué democracia estamos hablando?"*Revista Venezolana de Economía y Ciencias Sociales*, 12-1, 2006, pp. 89–99.

10 Enrique Dussel, *20 Tesis de politica* (Mexico City: Siglo XXI, 2006), p. 67; Guillermo O'Donnell, "Polyarchies and the (Un)Rule of Law in Latin America", paper presented at the Meeting of the Latin American Studies Association, LASA 1998, p. 6.

11 Instituto Nacional de Estadísticas (INE), January 2014, "Resumen de indicadores sociodemográficos," ine.gov.ve. The data are based on the same methodology employed by the United Nations Economic Commission for Latin America and the Caribbean, the World Bank, the United Nations Development Program, and the national statistics institutes of other countries.

formed from being one of the most unequal countries in Latin America in terms of income to being the third-most equal (after Costa Rica and Uruguay).[12] A national survey in Venezuela in 2008–2009 established that 80 percent of the population was eating three meals a day, and 16.2 percent even four meals a day.[13] The population has free healthcare and free access to education at all levels. Venezuela ranks among the top five countries in the world in terms of the percentage of the population studying at university level.

Protagonist participation by the population is specified in various articles of the Constitution, such as Article 62 in which the state is required to encourage participation in decision-making, and others that transfer functions and resources to organized communities, establish rights regarding associative forms of economy, status of neighborhood assemblies, and the like. Participatory and protagonist democracy therefore strengthens local communities and encourages the self-organization of the population. The popular takeover of the government during the 2002 coup and the 2002–2003 entrepreneurs' strike were particularly important manifestations of this. Starting in 2003, a powerful organizational dynamic was established in the neighborhoods around different social programs called "missions" addressing the most urgent problems of the marginalized and excluded populations. An economy of self-organization, as well as co- and self-management initiatives for businesses supported from above, grew stronger in 2004. And while some participation mechanisms have failed, new ones continue to appear and be experimented with.[14] Revolution is understood as a broad process of construction—an act of collective creation and invention, not a "seizure of power."

Venezuela's current president, Nicolas Maduro,[15] committed publicly to Chávez's program, and declared several times that the construction of communes was central to Venezuela's own path toward socialism. During

---

12   Ibid.

13   AVN and MinCI (Agencia Venezolana de Noticias and Ministerio de Comunicación e Información), "Consumo de kilocalorías del venezolano supera suficiencia energética de la FAO," MinCi, April 28, 2011, minci.gob.ve.

14   Steve Ellner, "Las estrategias 'desde arriba' y 'desde abajo' del movimiento de Hugo Chávez", *Cuadernos del Cendes* 23:62 (Caracas: UCV, 2006), pp. 73–93, p. 89.

15   Elected April 14, 2013, after Hugo Chávez died of cancer on March 5, 2013.

his electoral campaign he promised not to negotiate with the bourgeoisie, but to put popular power at the center of his politics. Initiatives for a better coordination of movement forces have proliferated, as have concrete struggles in communities and workplaces.

SELF-ORGANIZATION

Venezuela's self-organized groups are not restricted to the councils already mentioned. In fact, there are tens of thousands self-organized groups, including groups of indigenous people, Afro-Venezuelans, LGBTQ people, and environmental activists. There are also groups focusing on sports, several hundred independent or community radio stations, a dozen community TV stations, magazines, barter networks, local currencies, and many more.

Several huge, very well organized and consolidated popular movements exist. The Bolívar and Zamora Revolutionary Current (Corriente Revolucionaria Bolívar y Zamora, CRBZ) comprises the biggest peasants' movement, the Ezequiel Zamora National Peasant Front (Frente Nacional Campesino Ezequiel Zamora, FNCEZ)—which runs its own organic farming and political training system—the National Communal Simón Bolívar Front (Frente Nacional Comunal Simón Bolívar, FNCSB), which organizes communal councils, communes, and communal cities, the Simón Rodríguez Center for Social Studies and Education (Centro de Formación y Estudios Sociales Simon Rodríguez, CEFES), and the Movement for Workers' Popular Power (Movimiento Poder Popular Obrero, MPPO).

The Movement of Settlers (Movimiento de Pobladores, MDP) encompasses Urban Land Committees (Comités de Tierra Urbana, CTU), originally initiated for the zoning of "illegal" urban housing, and now active in planning housing and living environments; the Pioneer Camps (Campamientos de Pioneros), made up of families without homes struggling for urban land on which to build their houses collectively; the Tenants' Network (Red de Inquilinos), mobilizing against evictions, and the janitors' movement (Movimiento de Conserjes). In July 2011 the MDP signed eleven contracts for the administration of housing complexes in Caracas, providing 2,000 rented homes. Since 2004, there have been various workers' networks campaigning for workers' control. The movement consolidated its structure during the First National Encounter for Workers' Control and Workers Councils, in May 2011. A coordinating National Collective for Workers' Control was formed. Moreover there is the Network of Communards (Red Nacional de Comuneros, RNC). All of these popular movements and many more share the goal of building the communal state, and are an integral part of the Bolivarian process in Venezuela—but their structures are self-organized, and their discussions and decisions are autonomous. All are in a relationship of both cooperation and conflict with constituted power at all institutional levels.

Communal councils, communes, and the communal state

Communal councils have constructed a non-representative structure of direct participation that exists in parallel to the elected representative bodies of constituted power. Communal councils began forming in 2005 as an initiative from below. In various parts of Venezuela, rank-and-file organizations autonomously promoted forms of local self-administration named "local governments" or "communitarian governments." Chávez adopted this initiative, and the National Assembly approved the Law of Communal Councils in 2006. At this point, some 5,000 communal councils already existed. Communal councils in urban areas incorporate between 150 and 400 families; in rural areas, a minimum of twenty families; and in indigenous zones, at least ten families, various communal councils and other popular organizations can build a commune. A census carried out in September 2013 revealed the existence of 40,035 communal councils, and 1,401 existing communes or popular efforts toward their construction.[16] Most are directly financed by state institutions (thus avoiding interference from municipal administrations), without any entity having the authority to reject proposals presented by the councils. The relationship between the councils and

---

16   Gobierno Bolivariano de Venezuela, "Más de 70 mil organizaciones populares fueron censadas," September 17, 2013, mpcomunas.gob.ve. As of the end of 2013, some 500 communes had been officially registered by the Ministry for Communes.

established institutions, however, is not always harmonious; conflicts arise principally from the slowness of official power to respond to demands made by the councils, and from attempts at interference.

The communal councils are not a partisan initiative. Many count on the participation of neighbors considering themselves neither "Chavistas" nor opposition supporters. Even some middle- and upper-middle-class neighborhoods all over the country have formed communal councils dominated by the opposition. Only hardline opposition supporters in barrios boycott the communal councils.

At a higher level of self-government, there is the possibility of creating communes, which can be formed by combining various communal councils and other forms of self-organization in a specific territory. Participating councils themselves determine the geographical reach of their communes. Communes can develop medium- and long-term projects of greater scope, while decisions continue to be made in the assemblies of the communal councils.

Communal councils and communes tend to transcend the division between political and civil society—between those who govern and those who are governed. Hence, liberal analysts who support that division view the communal councils in a negative light, arguing that they are not independent civil society organizations, but rather are linked to the state. In fact, however, they constitute a parallel structure through which power and control are gradually drawn away from the state, in order for them to govern on their own.

In the context of the creation of communes and communal cities, it is important to distinguish between political–administrative (absolute) space and socio-cultural–economic (relational) space.[17] Communes reflect the latter; their boundaries do not necessarily correspond to existing political–administrative spaces. As these continue to exist, the institutionalization of the communal councils, communes, and communal cities develops and shapes the socio-cultural–economic space. Thus, the idea of council-based non-representative local self-organization creates a new "power-geometry." The concept of power in human geography, as elaborated by Doreen

---

17   David Harvey, "Space as a Keyword," in David Harvey, *A Critical Reader*, ed. Noel Castree and Derek Gregory (Malden, MA: Blackwell, 2006).

Massey, has been put "to positive political use" following the "recognition of the existence and significance, within Venezuela, of highly unequal, and thus undemocratic, power-geometries."[18]

Various communes can form communal cities, with administration and planning from below. The mechanism of the construction of communes and communal cities is flexible; they themselves define their tasks. Thus the construction of self-government begins with what the population itself considers most important. The first communal cities to have formed, for example, are rural, and are structured around agriculture. Organizing and constructing communes and communal cities have been easier in suburban and rural areas than in metropolitan areas, where common interests are harder to define. The councilist structures in various social sectors can be considered the foundation of the Venezuelan socialist project: they must cooperate and coordinate on a higher level in order to replace the bourgeois state with a communal state.

As Delbia, from the Commune the Seven Socialist Pillars, puts it: "To put into practice the commune and communal councils is to achieve the communal state we want—that the people take control of their projects and public policies, that it is oneself who exerts control regarding everything so that we can achieve the communal power we want."

The form that the communal state will take is an open question that will be resolved by creating councils in various areas. The political organization of the socialist societies of the twenty-first century—as a horizontal confederation of communities or as networks of social organizations,[19] has been formulated similarly, and without reference to Venezuela, by Gustavo Esteva in Oaxaca, Mexico. Esteva emphasizes socialism's original "communal impulse" before it was transformed into "collectivism, bureaucracy, and self-destruction." "The communities appear as an alternative because within them, unity is recovered between politics and place and the people take on a form in which they can exercise their power without having to surrender it to the State."[20]

---

18   Doreen Massey, "Concepts of Space and Power in Theory and in Political Practice," *Documents d'Analisis Geogràfica* 55 (2009), p. 20.

19   Gustavo Fernández Colón, "¿Verticalismo burocrático o protagonismo popular?," *Aporrea*, December 17, 2006, aporrea.org.

20   Gustavo Esteva, "Otra mirada, otra democracia," *Rebelión*, February 2, 2009.

Workers' control

The democratization of ownership and administration of the means of production is a declared goal of movements and government in Venezuela. Between 2001 and 2006, the Venezuelan government—in addition to asserting state control over the core of the oil industry—focused on promoting cooperatives for any type of company, including models of cooperatives co-administrated with the state or private entrepreneurs. The 1999 Constitution assigned the cooperatives a special role. They were conceived as contributing to a new social and economic balance, and thus received massive state assistance. The favorable conditions led to a boom in the number of cooperatives founded, only a third of which really started working. The National Cooperative Supervisory Institute, Sunacoop, certified 100,000 cooperatives as operating in 2013.[21] The initial idea that cooperatives would automatically produce for the satisfaction of social needs, and that their internal solidarity based on collective property would extend to their local communities, proved to be an error. Most cooperatives still followed the logic of capital, concentrating on the maximization of net revenue without supporting the surrounding communities.[22] Nevertheless, thousands of cooperatives were also founded by communities, workers, and movements with different goals.

In response to the employers' lockout of 2002–2003, the "entrepreneurs' strike," which had the stated intention of toppling the Chávez government, workers began the process of taking over workplaces abandoned by their owners. At first, the government relegated the cases to the labor courts, and then in January 2005 began expropriations. From July 2005, the government began to pay special attention to the situation of closed businesses, and since then hundreds of such

---

21   Dulce María Rodríguez, "67% de las cooperativas han dejado de funcionar," *El Nacional*, April 10, 2013, el-nacional.com.

22   Dario Azzellini, "From Cooperatives to Enterprises of Direct Social Property in the Venezuelan Process," in Camila Piñeiro Harnecker, ed., *Cooperatives and Socialism: A View from Cuba* (Basingstoke: Palgrave Macmillan, 2012), pp. 259–78; Dario Azzellini, "Economía solidaria en Venezuela: Del apoyo al cooperativismo tradicional a la construcción de ciclos comunales," in Sidney Lianza and Flávio Chedid Henriques, eds., *A Economia Solidária na América Latina: realidades nacionais e políticas públicas* (Rio de Janeiro: Pró Reitoria de Extensão UFRJ, 2012), pp. 147–60.

companies have been expropriated. Around one hundred of these had been occupied by workers. Since 2007, expropriated enterprises are officially supposed to be turned into "direct social property," under the direct control of workers and communities. In reality, most of them are not administered by workers and communities, but by state institutions. Working conditions have not fundamentally changed, and expropriations have not automatically produced co-management or workers' control—although dozens of worker-controlled factories exist, and initiatives and struggles for workers' control can be found in hundreds of companies and institutions.

The concept of "direct social property" is also supposed to apply to hundreds of new "socialist factories" built by the government as part of its industrialization strategy. The local communal councils select the workers, while the required professionals are drawn from state and government institutions. The aim is gradually to transfer the administration of the factories into the hands of organized workers and communities. But most state institutions involved do little to organize this process or prepare the employees, and this has generated growing conflict between workers and institutions.

Conflicts over working conditions, workers' rights, participation, co-management, and workers' control arose in 2012 and 2013 in numerous nationalized and state-owned factories. Class struggle has been strengthened, or is emerging, where it was previously weak or absent. The day-to-day experiences in enterprise management and the political training workers have often received through the same institutions—which paradoxically later prevented effective worker participation—have ultimately contributed to the formation of a movement for workers' control.

One of the main motivations for workers to push for workers' control relates to efficiency. Apart from better working conditions and a greater sense of dignity in their jobs, workers mainly demand workers' control because they see it as the only guarantee of lower production costs, and of production to satisfy the needs of the majority of the population. Their experience with the state bureaucracy has shown them that representatives of the state apparatus are often not qualified for their jobs—or, for various reasons based on corruption or internal power struggles, are not interested in efficient national production with workers' participation in management, nor in changing the relations of production.

In 2007, Chávez picked up the idea of "socialist workers' councils," which was already being discussed by many rank-and-file workers and by existing councils and workers' initiatives. In fact, there was a network with the same name: Socialist Workers' Councils (CST). Chávez presented CSTs as an example of good practice, and called on workers to form them at their workplaces. Nevertheless, since most institutions were opposed to workers' councils, only a few councils were formed at first—mainly in recovered factories.

Growing pressure from below led several government institutions to start to accept, or even promote, the creation of workers' councils in institutionally administered workplaces—even without the benefit of an enacted law on workers' councils. But while, on the one hand, the majority of institutions tried to prevent the constitution of workers' councils in their workplaces, in others, and in state-administered enterprises, the institutions often tried to assume the lead and constitute the CSTs themselves, reducing them to a representative authority dealing with work- and salary-related questions within the government bureaucracy. As a consequence, the CSTs turned into another site of struggle for workers' control.

The most successful attempt at democratization of ownership and administration of the means of production can be found in the Enterprises of Communal Social Property (EPSC), promoted to create local production units and community service enterprises. The EPSCs are the collective property of the communities, which decide on their organizational structure, the workers to be incorporated, and the eventual use of profits. Government enterprises and institutions have promoted the communal enterprises since 2009, and since 2013 several thousand EPSCs have been constituted. Most operate within community services like public transport, or are engaged in food production and processing (see Chapter 1).

VOICES

In Venezuela, thirty-four interviews were conducted between 2006 and 2013. Most people interviewed had no experience of political or social activism before the first election of Chávez in 1998, or even before the coup d'état in 2002. Most interviewees are self-organized and involved in the concrete construction of new structures where they live and/or work. This is true even for most institutional workers we interviewed, who are activists close to movements, or part of them. They do not represent a general institutional profile or approach in any way.

Crisis and rupture

The economic crisis starting in the 1980s led to an extreme impoverishment of the Venezuelan population and the pauperization of huge sectors. The economic crisis accompanied a political crisis. For the people of Venezuela, the rupture that has led to the current process of struggle and creation began on February 27, 1989, with the explosion of El Caracazo. The rebellion was caused by a situation of dramatically increasing poverty. There were shortages and speculation with regard to food and most basic necessities. These abysmal conditions had resulted from a program of austerity and structural adjustment following International Monetary Fund (IMF) guidelines. The final detonator was when on the morning of February 27, people went to ride their neighborhood bus and found that the fares had doubled overnight. Public rage was immediate. Throughout Caracas people responded by destroying buses, and then setting them alight. From there, people began to walk down the hills from the poor neighborhoods, taking what they needed and looting. The rebellion spread to all Venezuelan cities, involving more than one million people during almost one week. In response, the government ordered the police and the army to suppress the uprising, killing thousands. The Caracazo was a rupture. People suddenly realized their potential collective power, and that with it they could even chase out a government. But it also showed that if they could not build their own structures of self-administration, old forms of institutional power could again return. The middle ranks of the army were the ones ordered to carry out the massacre. The outcome enforced the conviction among the already secretly organized leftist "Bolivarians" in the military that it was necessary to act quickly to stop the regime. In February and November of 1992, there were two military uprisings coordinated with leftist groups and organizations from poor neighborhoods, and even some armed revolutionary militias and former guerrilla fighters. The civil-military uprisings failed but revolutionary change did no longer seem out of reach. Amid the crisis of traditional power, popular movements adopted increasingly autonomous stances and moved gradually from specific demands (such as asking for solutions to concrete problems) to demands for self-control, self-determination, self-management, and constituent power.[23]

Andrés Antillano, forty, social psychologist and criminologist, founder and activist of the CTU and the MDP, is from the barrio La Vega in Caracas.

Andrés, Comités de Tierra Urbana, La Vega, Caracas: The struggle for water had been one of the most important struggles in 1989–1990. The question of water is one of the most complex problems of the poor settlements in Caracas. The water comes more than 800 miles, and has to go up 1,000 meters in altitude. Therefore water was expensive, scarce, and unevenly distributed—middle-class residential areas always had water, the poor never had it. I remember that stage in my life where I learned to shower with a jar of water. At three o'clock in the morning a neighbor would shout that the water was coming, and we would all get up to fill any available bowl with water, since we never knew when it would be coming again. [So] we blocked the roundabout. That was our main form of struggle, we could hit the nerve of the city, because blocking here, you blocked a whole part of the city's southeast.

We blocked the roundabout, and it was almost like a ritual: the Hidrocapital water company people came and told us they could not solve our problem, and we would inevitably kidnap them. We said, "Oh, you are not responding to us," and we took them and brought them into the barrio, and they would not get out of there until we would get water. This means of struggle happened here in La Vega, and it happened as well in other barrios. It was almost cyclical—we protested, we would get water, the service would fail again, and you had to protest again. That led us in 1991 to raise in the Assembly of Barrios that the water question could no longer focus on whether it was coming or not, but had to be

---

23   "Constituent power" refers to the legitimate collective human ability to create something new, and to shape it without having to derive it from something that already exists, or submit to it to something that already exists.

about controlling the water, administrating the water, to be able to define who opens or closes the supply. If we had the ability to access that, we would increase our power. We began to mobilize for this struggle. The struggles for specific demands, instead of being political struggles, in the sense of a shallow definition of politics, turned into struggles for participation, struggles for control of the processes generating the problems. Then came the military uprising of February 4, which led to an intense politicization of popular struggles.

Jaqueline Hernández, forty-three years old, single mother of two children, is part of the financial committee of the communal council Emiliano Hernández in Caracas's poor neighborhood Magallanes de Catia.

Jaqueline, Emiliano Hernández communal council, Caracas: Never before were marginalized people who had only studied through elementary school taken into consideration. It was like a law here that you studied first to sixth grade, and you knew that getting out of sixth grade you had to work. This government cares that the people educate themselves. That's why, before, they kept us like that for forty years, because it was not convenient for them that one would know what was happening. Many of these opposition people had us stay on the ground under their boot. They called us "dirt people," "bad speaking," toothless, hordes. I came to know the Teresa Carreño Theater now, at forty-two years old, because going into the Teresa Carreño was a dream of many, and those who could get in there were very few—the wealthy. Today we all go into the Teresa Carreño.

Francisco Visconti Osorio is a former general who led the civil-military uprising in November 1992. He works for the National Institute of Agricultural and Livestock Farming Research (INIA) and is an advisor to the FNCSB.

Francisco: Following the basic philosophic principles of Bolivarianism, the party is a negation of the general will, since you don't respond anymore to achieving the general will of the collective but have to follow the lines given by the party. This denies the essence of participation.

Urban Land Committees

The CTUs were the first massive self-organization on a territorial level. They were originally initiated by the state, but have since been entirely appropriated from below, creating a space of autonomy. Andrés Antillano was among the founders of the first CTU, and has since been a CTU activist.

Andrés: The issue of the urban land committees is explained by the nature of the Venezuelan territorial structure. Venezuela is the most urbanized country on the continent after Uruguay. Its population is 87 percent urban, with brutal spatial segregation—60 percent of the population lives in barrios where people are in a situation of illegality. They occupied these spaces because there was no place for them in the city. These barrios are the result of urban exclusion and resistance to urban exclusion. [They] have problems with basic services, overcrowding, etc. But, at the same time, besides being a consequence of capitalist society, the barrios also express alternative values because the barrios are the result of the struggle of the people. We land committees are a new face of an old struggle against the segregation of the city, fighting for the right to the city. Who are the settlers? Those who are defined not by the activity they do, but by where they live, the territory they occupy. And that is a fundamental subject in the Venezuelan political process. The support for President Chávez from the barrios, has been the most important aspect of this process of change.

The regularization of land tenure was one of the main issues for the Assembly of Barrios in the late 1980s, early 1990s. We were generally threatened with eviction. Here in La Vega we had strong struggles around that in the 1990s, as in Pinto Salinas and other places, so we have been particularly sensitive. Then, in 2001, the Executive began to raise the issue of land tenure, and in early 2002 it issued a decree. Since then the land committees have met every Thursday. Initially, this dynamic was established as a space to discuss, to see how to start the process, etc., and then as a political space. It was very important that at the beginning there was a process of collective construction, interaction, and debate accompanying the whole proposal. But it was a proposal that starts from the state—a decree is an instrument of the state, but a decree that promotes self-organization of the people. So then we started meeting. We began to promote land committees with territorial organizations—the issue of territory is very important.

At the beginning we were just a few people in the meetings that started to promote land committees. Today there are about 6,000 CTUs throughout the country. We started with the regularization of land ownership. From there we started to aim at the transformation of the barrios in physical terms. That's where the different projects started, because there is no infrastructure, no services . . . The role of the land committees was to generate other processes, such as the medical program In The Barrio, or the educational programs, which were very important.

We began to ask the question of housing and habitat policy, denouncing the housing and habitat policies as more of the same—they were deeply neoliberal, they did not respond to the people's ideas. So we have been building a radical diagnosis and a proposal. We have a document titled "For a Revolutionary Housing and Habitat Policy," and another document called "For the Humanization of the City." These are documents we have been working on collectively in different spaces. We went from the regularization of land to what we call integral regularization. That has to do with the issue of physical regularization—i.e. the transformation of the barrio, water networks, and urban sanitation. That fellow who just walked by is from an environmental cooperative created by land committees to deal with the garbage problem, which is quite dramatic. We also work on the issue of urban regularization. We do urban spatial planning, recover the barrio's history, following our interests and our needs. We started to understand the struggle from the barrio as a struggle for the transformation of the barrio, for the inclusion of the barrio in the city.

The National Network of Communards

Atenea Jimenez, among the founders of the network, talks about the experiences with the network and the goals of their construction process. In 2013 the network connected 130 communes and communes under construction. She is engaged in building a commune in her neighborhood, Belomonte, in Caracas.

Atenea, National Network of Communards: The RNC was born out of an experience we began in 2008. We started to work with a team on the issue of the communes under direct instructions from the president of the Republic. We started to explore what commune experiences were evolving in the country from their own initiative. A mapping identified twenty-one pilot experiences. But since everything is complicated on a bureaucratic level, that took a year. Really interesting work was accomplished, and the communes made a substantial advance. The Ministry for the Communes was founded, and we were all kicked out. We decided to start a process of articulation from popular power. We were sixteen communes at that time. How could we could link together our work—not to work from the state, but from ourselves—with what we had progressed? How could we articulate that? Instruct, self-instruct, co-instruct, supporting the issue of endogenous development. We worked with popular education, the exchange of knowledge . . . We started in 2008 with sixteen, and right now there are over eighty national experiences in the country as part of the RNC—and in every activity we do, we add more experiences. We are united in pushing the process of building the commune without subordination to any kind of power other than the community itself . . .

Comrades we picked up from previous movements contributed a lot with their background—also because we have really practiced an exchange of knowledge, and this kind of economy of exchange pervades the whole process. Basically, understand that there is a diversity in the background of the communities, how to build organization, the modus operandi, and even everyday reasoning . . . because in the east, for example, there is a fishing culture where they have a completely different dynamic compared to that of the Andes.

We reflected on how to build a commune, what categories we should handle, always understanding that each experience has particularities, and what they do is enrich the process. Through knowledge-sharing, we have tried to collect and systematize what each communitarian experience was doing, so as to enrich the process. And we did a very important thing—I think it was fundamental: we exchanged experiences among communes on site. We visited other spaces, we looked at their strengths, we shared the challenges they faced and how they could be overcome. How did they suddenly avoid any weakness, bypass bureaucratic obstacles? And how did they strengthen themselves ideologically? There are a number of communes that have advanced a lot ideologically, but very little in practical ways or popular participation. There is a tendency that, when there are politically advanced leaders, like former guerrillas or others, then the people just watched them organizing, but it was not an expression of what people felt.

Our method allows the sharing of experiences, so people can live it beyond being just told. Every time we do an exchange visit or there is a meeting in the commune, there is an exchange of knowledge regarding the practical and everyday life. This has created spaces of collective construction, always understanding there are many questions for which there will be no agreement, because it is not possible. But we continue to work, debate, and build. This space of respect has been very important. We understand there have been crucial historical processes for each communal enterprise, for every commune, and they must be respected, but we must also learn from their successes and experiences, and perhaps also from mistakes. All these experiences have nurtured us.

Participatory and protagonistic democracy

The new culture of participation also follows the Zapatista logic of "leading by obeying," and a new vision and practice of gender. Participation is often described as "horizontal." Although participation has been a central goal of movements since the late 1980s and early 1990s, it is something that has had to be learned. Participation is a process. The children of the Emiliano Hernández communal council adopted the methods they observed, and organized several demonstrations. One was to protest the intention of well-liked activist Alexander to move to a different neighborhood. The children changed the popular chant "¡Uh Ah, Chávez no se va!" ("Chávez will not leave!") to "¡Uh Ah, Alex no se va!" In a different mobilization, the children demonstrated to demand a sports field.

Delbia Rosa Avilés, forty-five, housewife and worker in popular construction community council La Floresta, the Seven Socialist Pillars commune, Anaco, Anzoátegui.

Delbia, Comuna Los 7 Pilares Socialistas, Anaco: I have never been a member of a party. I went to vote, but not because I had an ideal . . . All my life I was a working woman, my life slipped away working in a private company, and it was hard because I worked rotating shifts: six to two, two to ten, night and day . . . that was in Caracas. Here I got involved about two years ago when I started working on the integration of the communal council. It was the need to see the change. You think things could be different. One day I said to myself: How do things change if one does not contribute? The only way to change things is that you participate. If you do not participate, you cannot change. I started to get involved, and I fell more and more in love with the process, and here I stay because I really do not see any other alternative.

Talía Álvarez, sixty-two, is a retired teacher and started participating with the Bolivarian movement before 1998. She is an activist of the Housing Committee of the Las Quintas communal council in Artigas, Caracas, a formerly middle-class neighborhood that became increasingly impoverished in the 1980s.

Talía, Las Quintas communal council, Caracas: Participatory and protagonistic democracy—that means that the people who were ignored or were only represented by someone assume power. It is what is missing in our constitution—a sixth power, popular power. I understand that we are only at the beginning, but what you can see is wonderful. Imagine all the ministries, city halls, and local representations disappear, and that everything is in the hands of the community—that it is for the community to decide, administer, and plan its own resources. Because who knows better than we ourselves what happens in our community?

Wilson Moya, forty-five, accountant, has a small garage for car repairs. He participates in the financial committee of the communal council Emiliano Hernández, Caracos.

Wilson, Emiliano Hernández communal council, Caracas: A protagonistic democracy means we all participate. It is something horizontal. No one has a rank, or anything like that, and it is protagonistic because we are the ones setting the tone . . . We all participate voluntarily, not because we are commanded by anyone. We don't have bosses.

Merzolena Rodriguez, forty-four, communal council, the Seven Socialist Pillars commune.

Merzolena, Comuna 7 Pilares Socialista, Anaco, Anzoátegui: All decisions of the community councils and the commune are made in assembly. It is preferable, better than having a boss. So we all have the right to take a stand. They see what can be done and decide if they agree with what is being proposed. We all speak, we all give our opinion. No one is denied the right to speak, and we are all heard. It is preferable that way. We have no bosses at all; we are our own bosses. We are not workers in a capitalist enterprise, we are workers for ourselves—we work to build and bring that to other communities.

Atenea, Red Nacional de Comuneros y Comuneras: In Venezuela, participatory and protagonistic democracy is advancing—that's the path. The point is to give it content. How is this democracy? In many cases it is not exercised right now. It is a process—it is under construction. There are spaces in which to exercise direct democracy, but there are others where that is not appropriate, such as if there is a confederation of communes . . . Surely there will be a few debates in the assembly—it will lead to electing delegates for higher levels of coordination because it is also an issue connected to scale. But we can definitely say that most of the decisions are made in assemblies—they work through what the people decide there. One or the other will be delegated to execute decisions. What we have to do is generate progressively larger spaces of decision-making.

In reality, the spokesperson's role is sometimes relative. You get elected spokesperson of a commune, and you go to a meeting where there will be other opinions. And when things are decided you are giving your opinion as delegated spokesperson, but you will also have to give opinions immediately, when you cannot consult, so it is not absolute. Therefore, we must deal further with the question of spokespeople—who are the most appropriate spokespeople and what are their profiles. It is also an exercise in the construction of collective consciousness in the exercise of "power to" and democracy, because we can decide which characteristics the delegates should have. But if there is not a certain level of consciousness to build this democratic exercise, then it does not make any sense . . . For example, communal council spokespeople are not representatives . . . but when you are delegated as spokesperson and the community does not participate, you end up being a representative. The idea is that we grow in awareness of how democracy is exercised in our daily practices, and it is a matter of conscience that democracy is assumed as such, and that it will be built with an ongoing fine-tuning mechanism.

Communal councils

> *Communities have appropriated the communal councils, and use them as a self-organization mechanism for the improvement of their living conditions. They struggle to impose their will against institutional impositions, and defend their self-organization against any attempts at co-optation. Communal councils are not seen as an appendix of constituted power but as autonomous bodies that do not depend on any institution or the president. The communal councils' activists consider state funding neither a problem nor a gift, but a legitimate and unconditional right.*

Talía, Las Quintas communal council, Caracas: Communal councils are not comparable to the old condominium boards or the neighborhood associations; they are something entirely different. Communal councils are an expression that I think is going to be the backbone of socialism. I think the communal councils are the bull's eye of future socialism. Of course we are just starting—we are all products of the Fourth Republic, those forty-something years of education, developing vices—bureaucracy, laziness, indifference, apathy, individualism . . . It is not easy to build, but that's it. Communities discussing budgets . . . I think I am crazy! Peasants planning roads, making their own electricity network or direct gas system—a quick training, and there they go. Before you were taught that the technician is essential, and that is not the case—same thing in the oil company, saved by the workers when the managers went on strike . . . The labor movement, self-management, co-management, endogenous development—all these are key issues for the future we are glimpsing. That's the right way.

Luz Herrera, in her late forties, is director of the training commission for communal councils, at Caracas City Hall Policy Department.

Luz, support for Consejos Comunales: What people do with their communal councils goes beyond the law. They incorporate elements. For example, the law says you have to organize one informative assembly to elect a provisional promoter committee, and then later elect a promoter committee, both to organize the process of building the communal council. And after that you have to hold your elections within ninety days, and they are done in an assembly. When a communal council is formed, they don't have just one informative assembly—they have up to ten, until you manage to have a consolidated group. Then the provisional promoter committee becomes the regular promoter committee. They don't elect a new committee, since this has been working already. The only elections are the elections of spokespeople, and they do not take place in a neighborhood assembly but are a full day of ballot-box elections, where you mobilize the entire population. No election is done in assembly, but the law says it has to be in assembly. If we stuck to the law, all communal councils would be no good. But who gives legitimacy to the council? It is the people! People say how they will hold their election, and that is how they do it. Other things happen as well regarding the committees—which committees are formed, how they are formed, how the control of finances works, and how the community bank works: all that is transformed by the people according to their reality. You don't hear the same story from all communal councils— they are all different ... We stick with the people and not with the conceptual, with what is written. What is written is the product of systematizing previous experiences and turning that into a law, which is not bad, but it does not reflect what exists right now.

Building community

The community does not exist automatically—it is a process of active construction. The commitment of volunteers to work for the community is honored and recognized by the community, which usually supports the spokespeople in different ways. Examples for the support given by the community to spokespeople range from taking care of their children to *cooking for them and their families. The most advanced example of community solidarity we found was in the Emiliano Hernández communal council, where the community decided after several weeks of discussions to use more than US$70,000 left over from the remodeling of more than one hundred houses and the replacement of fifteen shacks with houses to buy a four-story building and give each of the four women most active in the communal council an apartment, since they did not have their own houses.*

Delbia, Comuna Los 7 Pilares Socialistas, Anaco: My life has changed a lot since I got into community activities . . . It was a 180-degree turn. I lived all my life in Caracas, and now only ten years here in Anaco. I was a housewife and was never involved in anything like this process. I dedicated myself to my children and my husband. That was my day-to-day life. As I started working on this things changed, because this means dedication. While I'm here at this meeting of communes for three days, my family is there. But I manage to work with the commune, despite the demands of the family: "You are on the streets the whole day! You don't even stop by! We don't see you anymore!" I have tried to make them understand that it is a way to achieve change for their future. We think that there can be a different country for them, so they can live in a better Venezuela, that they can really be free men and women. That is the dream one has. And there are learning processes, because aside from being in these activities, we also have political studies where we sit down to discuss. We work with the magazine *Poliética*—we discuss many articles for *Poliética*, on Saturdays. At the commune meeting each communal council in the community makes some time to discuss the most relevant aspects.

Luisa Morales, late forties, worker, Inveval valve factory, Carrizal, Miranda.

Luisa, Inveval, Carrizal: I've changed a lot. I am no longer a passive person, dedicated simply to work, study, my daughter, and to ensuring that my parents are in good health . . . No, now I think that one's mission in life should be much more transcendent. You have to contribute more—you have to worry more about others than about yourself. You do not know if the child next door ate, if the lady is OK, if the guy has work . . . you have to stop being selfish, and I've learned that—not to think only about myself. I have learned to see beyond, to get involved in some way.

Adys Figuera León, thirty-three, is a computer scientist and popular power trainer, something similar to an organizer in the US.

Adys, Comuna Los 7 Pilares Socialistas, Anaco: My life has changed a lot. I started in 2007 with popular education. You see people suddenly wake up—housewives who have never done anything political—and they begin to participate and make a change, and you change too. Your way of life changes too. How do I feel? Happy, because we will achieve the goal. We may not see the communal state as ready-made socialism, but we know that our children will see a better Venezuela, better people. Because in Venezuela, as in the rest of the world, the culture we have is the culture we have been taught. We have to change this culture. A proverb says that an old parrot cannot learn anymore how to talk. It is a lie.

Communes

The construction of communes is a step into unknown territory—a process of invention and creation based on people's needs and desires. Various activists involved in different ways in the construction of communes speak below about this process, and the redefinition of the state based on a system of communes. Finally, communards from the Seven Socialist Pillars commune describe their process of construction.

Atenea, RNC: Following a call from Chávez in 2007, every community started to debate how the commune should be. Several communal councils built a commune—but there were also historical popular groups and organizations that were not coordinating with the communal councils, but could not be excluded from the commune. The debate took place in almost all cases, and the agreement was that, beyond the communal councils, all these movements should also be organically coordinated in the commune.

There was also the risk that the commune would replace the

municipality or parish in terms of political and administrative organization, and our proposal is that it is not a space like that, because otherwise it would be as in many countries—just another instance of the liberal bourgeois state. It would change the name while the functioning remained the same. We started building with this perspective, and we began also to study other historical experiences of communes. We built a space to talk, and also invite international guests who have thought about the subject. We started thinking how to work the whole country into communes. If it is a process of construction, it means to be able to activate the constituent popular power, which is in the constitution, which is creative, which allows you to create spaces and create a number of things collectively—and people started to say, "Let's build the communes."

Juan Carlos Pinto, in his mid-thirties, is an activist for the FNCSB in Barinas, southwest Venezuela, and supports the construction of communes. Carmelo González, in his early thirties, is an employee of the Autonomous Municipal Institute for the Communes of the city of Barinas.

Juan Carlos, FNCSB, Barinas: The issue of people's power deals with the ability of the people to take up the reins actively—it is this ability, this power to take action and to take control. And "popular" points to the pueblo, the grassroots. It's the only way for us to participate, to empower and to appropriate this new institutional structure, which ultimately means the democratization of the state. This is the popular democratization in which the people adopt this new institutional arrangement and establish it in order to build up socialism. For this reason, it's important that the people acquire the various tools.

The most important thing is for the entire community to participate in building up the commune from the very beginning. Usually the institutions of the state come together and say, "This is the project, this is the commune, this is ready," and they present everything. And then you ask yourself, "When was this project ever discussed at all?" This destroys the essence, because the essence is the participation of the people, and the people are writing their own history.

Carmelo González, Autonomous Municipal Institute for the Communes, Barinas, during a community workshop to support the building of a commune: Water, electricity, telephones, and the establishment of the EPS [social production company]—these are matters that are supposed to be managed by the assembly. This is your power, and not ours as administrative officials. You have the opportunity to acquire the power. This is something new. This is the creation of a new kind of socialism in which there is real participation, which doesn't exist anywhere so far. If the commune becomes a reality in the whole country, in Barinas, in Venezuela, then we can attempt to construct a communal government in transition toward socialism, toward the new geometry of power. All of these forums and talks are also meant to bring the information into your communities . . . because discussions create participation, and participation will enable you to create government. The government is not who has the power. The power is in your hands, in the possibility that you could build, create, establish governments, and therefore create this model of socialism . . . We intend to learn collectively from what you know, because that is more than we do. It's the knowledge of the people that is expressed right now.

Atenea, RNC, Caracas: The first thematic meeting we organized with the RCN was about communal economy. We have cared much about how to move forward to a productive economy. No commune can be autonomous if it has no production of wealth that can be distributed first of all among its members. If we have a commune that depends on a third party, a governor, a mayor, or whoever, it does not depend on its own production of goods and services and wealth, then it is not a commune. The questions are: How do we think about these new social economic relations that exist in the commune? How is the surplus distributed? What are the social relationships in those enterprises of social or communal property? The other important issue is that you cannot separate the question of workers' control from the commune. There must be workers' control of the companies that are in the commune and the ones to be built. And not only the workers decide, but also the commune decides how they will operate, what the production process is like, and what is to be done with the surplus. The management is socialist because the commune decides.

Comuna Los 7 Pilares Socialistas, Anaco, Estado Anzoátegui

The Seven Socialist Pillars commune is situated in eastern Venezuela, in the state of Anzoátegui, in the Anaco municipality. Anaco is a natural gas extraction site. The commune is part of RCN. Its story is told by three communard women—Adys Figuera León, thirty-three, computer scientist and popular power facilitator; Delbia Rosa Avilés, forty-five, housewife and worker in popular construction; and Merzolena Rodríguez, forty-four.

Adys: The commune arose out of the need for unity among the communal councils. We say the commune is in development because we want to develop the communes' productivity so they can be truly a communal self-government. Our commune is composed of forty-two communal councils so far. Each community has 1,500 to 1,600 people. We are more than 50,000 inhabitants.

Delbia: The decisions in the commune and communal councils are made in assemblies. We meet every Saturday from 9 a.m., for as long as we need and want to, and decide the commune plan. During the week there is planning for everything to be done, and on Saturday we gather to make further decisions.

Adys: All communal councils participate. Spokespersons for all communal councils are present. Moreover, everybody can participate in the Saturday assemblies, not just spokespeople—people from the community, anyone who wants can attend the assembly, get involved and participate. There is good participation. Everyone likes to participate. We explain, and everyone gives his opinion and suggestions regarding what we are doing. You know some people are a little ashamed, but because of the way we do it, people who had never participated and were new have become active, attending the assemblies and joining all the others.

It all started when, in 2010, the mayor of Anaco grouped the commune councils by sector, and declared seventeen communes. Each director of the city government was appointed representative of one of the communes. That created huge discontent within the municipality. Nevertheless, the meetings with the assigned municipality directors continued. The only commune that did not accept this imposition at the time was our commune. We did not even have a name . . . We did not accept any of the mayor's imposed directors. We started to work in the same communal councils that they chose at the time to form the commune. We did surveys, we continued to meet, all contributed in workgroups. We did not limit ourselves to only seven communal councils of the pretended Commune 2, but extended our work to the entire municipality. The geographic space of a commune is declared after the integration of all those who want to be part of the commune. We encountered huge obstacles during the whole process—communities withdrew, then joined again.

Merzolena: We decided to form a commune to achieve independence, be economically free. The idea is to produce our own consumption and lower costs. Doing it in the commune means supporting each other, the communal network . . . We have to change the way of life we have had until now.

Adys: If we are not owners of our production system, how can we be a commune? It's like more of the same. We will continue to depend on the same institutions, and that's not the idea. The idea is to let go of mom and dad, mayor, governor, and be ourselves—owners of our means of production. In fact, none of us develops projects to put a sidewalk in our communities, because we know that we can build the sidewalks later with our socio-productive projects. So the focus has been on socio-productive projects.

We have already realized some projects. We have the financial resources and they are under implementation. The most important is the tile factory, which is a result precisely of an encounter we had at the meeting of the RCN in Carora. We visited their all-artisan tile production and took the idea to Anaco because Anaco has the raw material—clay. We began to explore this in relation to a different project we were developing at the time—a factory of prefabricated house panels. The roof of the house needs tiles. The tile production matched the productive project we were developing. We got in touch with some tile-production specialists in Rio Caribe. They came, and we went to different communities with workshops. The first funding we looked for was to build the ovens—not like those in Carora, which are artisan ovens. We designed gas ovens. We will start with huge gas cylinders while we move forward to connect up to the gas network. Anaco is a gas city, but we have no gas in our sectors. Our project is not based on large structures. The ovens are built in the communities. We will bring the material to build them, and what we need is a space to place the oven and a space to store the production. Regarding the factory for prefabricated houses, we were working with the Ministry of Science and Technology and with people of our communities—engineers, turners, masons, etc. And we have elaborated the plans to produce the prefabricated panels to replace the cement blocks.

The waste from the production of clay tiles after burning becomes a lightweight material that will be processed for further use in the production of the panels. The panels we are producing right now are artisan, not with the molds we need, because the funding we need for the molds is very high, almost 15 million bolivars [US$3.5 million].

Delbia: That is because the house factory project is huge. It consists not only of the tile factory and the molds factory, there is also the production of the steel structure kit . . . Now we are building the first six ovens, distributed through various groups of communal councils. With the ovens, we will generate 1,326 workplaces.

Adys: The idea is to keep expanding the production of ovens and take them to other communities. It is not only the commune—we work with the perspective of the economic transformation of the whole municipality, in order to bring welfare to all communities. We are talking about a process of integration. A communal carpenters' workshop is also part of the project, as well as other elements. So that we build houses and the company is owned by the community, not by private owners and administered by the community through communal councils and communes. That's what we want.

Adys, eighteen months later in late 2013: The community is still not registered. We have already fulfilled the steps established by the law and demanded by the Fundacomunal [state institution supporting communal councils and communes]. We fought a tough political struggle in the municipality, but we are working and organizing ourselves. We are legitimized by the people. We meet every Saturday as a commune, and are building popular power. The struggle has been hard, since the old does not want to die and the new is still not totally born. There are problems especially with funds, since the municipal government is bureaucratized. The Ministry of the communes has not been helpful. But radical changes are occurring in the Ministry that were needed. We are waiting for registration, and continue to work and organize ourselves.

Autonomy and the state

The greater the number of self-organized initiatives emerge, and the more participation and development of constituent power move forward, the more conflicts with constituted power emerge—particularly in production and regarding matters of autonomy and state control. The deepening of social transformation has increased the number of points where the logics of power from above and from below confront one another. The strengthening and extension of the institutions and the presence of the state led simultaneously to a growing bureaucratization, which works against opening up and transformation, and tends toward the institutional administration of social processes.

Andrés, CTU, Caracas: We learned that the problem of popular power is not a problem of managing resources. We have told the Housing Ministry that our fundamental problem is not whether they will give us resources and fund our projects, but that we want to define housing policies, and that's part of the dispute we have today with the Ministry. We have always said that we must move forward in the construction of a new society—with the state, without the state, and against the state. The relationship with the state is not defined by us but by the state's willingness to subordinate itself to the interests of the people.

Josefina Cadet, forty-nine, trained as a computer specialist, but gave up her job and became a taxi driver in order to have time for her political activism. She is from the Agua Viva communal council of the Cacique Terepaima Eco-Tourism and Artisanal Commune, which brings together twenty-two communal councils. Josefina is also active in the RCN.

Josefina, Comuna Ecoturística Artesanal Cacique Terepaima, Lara: We managed to force the registration of forty-two communes in the state of Lara. That struggle started the whole commune-registration process on a national level in 2012. We began with several communes meeting to study ourselves, to see what we had in common, and we concluded that for all struggles that deserved a team effort—among these was the struggle regarding the problem that state resources for farmers had not been distributed—we had to build strategies to register the communes officially. We elaborated all standards and procedures. Those who knew about standards worked on the procedures, and those who knew about strategy set up a plan. We did not omit one document. We did the work required by the Ministry, all of it. The dudes at the Ministry did not even have a form in order to receive our documents. We read that law from top to bottom, so that we did not make any mistakes. We found some lawyers from the PSUV who helped draft the charter so that it had not a single mistake . . .

We decided on a date for the big popular party. We never imposed on anyone to form a commune. We had planned to have fifteen, and we had nine. All nine showed up with their papers—with the agreement we had reached, with the same founding charter, with the same documents, everyone with their folders. The rest of us went to accompany them, popular movements participated, and we set up a march. The communes of Torres, Urdaneta, and Irribarren participated, as well as the commune of Palavecino in Yaracuy and a commune from Portuguesa. We agreed on implementing the same procedure to accompany the communes in the states of Portuguesa and Yaracuy. We announced we would register the communes on a certain date. We called the press, called everyone, and went to register our communes. We assembled on the street. Fundacomunal had to come out to receive our documents, and the nine communes went in to register. That was on November 21, 2011. With this action, we opened nationwide registration of communes. We've been monitoring and controlling it—they had to implement and activate all procedures. Then we went to accompany the commune in Portuguesa. There was a certain reluctance to register it. We blocked the place . . . and they had to receive us. It was televised, and the commune is now registered.

Workers' control

The state-owned aluminum producer, Alcasa, started a process of workers' co-administration with the goal of workers' control in 2005–2007, and again in 2010–2011. Though the workers did not succeed, the movement in Alcasa persists, and the experiences gained were crucial for struggles and experiences of workers' control in other companies of the state-owned holding of basic industries CVG (Corporación Venezolana de Guayana).

Three interviews were conducted in Alcasa—all with workers' control activists. The two workers, Osvaldo León, in his late fifties, and Carlos Agüero, in his mid-fifties, are active in the collective for workers' control, and participants in the Alcasa workers' education center, Centro de Formación Negro Primero. Elio Sayago, in his mid-fifties, an environmental technician, belonged to the Board of Directors of Alcasa during the first workers' control experiment, and was president of Alcasa during the second.

The paper factory Invepal, Morón, state of Carabobo, was occupied by the workers in 2002, and nationalized after a workers' struggle. Huge investments were necessary to restart production. The model of co-managing Invepal with the state through a workers' cooperative failed. Financial and contractual irregularities prompted the intervention of the ministry. Today there is worker participation on different levels, but no workers' control in Invepal.

In Invepal we spoke with Rowan Jímenez, in his mid-forties, a worker and activist in Invepal and with the communities.

Elio Sayago, Alcasa worker: What we need right now is that our union leaders and the other comrades understand that the leadership must aim for the workers to take a leading role—to make sure that the workers' knowledge really guarantees control. How are we, as union leaders, able to get the knowledge and wisdom of our people, in these moments, to go beyond the traditional union demands? And we in these moments have the historic opportunity to construct society, to define our own destiny.

Osvaldo, Alcasa worker: Workers' co-administration represented huge gains in consciousness. Just the fact that hundreds of workers participated actively in the process of transformation of Alcasa is very important. The fact that they spoke out in assemblies and discussed directly with the company's management—something that had never happened before in this plant—is also an important lesson. The roundtables did not work out, and the dense bureaucracy led to the current situation of co-administration—one that is close to being paralyzed . . . but still, with great experiences and progress. The workers learned that it is possible to manage and control the whole production process by themselves—a great lesson! We had always been told that that was impossible.

The valve factory Inveval, Carrizal, state of Miranda, was occupied by the workers in early 2003. Five workers were interviewed in Inveval, among them Rubencio Valero, in his late fifties.

Rubencio, Inveval worker: The community helped us a lot when we occupied. We were asking for financial support right down here on the street, on Fridays and Saturdays, when people would get paid. And they gave us money. We were collecting money for coffee and water, and the community helped us a lot. Right now we help the community in the education programs by offering the factory as learning space, and there are men and women from the community studying here in the factory.

Rowan, Invepal worker, Morón: The project of communal paper stores is well underway, and there are four stores opened, most recently, in September 2013, in the state of Barinas, where 380 people benefited from it just on the first day. The communal paper stores are run by a communal council, supported by a local institution or municipal government, because of the amount of money involved—all this with a signed agreement. Invepal hands over the material and sets the sale price of each item. We also monitor to ensure compliance with the agreement. Talking to one person at a store, I was told that the products sell very quickly due to price, and that they will make a social contribution to the community because of the profit from the sale. Similarly, they are vigilant not to sell large quantities to individuals, to fight against speculation.

Inveval

The valve factory Inveval is a good example of an enduring workers' struggle that has achieved workers' control, and submitted the factory to different criteria than those of capitalist productivity and efficiency. What initially appeared to be a solution to their problems was later to develop into a shift in the struggle toward a conflict with the state institutions. The expropriation in 2005 was followed by months of discussions and disagreements with the representatives of the responsible ministry about the enterprises' status. After tough negotiations and eight different proposals rejected by one side or the other, the enterprise was re-established as a stock company with 51 percent state ownership and 49 percent employee ownership in a joint cooperative. All the important decisions that affect the factory were to be made in the weekly cooperative assembly.

For nearly two years the Inveval workers tried to manage the factory on their own, without being guided by capitalist logics, following the conditions of the newly conceived model of a co-management between state and cooperative. They came to the conclusion that the legal framework made direct administration by all the workers impossible. Moreover, the workers noticed how their situation as owners pushed them toward assuming capitalist logic. The cooperative had not just a share of the factory but also of the debt. The workers realized that they were forced to adopt the logic of living to work and pay the debt.

So the workers of Inveval took up Chávez's January 2007 proposal to strengthen the revolution through the formation of workers' councils. In the council they have created several commissions, dealing with the various functions of the organization. Each commission has to produce reports of its work and proposals, and present them to the council. The cooperative was dissolved by the workers. Inveval was transferred into full social ownership, and is managed entirely by the workers.

Five Inveval workers were interviewed over the course of several years: José Quintero, thirty-one; Julio González, in his late forties; Luisa Morales, thirty-nine; Nelson Rodríguez, in his early thirties; and Rubencio Valero, in his late fifties. All of them became politically active because of the circumstances of the transformation process; none had previous experience to rely on.

Luisa: It all started when the owner of the company joined the oil strike to topple Chávez in December 2002. He was one of the leaders of the opposition coordination. We returned to work on January 6, 2003, and the doors were closed. Only executive staff could go in. In the second week of March, the owner came, responding to the pressure of the workers at the factory gates. The guy had the nerve to propose we form a cooperative in which he would have a 90 percent stake and we would have 10 percent, but assume all the workload. We did not reach any agreement, and he began to dismiss workers. Of the nearly one hundred workers on the staff, there were sixty of us who did not accept the dismissal.

Almost a year later, the labor court decided he had to employ us again and pay all lost wages. But, as the owner is definitely not a serious person, we decided to take over the company. That was in May 2003. The lady in the kiosk outside the factory told us that they were taking out some trucks and machinery, so we occupied the factory at six o'clock in the morning. The security guard of course did not want to let us in, so we jumped the fence. We lasted about a year and a half installed here in the factory without entering the buildings. We asked unions in nearby factories for cooperation. City Hall helped us with mineral water and medical care. Most of the neighbors supported us with food. The owner of the company took us to court, and the judge came in person to evict us—but it failed. The police did not support the judge, nor did the mayor.

Over time, however, many workers had to leave the occupation to earn money. In December 2004 there was only one person here, and the company took advantage of that and started to take out some valves. We—a group of workers—met and decided to do a second recuperation, but more organized, to take over the facilities the way it should be—have access to the offices and the whole plant. When we got there we found the general manager of the company, and asked him very decently for the keys. The gentleman said he would not give us the keys, so the comrades told him, "Well, if you do not turn over the key you will not get out of here." So in the end he reluctantly handed over the keys.

The comrades inspected the facilities. They had removed all computer equipment, a number of valves, and materials. A group of comrades related to administration went to several meetings with the ministry and the National Assembly, and they told us about the mechanism to request expropriation, because there is a legal mechanism. And we started to broadcast through community radio stations, in the communities, and then in state media, that what we wanted was the expropriation of the company—that we, the workers, were in the factory and we were fighting for its expropriation.

Julio: As this is a new process and we as workers are learning and building, there have been times when agreement has not been easy. There have been times when the differences are big, and you do not reach any consensus. We workers are clear that it is about the general good of the company, and ideas are discussed until we reach consensus. If there is no consensus, the assembly is suspended and a new meeting is prepared.

Luisa: In early 2005 we delivered all documents proving mismanagement by the owner. In late April 2005, expropriation in the name of the "common public interest" took place. A few months later we got resources to start the recuperation—to change ceilings, paint walls, restore desks, clean, and sweep, and all the work that had to be done. It took us nine months to complete the recuperation process. We started with the repair and maintenance of valves, but with a perspective to start production.

Julio: In the workers' assembly we began to assign responsibilities—not positions, but responsibilities for every area. We wanted to break up the social division of labor and democratize knowledge, so each one of us was preparing. We had to rotate work. When we worked with the previous owner, we saw that the managers took all the credit, while it was the worker who came up with the innovation, who worked day after day on the machine—you know? We are the ones who know how the company and production processes evolve.

Luisa: We declare and believe something when we are inside the plant, but when we leave it we clash with a different world, which hasn't changed. Inveval is identified as a stock company. So everything true for a stock company is true for Inveval: it has to be competitive on the market to sell valves. So what is the real change, that we administer it? That's not the important aspect of the whole issue. The important aspect is that the whole work organization should be social.

Julio: What the cooperative does is feed capitalism, because it's created as part of the capitalist system, and that's what we don't want here. We didn't kick out one capitalist to create sixty new ones.

In early 2007 we began to implement the factory council to build a workers' administration. The prior work organization scheme was vertical—its functioning was hierarchical. The organizational structure we developed is as horizontal as possible—to 100 percent. We are sixty-one workers, and the workers' assembly is the highest authority. It is followed by the factory council, which comprises thirty-two workers, including the directors and coordinators of each area. Those who make up the factory council are elected for one year. The workers' assembly may revoke them at any time, or they can be confirmed again for one year. This allows us not to bureaucratize ourselves in the workplace, and it allows us to break the social division of labor. For example, I was ratified, and today I am in the marketing area; tomorrow I might be at a machine or on a different task, according to my knowledge. We have to be clear: you cannot put people in a workplace they don't know, otherwise the work is not done as it should be done.

Rubencio: Relations between the workers have changed considerably. There are no employees anymore—all are equal, and all are paid the same. If we have to contribute something for any cause, we will do it together.

Julio: People are being trained to have knowledge in all areas. There are a large number of comrades studying in universities, and some who are in missions [adult school programs] we have right here in our facilities, Mission Robinson [elementary school] and Ribas [high school], because almost 40 percent of workers are between forty and fifty years of age. Several comrades have already graduated here, and are waiting to enter universities and continue studying to provide knowledge to our organization. Twenty-two are in the Mission Ribas right now. Ten are going to college. Some are studying higher technical degrees, and others bachelor's degrees.

Nelson: Participative and socialist administration, factory council, socialist enterprise, revolutionary government, and communal council. That is how we have been structuring and how companies are administered. We came to the conclusion that, through the factory council, we made a quantum leap to the management under a socialist model.